LOWE'S®

W9-BPJ-630

BUILDER PORTFOLIO
EASY to BUILD
PLANS

CREATIVE HOMEOWNER®, Upper Saddle River, New Jersey

COPYRIGHT © 2012

CRE▲TIVE
HOMEOWNER®

A Division of Federal Marketing Corp.
Upper Saddle River, NJ

Home Plans Editor: Kenneth D. Stuts, CPBD

Design and Layout: Kroha Direct (David Kroha, Cindy DiPierdomenico, Judith Kroha)

Cover Design: David Geer

Vice President and Publisher: Timothy O. Bakke
Production Coordinator: Sara M. Markowitz

Current Printing (last digit)
10 9 8 7 6 5 4 3 2 1

Manufactured in the United States of America

Builder Portfolio: Easy-to-Build Plans
Library of Congress Control Number: 2010943157
ISBN-10: 1-58011-527-6
ISBN-13: 978-1-58011-527-8

CREATIVE HOMEOWNER®
A Division of Federal Marketing Corp.
24 Park Way
Upper Saddle River, NJ 07458
www.creativehomeowner.com

CREDITS

Front cover: *Kim Jin Hong Photo Studio/CH*, **page 1:** plan 731057, page 65 **page 3:** *top* plan 731039, page 96; *center* top plan 731041, page 104; *center* bottom plan 731147, page 230; *bottom* plan 731137, page 158 **page 4:** 731028, page 135; **page 5:** John Parsekian/CH; **page 12:** 731159, page 159; **page 231:** plan 731033, page 72 **page 235:** *top* plan 731051, page 38; *center* plan 731038, page 78; *bottom* plan 731061, page 30 **page 240:** *top* plan 731060, page 20; *center* plan 731007, page 70; *bottom* plan 731048, page 56

Note: The homes as shown in the photographs and renderings in this book may differ from the actual blueprints. When studying the house of your choice, please check the floor plans carefully.

Contents

THE LOWE'S EASY-TO-BUILD DIFFERENCE

Professionally designed blueprints are a great way to save money and expedite the construction process. Unfortunately, in choosing a home plan you generally only have two things to go by – a front elevation and a generic floor plan. While this level of detail seems to satisfy many nonprofessionals, *Builders Know Better.* They also know they have a lot of questions. How is this project framed? What type of foundation does it have? Will it work with my site?

The simple truth is that most home plans are design driven, and the framing method, cost of construction, and use of sustainable materials are afterthoughts—if addressed at all.

The Lowe's *Builder Portfolio: Easy-To-Build Plans* **reverses that process.** Each Lowe's *Easy-To-Build* series structure is a collaboration of some of the nation's top builders, estimators, designers, and framers to design buildings that are **SIMPLE, STURDY,** and **EASY-TO-BUILD.** All designs feature:

- **Standard stock supplies–no exotic methods or materials**
- **Uniform platform framing that equals strength plus speed**
- **Fully IRC-compliant techniques**
- **130-mph wind resistance using SPF lumber**

From Start to Finish

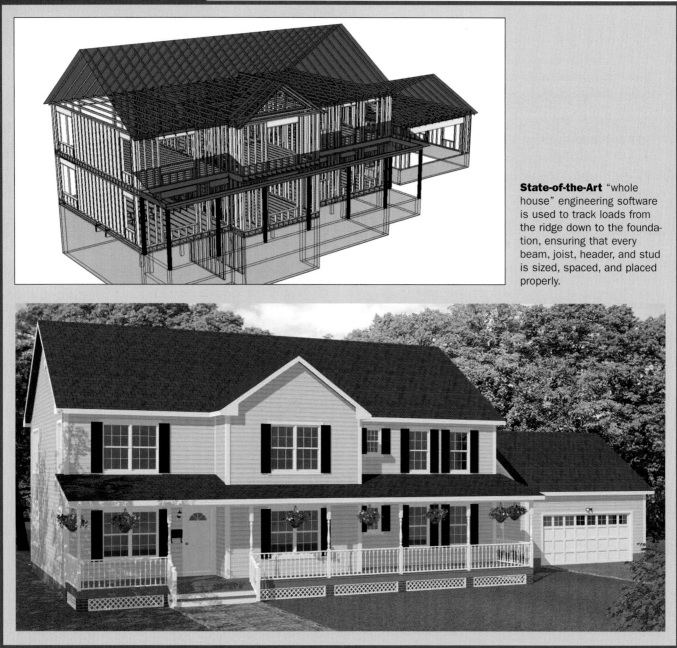

State-of-the-Art "whole house" engineering software is used to track loads from the ridge down to the foundation, ensuring that every beam, joist, header, and stud is sized, spaced, and placed properly.

PLAN–BUILD–OWN

Construction is a three-phase process. These plans have built-in cost savings.

PLAN Purchase

LOWE'S Commercial SERVICES $345 Gift Card

For details please visit our Lowes for Pros Website
www.lowesforpros.com/BlueprintEstimates

EVERYDAY**LOW PRICES** GUARANTEED

Lowe's Blueprint Estimates Rebate Program

The Best Products at the Best Prices for Your Dream Home

When you purchase a blueprint estimate from Lowe's you are eligible to receive a gift card equal to the value of your estimate once you meet pre-determined purchase amounts for materials and supplies. When you receive your blueprints back from Accurate Estimates you will receive instructions on how to request your gift card at www.LowesForPros.com. You will need to enter the invoice numbers from your purchases and specify the address where you would like to receive your gift card. The gift card is valid one year from the date of receipt and please allow 2 – 3 weeks for delivery.

Let's Build Something Together™

LOWE'S

Save up to $500 on your building material purchase

For details please visit our New Mover's Website
www.LowesMoving.com/CHO

EVERYDAY**LOW PRICES** GUARANTEED

The Lowe's Advantage

The Best Products at the Best Prices for Your Dream Home

Your neighborhood Lowe's store is here to help. Think of Lowe's for building materials, finish materials, appliances, and more—as well as inspirational decorating ideas from our Design Centers. We have the right product for the job, offered by knowledgeable and friendly sales associates. Stop by your local Lowe's store or visit Lowes.com.

Let's Build Something Together™

$845.00 in Lowe's Gift Cards for "Starters" actually covers the entire cost of most plan packages*

Lowe's Everyday Low Prices, *Guaranteed*

When you buy your materials at Lowe's.

PLUS:

- $345.00 Accurate Estimate included at no extra cost
- $300.00 Structural Pages included at no extra cost
- $155.00 Free Garage Plan included at no extra cost
- Adds up to $1,645.00 in value savings right off the bat
- Best and most complete plan available

- 14 sheets per set versus typical 7 or 8 sheets
- Multi-level quality control
- Low-Cost modifications
- Best material prices
- Financing available

BUILD to Last

- Three foundation types to suit your site
- Construction-ready framing diagrams, which eliminate guesswork and save time

- Professional presentation and level of detail, which put you ahead of other bidders
- Easy-to-install and durable exterior siding and roofing materials

OWN with Confidence

- Low-maintenance finishes
- Energy-efficient vapor barrier & insulation envelope

- Energy-efficient windows and doors
- Lowe's Appliance Advantage on Energy Star

Lowe's Builder-Support Program

Get What You Need. When You Need It.

Since opening our first store in 1946, Lowe's has learned a lot about meeting the needs of commercial business customers. Our in-store services are designed to help save you time and money, and make your business run smoother. Our goal is to get you out of the store and back on the job faster. Everything you need to make Lowe's Commercial Services work harder for you is available at the **Lowe's Commercial Desk.**

Just having the best blueprint is not enough. You need a complete strategy! The Lowe's *Builder Portfolio: Easy-To-Build Plans* is the centerpiece of the **Lowe's Builder-Support Program** which is a totally integrated program designed to be there to help you along every step of the way.

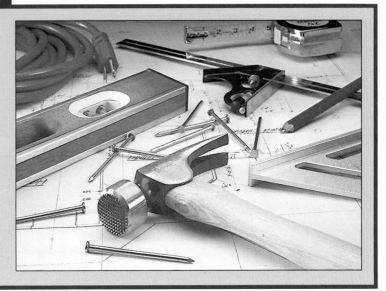

"FREE" *
Garage Plans

*Only with plans purchased from this book, except Study Sets.

Any plan purchased from this book qualifies for a free detached garage plan. If your building lot has room for a detached garage, please select one pictured here or on pages 8 and 9 for **FREE**.

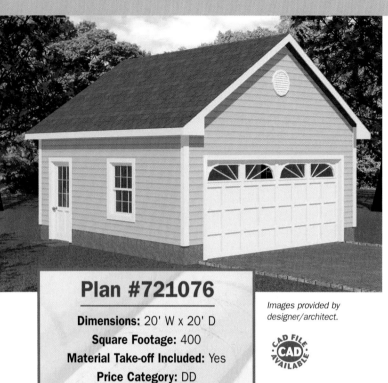

Plan #721076

Dimensions: 20' W x 20' D

Square Footage: 400

Material Take-off Included: Yes

Price Category: DD

Images provided by designer/architect.

CAD FILE AVAILABLE

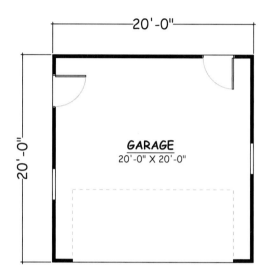

20'-0"

20'-0"

GARAGE
20'-0" X 20'-0"

Copyright by designer/architect.

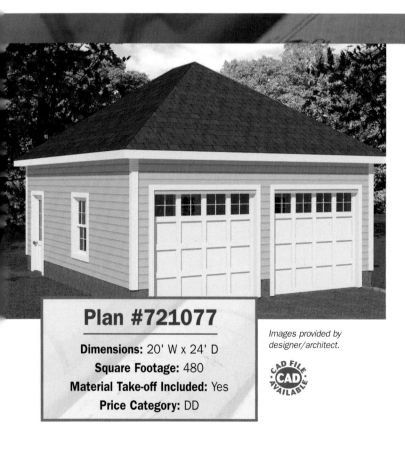

Plan #721077

Dimensions: 20' W x 24' D

Square Footage: 480

Material Take-off Included: Yes

Price Category: DD

Images provided by designer/architect.

CAD FILE AVAILABLE

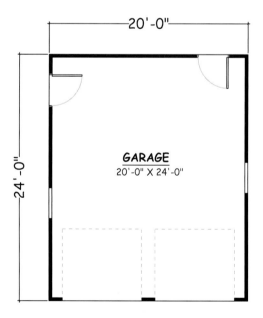

20'-0"

24'-0"

GARAGE
20'-0" X 24'-0"

Copyright by designer/architect.

- Select a garage plan with a style to match your plan.
- A Material Take-off is included with all **FREE** garage plans. See page 234 for more details.
- If you need even more storage space, all garage plans are also for sale. See page 237 for pricing.

- Customers who *purchase* a garage plan recieve a Material Take-off, a $125 value. In addition, if you buy a minimum of $2,000 in merchandise from Lowe's, you will be eligible to receive a $125 Lowe's gift card. More details will be included in your plan package.

Plan #721078

Dimensions: 22' W x 24' D
Square Footage: 528
Material Take-off Included: Yes
Price Category: DD

Images provided by designer/architect.

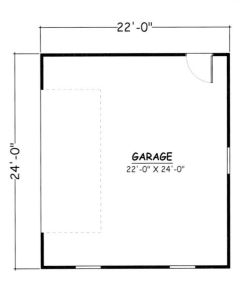

Copyright by designer/architect.

Plan #721079

Dimensions: 20' W x 24' D
Square Footage: 480
Material Take-off Included: Yes
Price Category: DD

Images provided by designer/architect.

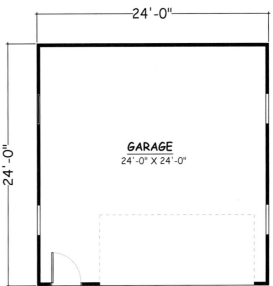

Copyright by designer/architect.

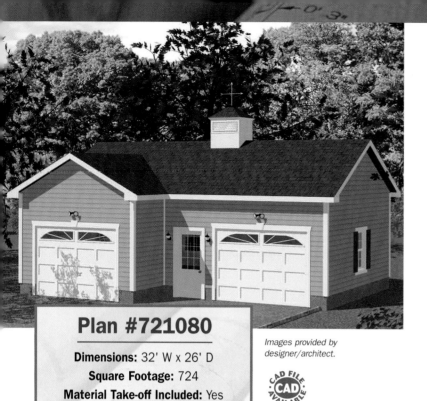

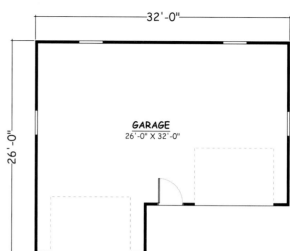

32'-0"

26'-0"

GARAGE
26'-0" X 32'-0"

Plan #721080

Dimensions: 32' W x 26' D

Square Footage: 724

Material Take-off Included: Yes

Price Category: DD

Images provided by designer/architect.

CAD FILE AVAILABLE

Copyright by designer/architect.

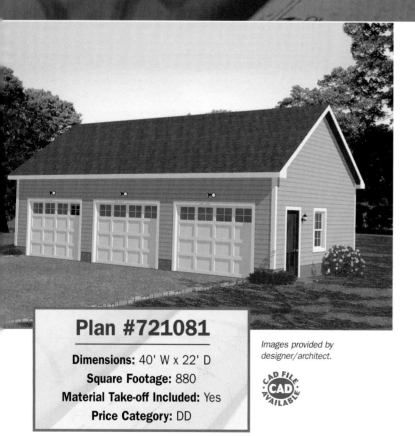

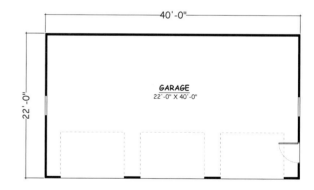

40'-0"

22'-0"

GARAGE
22'-0" X 40'-0"

Plan #721081

Dimensions: 40' W x 22' D

Square Footage: 880

Material Take-off Included: Yes

Price Category: DD

Images provided by designer/architect.

CAD FILE AVAILABLE

Copyright by designer/architect.

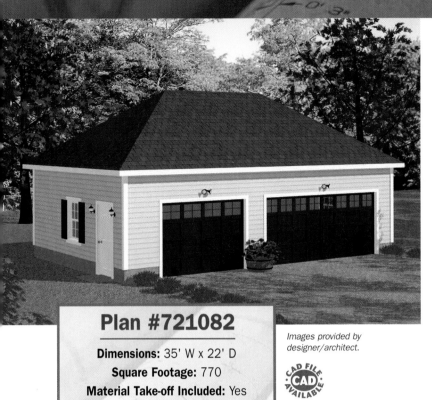

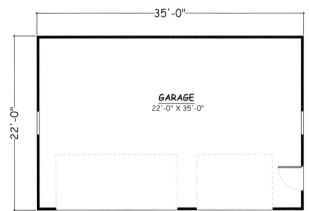

GARAGE
22'-0" X 35'-0"

35'-0"

22'-0"

Plan #721082

Dimensions: 35' W x 22' D

Square Footage: 770

Material Take-off Included: Yes

Price Category: DD

Images provided by designer/architect.

CAD FILE AVAILABLE

Copyright by designer/architect.

24'-0"

22'-0"

GARAGE
22'-0" X 16'-0"

PORCH
22'-0" X 8'-0"

Plan #721083

Dimensions: 24' W x 22' D

Square Footage: 352

Material Take-off Included: Yes

Price Category: DD

Images provided by designer/architect.

CAD FILE AVAILABLE

Copyright by designer/architect.

BEST SELLERS

Single Family Plan 731033 see page 72

Single Family Plan 731051 see page 38

Single Family Plan 731038 see page 78

AND HIGHLIGHTS

Multiamily Plan 731120 see page 188

Office Plan 731148 see page 221

Ten Steps You Should Do Before Submitting Your Plans For a Permit

1. Check Your Plans to Make Sure That You Received What You Ordered

You should immediately check your plans to make sure that you received exactly what you ordered. All plans are checked for content prior to shipping, but mistakes can happen. If you find an error in your plans call 1-800-523-6789. All plans are drawn on a particular type of foundation and all details of the plan will illustrate that particular foundation. If you ordered an alternate foundation type. It should be included immediately after the original foundation. Tell your sub-contractor which foundation you wish to use and disregard the other foundation.

2. Check to Make Sure You Have Purchased the Proper Plan License

If you purchased prints, your plan will have a round red stamp stating, "If this stamp is not red it is an illegal set of plans." This license grants the purchaser the right to build one building using these construction drawings. It is illegal to make copies, doing so is punishable up to $150,000 per offense plus attorney fees. If you need more prints, call 1-800-523-6789. The House Plans Market Association monitors the building industry for illegal prints.

It is also illegal to modify or redraw the plan if you purchased a print. If you purchased prints and need to modify the plan, you can upgrade to the reproducible master, PDF file or CAD file—call 1-800-523-6789. If you purchased a reproducible master or CAD file you have the right to modify the plan and make up to 10 copies. A reproducible master or CAD files comes with a license that you must surrender to the printer or architect making your changes.

3. Complete the "Owner Selection" Portion of the Building Process

The working drawings are very complete, but there are items that you must decide upon. For example, the plans show a toilet in the bathroom, but there are hundreds of models from which to choose. Your individual selection should be made based upon the color, style, and price you wish to pay. This same thing is true for all of the plumbing fixtures, light fixtures, appliances, and interior finishes (for the floors. walls and ceilings) and the exterior finishes. The selection of these items are required in order to obtain accurate competitive bids for the construction of your home

4. Complete Your Permit Package by Adding Other Documents That May Be Required

Your permit department, lender, and builder will need other drawings or documents that must be obtained locally. These items are explained in the next three items.

5. Obtain a Heating & Cooling Calculation and Layout

The heating and cooling system must be calculated and designed for your exact home and your location. Even the orientation of your home can affect the system size. This service is normally provided free of charge by the mechanical company that is supplying the equipment and installation. However, to get an unbiased calculation and equipment recommendation, we suggest employing the services of a mechanical engineer.

6. Obtain a Site Plan

A site plan is a document that shows the relationship of your home to your property. It may be as simple as the document your surveyor provides, or it can be a complex collection of drawings such as those prepared by a landscape architect. Typically, the document prepared by a surveyor will only show the property boundaries and the footprint of the home. Landscape architects can provide planning and drawings for all site amenities, such as driveways and walkways, outdoor structures such as pools, planting plans, irrigation plans, and outdoor lighting.

7. Obtain Earthquake or Hurricane Engineering if You Are Planning to Build in an Earthquake or Hurricane Zone

If you are building in an earthquake or hurricane zone, your permit department will most likely require you to submit calculations and drawings to illustrate the ability of your home to withstand those forces. This information is never included with pre-drawn plans because it would penalize the vast majority of plan purchasers who do not build in those zones. A structural engineer licensed by the state where you are building usually provides this information.

8. Review Your Plan to See Whether Modifications Are Needed

These plans have been designed to assumed conditions and do not address the individual site where you are building. Conditions can vary greatly, including soil conditions, wind and snow loads, and temperature, and any one of these conditions may require some modifications of your plan. For example, if you live in an area that receives snow, structural changes may be necessary. We suggest:

(i)Have your soil tested by a soil-testing laboratory so that sub-surface conditions can be determined at your specific building site. The findings of the soil-testing laboratory should be reviewed by a structural engineer to determine if the existing plan foundation is suitable or if modifications are needed.

(ii)Have your entire plan reviewed by a structural engineer to determine if other design elements, such as load bearing beams, are sized appropriately for the conditions that exist at your site.

Now that you have the complete plan, you may discover items that you wish to modify to suit your own personal taste or decor. To change the drawings, you must have the reproducible masters, PDF files or CAD files (see item 2). We can make the changes for you. For complete information regarding modifications, including our fees, go to www.ultimateplans.com and click the "resources" button on the home page; then click on "our custom services."

9. Record Your Blueprint License Number

Record your blueprint license number for easy reference. If you or your builder should need technical support, the license number is required.

10. Keep One Set of Plans as Long as You Own the Home

Be sure to file one copy of your home plan away for safe keeping. You may need a copy in the future if you remodel or sell the home. By filing a copy away for safe keeping, you can avoid the cost of having to purchase plans later.

Images provided by designer/architect.

Plan # 731063

Dimensions: 56' W x 32' D

Levels: 1

Heated Square Footage: 1,030

Bedrooms: 3

Bathrooms: 1½

Foundation: Crawl space, slab, or basement

Material Take-off Included: Yes

Price Category: B

This home's spacious front porch is a wonderful place to greet visitors.

Features:

- Porch: A perfect place for a set of rockers, this wraparound front porch will be favorite place for the family to gather on warm summer evenings.

- Foyer: With two coat closets and a powder room, this spacious foyer provides an elegant entrance into the home.

- Dining Room: Enter this lovely dining room directly from the foyer, living room, or kitchen—a set of double windows provides lots of natural light.

Copyright by designer/architect.

- Kitchen: This large kitchen features a breakfast bar and is open to the living room, encouraging family interaction during meal preparation. It is just steps away from a utility room that houses a washer and dryer, allowing for the multitasking that is required in today's active lifestyles.

- Deck: The home's entertaining and living space are expanded when you step through a set of sliding glass doors from the living room onto this lovely rear deck.

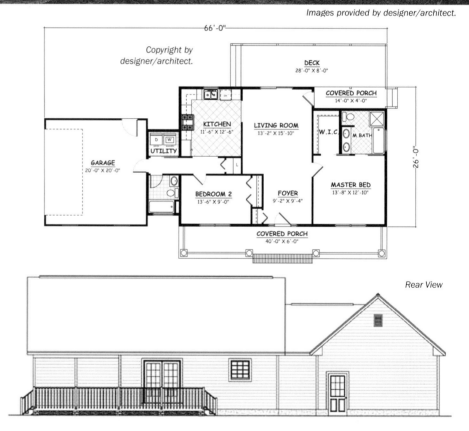

Images provided by designer/architect.

Plan # 731046

Dimensions: 66' W x 26' D

Levels: 1

Heated Square Footage: 1,085

Bedrooms: 2

Bathrooms: 2

Foundation: Crawl space, slab, or basement

Material Take-off Included: Yes

Price Category: B

The stately columns at the front porch, along with transom windows, give this home its curb appeal.

Features:

- Front Porch: This lovely entry porch offers shelter from the elements, while being wide enough to accommodate a small seating area.

- Living Room: This living room truly invites indoor and outdoor entertaining. Open to the foyer and connected to the kitchen through a cased opening, it features a set of sliding glass doors that open onto a rear deck and French doors that lead to a porch.

- Kitchen: Steps away from a utility room is this eat-in kitchen that contains ample counter space. Open to the living room, traffic flow will appear seamless.

- Deck: This amply sized deck at the rear of the house has a small covered area that provides some shade during the hottest parts of the day.

- Master Suite: Situated away from the additional bedrooms is this lovely master suite. The suite features a large walk-in closet and a private bathroom, which houses a tub, a separate shower, and a dual-sink vanity.

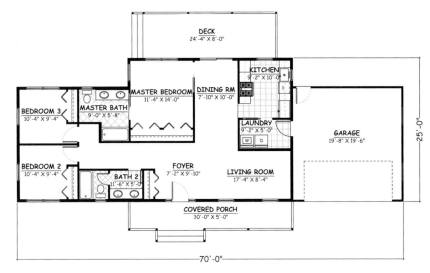

Images provided by designer/architect.

Plan # 731085

Dimensions: 70' W x 25' D
Levels: 1
Heated Square Footage: 1,150
Bedrooms: 3
Bathrooms: 2½
Foundation: Crawl space, slab, or basement
Material Take-off Included: Yes
Price Category: B

- Kitchen: Efficiently designed, this kitchen is also adjacent to a utility room that houses the washer and dryer, allowing for the multitasking required with today's active families.

- Master Suite: This master suite, which includes a private bathroom, is given a touch more privacy as it is set apart from the secondary bedrooms in the home.

You'll love the many wonderful spaces in this home, including the spacious front porch.

Features:

- Front Porch: This charming porch graces the front of the home. The porch is wide enough to allow for a small seating area, perfect for enjoying warm summer evenings.

- Entry Foyer: From the entry porch, enter this foyer that is open to the living room, making you immediately feel welcome.

- Dining Room: Next to the kitchen is this lovely dining room that features a sliding glass door leading to a large rear deck.

Copyright by designer/architect.

Images provided by designer/architect.

Plan # 731096

Dimensions: 40' W x 44' D

Levels: 1

Heated Square Footage: 1,198

Bedrooms: 3

Bathrooms: 2

Foundation: Crawl space, slab, or basement

Material Take-off Included: Yes

Price Category: B

This moderately sized home features clean and simple lines and is filled with many amenities to fit the lifestyle of a busy family.

Features:

- Front Porch: Large enough to fit a small seating area, this expansive front porch will offer you shelter from the elements while providing you with a place to sit and relax in the evenings.

- Dining Room: Connected to the kitchen and living room, this dining room will be used for everyday dining as well as an occasional dinner party. A sliding glass door at the rear of the room provides additional light and leads to the backyard.

- Kitchen: This kitchen features include a double-sink and snack bar, surely pleasing the family cook. The snack bar is the perfect spot for informal meals.

- Master Suite: At the end of the day, relax in this lovely master suite, which features a large walk-in closet and a private bathroom. The bathroom has amenities such as a whirlpool tub and a dual-sink vanity that is certain to leave you feeling refreshed.

- Secondary Bedrooms: Flanking the spacious foyer are two additional bedrooms and a full bathroom.

Copyright by designer/architect.

Images provided by designer/architect.

Plan # 731047

Dimensions: 72'8" W x 26' D

Levels: 1

Heated Square Footage: 1,200

Bedrooms: 3

Bathrooms: 2

Foundation: Crawl space, slab, or basement

Material Take-off Included: Yes

Price Category: B

Thoughtful design gives this well-balanced home a feeling of spaciousness.

Features:

- **Living Room:** Open to the kitchen, this living room features a sliding glass door leading to the rear deck, giving the room an open and airy feeling. The spaciousness and location will ensure that it will become the central gathering spot for all.

- **Kitchen:** With ample counter and cabinet space, and a pantry that will provide plenty of extra storage space, this kitchen will delight the family cook. The snack bar will invite the family to converse while the meals are being prepared.

- **Master Suite:** Secluded from the main part of the home is this lovely master suite. A private bathroom along with

Copyright by designer/architect.

Rear View

with his and her walk-in closets, provides convenience and a touch of luxury.

- **Master Bath:** Amenities such as a sunlit whirlpool tub, a separate shower, a separate toilet room, and a dual-sink

vanity are sure to help you relax and unwind after a long day.

- **Secondary Bedrooms:** Two additional bedrooms, a full bathroom, and a utility room complete the private areas of the home.

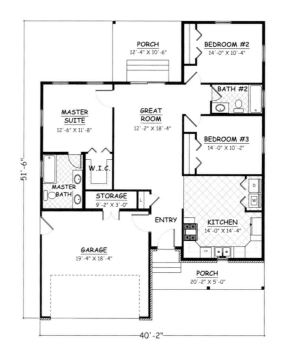

Images provided by designer/architect.

Plan # 731071

Dimensions: 40'2" W x 51'6" D

Levels: 1

Heated Square Footage: 1,224

Bedrooms: 3

Bathrooms: 2

Foundation: Crawl space, slab, or basement

Material Take-off Included: Yes

Price Category: B

This quaint home features dormers and an entry porch with stately columns.

Features:

- Great Room: This centrally located great room is sure to be the main gathering spot for the entire family. At the rear of the room is a sliding glass door that brings you to a rear porch, making outdoor living part of the everyday.

- Kitchen: Mealtime prep will be a joy in this spacious kitchen. Today's active family will appreciate the attached utility area that houses the washer and dryer, making multitasking easy.

- Master Suite: Comfort and privacy are featured in this master suite, which is situated apart from the other bedrooms in the home.

- Bedrooms: Completing the home are an additional two bedrooms and a full bathroom.

Copyright by designer/architect.

Images provided by designer/architect.

Plan # 731053

Dimensions: 56'6" W x 50' D

Levels: 1

Heated Square Footage: 1,226

Bedrooms: 3

Bathrooms: 2

Foundation: Crawl space, slab, or basement

Material Take-off Included: Yes

Price Category: B

This lovely three-bedroom ranch includes a number of amenities any family will love.

Features:

- **Front Porch:** Columns add a touch of elegance to this entry porch.

- **Family Room:** Step through the front door and be welcomed immediately into the heart of the home. Gracious in nature and connected to the dining room and kitchen, this family room will surely be the gathering spot for all.

- **Kitchen:** Open to the dining room and located close to the expansive family room, this spacious kitchen makes organization and meal preparation simple.

Copyright by designer/architect.

- **Master Suite:** At the rear of the home is this lovely master suite, which features a private bathroom with a double vanity for comfort. The suite also has French doors that lead to a generously sized deck, offering you a secluded area for morning coffee or enjoying a summer evening.

- **Secondary Bedrooms:** Rounding out the home are two additional bedrooms and a centrally located full bathroom.

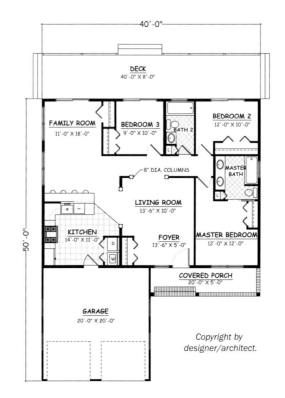

Images provided by designer/architect.

Plan # 731060

Dimensions: 40' W x 50' D

Levels: 1

Heated Square Footage: 1,200

Bedrooms: 3

Bathrooms: 2

Foundation: Crawl space, slab, or basement

Material Take-off Included: Yes

Price Category: B

This lovely traditional-styled home features amenities the whole family will love.

Features:

- Front Porch: Sturdy columns and brick accents adorn this front covered porch.

- Living Room: Columns at each of its entryways add touches of elegance and grace to this modestly sized living room.

- Kitchen: This tidy and well-designed kitchen features a large countertop eating area that is open to the family room allows for interaction between the cook and the rest of the family during the preparation of meals.

40'-0"

DECK
40'-0" X 8'-0"

FAMILY ROOM
11'-0" X 18'-0"

BEDROOM 3
9'-0" X 10'-0"

BATH 2

BEDROOM 2
12'-0" X 10'-0"

MASTER BATH

8" DIA. COLUMNS

LIVING ROOM
13'-6" X 10'-0"

50'-0"

KITCHEN
14'-0" X 11'-0"

FOYER
13'-6" X 5'-0"

MASTER BEDROOM
12'-0" X 12'-0"

COVERED PORCH
20'-0" X 5'-0"

GARAGE
20'-0" X 20'-0"

Copyright by designer/architect.

Rear View

Left Elevation

Right Elevation

- Rear Deck: A wonderful outdoor space, this rear deck spans the length of the home, connecting the family with nature. Along with the family room,

each of the secondary bedrooms in the home features a sliding glass door leading out to the deck.

- Master Suite: Comfort and privacy are added to this lovely master suite with the inclusion of a private bathroom that features a dual-sink vanity.

Flooring Buying Guide

Carpeting

Carpet is both a comfortable and fashionable choice for a home. It is quiet, insulates well from cold, and comes in a wide variety of colors. When choosing carpet, you have many different materials and styles available to choose from, and the decision can be somewhat daunting at times. This buying guide is designed to give you the facts you need to make an informed choice when you decide to carpet the floors.

Types

- **Fiber** is the carpet material itself. Single fibers are spun together to create two-, three-, or four-ply yarn, which is then attached to a woven backing.
- **Pile** refers to the height of the fiber.
- **Density** is the measure of how closely packed the strands of fiber are to one another. The higher the density, the stronger the carpet.
- **Carpet** weight is measured in ounces per square yard. Face weight refers to the amount of fiber on the surface of the carpet, while total weight includes the backing and latex as well. High face weight is a good indication of quality. Note: when using weight to compare carpets, make sure you're comparing similar materials, like nylon to nylon, not nylon to polyester.
- **Texture** comes from the style in which fibers are looped, twisted, or cut. This determines the look and feel of the carpet and plays a large role in its durability.

Fibers

Carpet fibers are made from either natural materials, like wool, or synthetic materials, like nylon, olefin, acrylic, and polyester. Each different material brings unique characteristics to carpet.

- **Wool** offers a deep, rich look and feel with excellent resilience and durability. It is naturally stain resistant and resists soil and dirt due to how tightly packed the fibers are. For these reasons, wool carpet tends to run higher in price than the synthetic options.
- **Nylon** is the most common carpet material. It's the strongest fiber, making it an excellent choice for heavy traffic areas. It's also the most durable of the synthetics; it is easy to clean and maintain. Nylon is soil- and mildew-resistant, resilient, and non-allergenic. However, some nylon may pill and be prone to static.

- **Olefin** (Polypropylene) was originally for outdoor carpeting and basements due to its resistance to moisture, mildew, water damage, staining, pilling, shedding, and static. Now it's more widely used for its durability and wool-like feel and appearance. Olefin is dyed before it's made into a fiber and therefore is colorfast, though some olefin can flatten and fade in direct sunlight.
- **Polyester** is not as durable as nylon, but it's quite stain-resistant. Polyester offers a wide selection of textures and colors, and while it's susceptible to pilling and shedding, it's non-allergenic, sheds moisture, resists moths and mildew, and cleans easily.
- **Acrylic** is the closest to wool of any of the synthetics. Acrylic is manufactured primarily for commercial use. It offers soil resistance, excellent cleanability, and resistance to static, moths, and mildew. Acrylic is available in a wide choice of colors and is less likely to fade in bright sunlight than nylon or polyester.

Treatments

Carpet is available with stain-resistant fibers and finishes, which are ideal for homes with children and pets. Treatments are supplemental to the natural resistence of the carpet fibers. The most effective treatments are integrated as part of the manufacturing process. Finishes applied later are not as long-lasting. One example of an effective carpet treatment is heat setting, which is a manufacturing process that reinforces the twists of the yarn plies to add durability.

Pile

CUT PILE fiber ends are cut evenly. There are several types of cut pile:

- **Saxony** is a popular carpet of dense, level-cut pile clipped to about ½ inch high. The closely packed yarns give a soft,

smooth surface, which is perfect in formal settings. A smooth-finished saxony is often referred to as plush. Saxony carpet is highly susceptible to showing seams, footprints, and vacuum marks.
- **Textured** isn't as densely tufted as a saxony but is equally known for its very soft feel. Two-toned yarn and an uneven surface give it a casual look suited to any room. Its tight-twist construction helps resist soil, so it's often a good choice for family rooms and kitchens. This is the most popular carpet option and the one you see most often in homes.
- **Frieze** carpets have a short, durable, twisted pile fiber well suited to busy areas, often used for commercial purposes. The fibers of a frieze carpet curl in different directions, so they hide footprints and other common carpet marks. Frieze yields a somewhat informal look.

LOOP PILE yarns are looped and fastened to the backing. These are very durable carpets and usually a good choice for high-traffic areas. There are two types of loop pile carpeting:

- **Berber** features large, uncut loops of natural-tone fibers, varying in size and usually made from wool, nylon, or olefin. It is denser than most other carpets and very stain resistant. This is not a good choice for houses with animals, though, as their claws can snag on the fibers.
- **Level loop** refers to tufted, uncut loops of equal height, resulting in a very smooth surface. It's durable, easy to maintain, and a great carpet for high-traffic areas and informal rooms. Level loop is, however, known to be harder and more stiff than the other carpet options.

CUT AND LOOP offers a combination of the above, allowing more options of textures and patterns. Cut and loop achieves a sculptured pattern with varied levels of uncut low loops and sheared top loops. The pattern looks as if it's been cut into the carpet and usually features several tones from the same color family. The change in color helps disguise wear and soiling. Cut and loop doesn't necessarily hold up as well as loop pile, but it is considerably softer.

Tiles

Peel-and-stick carpet tiles have become an excellent do-it-yourself flooring method. New technology has provided carpet squares that are easy to install, clean, and maintain. The adhesive system keeps the carpet in place and eliminates curling. Builders can mix and match colors and patterns to suit the décor of the house.

Alternatives

Area rugs are also a popular floorcovering alternative. A variety of materials, sizes, shapes, and colors is available to complement the new floor.

Padding

Padding is just as important as the carpet itself—in some ways even more so. Although it's not visible, the cushioning layer is critical to a quality carpet installation. Installing the proper backing cushions the foot, insulates from cold and noise, and increases the life of the carpet. Always use a quality backing, but remember that thicker is not always better. A floor that's too soft can be dangerous, especially to those whose steps may be a bit unstable at times. When foot testing a carpet in the showroom, test it with a padding sample underneath. Also be sure to follow the manufacturer guidelines as to which padding to choose. Different kinds of carpet require different padding, and oftentimes the carpet will not wear properly with the wrong kind of padding.

Hardwood Flooring

In addition to adding warmth and beauty to a room, hardwood floors are also a great way to increase the value of the home. There are many different styles of hardwood flooring to choose from, including domestic and exotic species, bamboo, and cork.

You can buy prefinished hardwood floors that are already stained and finished with a coating that is stronger than most site-applied finishes. There are also coordinating mouldings that are stained and prefinished to coordinate with the floor you select. If you prefer to finish your new flooring on-site, unfinished flooring is an option.

Choosing the right flooring is as easy as 1, 2, 3. We make it easy to get the floor that's right for both you and your project. All you need to do is choose your construction, style, and installation method. It's that simple.

Hardwood Construction

Hardwood floors can be installed on any level of the home and are available in multiple constructions to allow for installation flexibility over different subfloors and to mitigate moisture. Identify your subfloor and level of the home to determine what construction of hardwood to install.

It's important to take moisture into consideration when you're installing hardwood floors because changes in moisture can create issues such as warping and gapping. To mitigate the effects of moisture, keep moisture levels within manufacturer recommendations and choose the right construction of hardwood flooring and installation materials. For an added layer of protection against moisture damage, install a moisture barrier. It is not recommended that you install hardwood flooring in full baths due to fluctuating moisture conditions. There are three primary subfloors over which you can install:

- Basement or concrete below ground level
- Concrete at ground level
- Plywood subfloor at or above ground level

Hardwood Floor Construction

¾-in. Solid

This is a ¾-in.-thick solid piece of hardwood floor and is what customers traditionally think of for hardwood floors. Because solid floors expand more when exposed to moisture than engineered floors, you can only install them over a plywood subfloor at or above ground level. If you have a crawl space, it's a good idea to put a moisture barrier underneath the crawl space to help control moisture coming through the ground into your home.

*Most solid floors can be sanded and refinished. Check manufacturer's warranty.

⁵⁄₁₆-in. Solid

A thinner version of the ¾-in. hardwood floor. Because it's solid, you cannot install it in the basement or on concrete below ground level, but it's thin enough to glue down to concrete at ground level or install over plywood at or above ground level. Urethane adhesives are required, and moisture barriers are recommended for gluing down ⁵⁄₁₆-in. solids.

*Most solid floors can be sanded and refinished. Check manufacturer's warranty.

Engineered Hardwood

Engineered floors are as much of a hardwood floor as a ¾-in. solid floor. In fact, engineered floors were designed for installation over concrete and to help mitigate potential moisture issues. The cross-layer construction prevents the floor from expanding as much as a ¾-in. or ⁵⁄₁₆-in. solid floor when exposed to moisture. Therefore, you can install engineered anywhere in the home, including the basement. Engineered floors are also more environmentally friendly and less expensive than solid floors because the veneer is only a few millimeters thick instead of ¾-in. thick. The real hardwood veneer of engineered floors differs from laminate, which has a printed paper veneer.

*Some engineered floors can also be sanded and refinished. Check manufacturer's warranty.

Locking Hardwood

A locking, or floating, floor is an engineered floor but with the added advantage of a locking tongue-and-groove system. It's the perfect easy installation flooring solution because nails, staples, and glue are not required. All you have to do is roll out the moisture barrier underlayment and lock the planks into place.

*Some locking floors can be sanded and refinished.

Hardwood Flooring Types

Hardwood floors are available in a wide selection that can match anyone's style. When considering a hardwood floor that is right for you, consider the following factors:

Species. There are domestic species like oak, maple, and cherry, as well as exotic species like bamboo, brazilian cherry, and cork. Each species has a distinct grain pattern. For example, oak has an exaggerated grain whereas maple's is very subtle. Exotics are very popular because of their distinct grain patterns and color.

Different species also have varying degrees of hardness. Hardwood floors are a natural product and are susceptible to dents. (Dents are not covered under manufacturer warranties unless specifically stated.) If you expect that your floors will take a lot of abuse, consider a species at least as hard as red oak based on the hardness table to the right.

Color. Most domestic species of wood come in a variety of stained colors. Most exotic species, on the other hand, are not stained because their natural color is very popular. Many exotic species are photosensitive and need exposure to sunlight to achieve their desired rich color.

Width. Wider floors over 3 inches are gaining popularity. Widths can easily change the look of a floor because the wider the plank, the fewer the seams that can be seen in the floor. Wider widths also showcase the natural beauty of the wood, especially hickory and tigerwood.

Texture. There are many types of texture to choose from, including smooth, hand-scraped, distressed, and wirebrushed.

Janka Hardness Rating

The relative hardness of wood species is measured using the Janka Hardness Rating. This test measure the force needed to embed a steel ball (.444 inch in diameter) to half its diameter in the piece of ¾-in. solid wood being tested. The higher the number, the harder the wood. This means the wood is more resistant to indentations.

Wood Species	Janka Rating
Ipe, Brazilian Walnut, Lapacho	3,684
Cumaru, Brazilian Teak	3,540
Brazilian Cherry, Jatoba	2,350
Santos Mahogany, Cabreuva	2,220
Amendiom	1,912
Tigerwood	1,850
Hickory/Pecan	1,820
Acacia	1,750
Kempas	1,710
Timborana	1,570
Sapele	1,510
Maple, hard	1,450
Bamboo, natural	1,380
Australian Cypress	1,375
Oak, white	1,360
Ash, white	1,320
Beech, American	1,300
Oak, red	1,290
Birch, yellow	1,260
Walnut, black	1,010
Cherry, black	950
Cedar	900
Pine, southern yellow	690
Balsa	100

Choose Your Hardwood Construction

Here is a quick overview of the different ways to install hardwood flooring:

Locking. Nails, staples, and glue are not required. All you have to do is roll out the moisture barrier underlayment for moisture protection and then float the floor over the subfloor by locking the planks together.

Glue. Gluing involves troweling glue on the floor and setting the planks into the glue. Lowe's offers adhesive systems that incorporate a moisture barrier to help mitigate moisture-related issues.

Nail. Nailing involves driving a nail at an angle through the tongue of the hardwood floor into the wood subfloor. The nail is then hidden by the groove of the next row of boards.

Staple. Using staples is simliar to the nailing process.

Things to Consider

Defects. Make sure you know the defect rate of the wood you are buying. If the rate is over 50 percent, you will need to buy almost twice as much as a wood that is rated 95 percent defect free. Wood with high defect rates can also create issues with installation.

Grade. The wood's appearance determines its grade. All grades can be equally defect free, but each grade offers a distinct look. Clear and select grades are the cleanest looks with minimal knots and color variations. Millwood and cabin grades will allow all of the characteristics of the species to show, shuch as knots, streaks, and color variations.

Laminate Flooring Buying Guide

There's no way to prevent spills, stains, and heavy traffic, but you won't have to worry about the damage anymore with new laminate flooring. It would be difficult to find a flooring product that is tougher and more versatile than laminate. Laminate flooring is available in a variety of colors and finishes and is extremely simple to install.

How Laminate Flooring is Made

Laminate flooring shouldn't be confused with engineered-wood flooring. Both are made of layers of material laminated together for strength. Laminate floors use several materials such as resin, wood fiber, and kraft paper (materials vary by manufacturer) compacted under pressure to create the final product. The flooring is made into planks.

The surface of a laminate plank is actually an image printed from film onto a thin decorative layer, which is then treated with a wear layer. The high resolution of the film allows an extremely authentic appearance. The finished material is similar in feel to a kitchen countertop. A variety of finishes is available, from wood grain to color.

Most laminates are coated with aluminum oxide, which is where it gets its strength. Laminates are known to be very durable, water-resistant, and dent-resistant. They also resist wear better than hardwoods.

Installing Laminate Flooring

Laminate floors are floating floors, meaning that they aren't attached to the subfloor. The flooring is sold as tongue-and-groove planks where the planks simply lock together.

Laminate flooring can be installed on all grade levels. Because it's durable and easy to clean, it's a perfect floor for kitchens, bathrooms, laundry rooms—any room that has a lot of traffic. With proper preparation, installation is possible over concrete, vinyl, tile, and even some carpet.

Tile-Flooring Buying Guide

Choose the Best Tile for the Home

Tile continues to grow in popularity as a floor covering, with good reason—it has a natural, handcrafted look that's durable and easy to care for. Tile also works well in areas with high foot traffic and is especially suited to entry areas where water and dirt enter the house. The design patterns, with all of the possible combinations of size, texture, and color, are limitless.

Selecting Tile

Finding a tile you like is easy. Just make sure it's the right one for your project, and choose a tile that's rated for the area where you plan to install it. Entryways need a hard, abrasion-resistant, moisture-proof tile. Baths require a moisture-proof, non-slip material. Slip-resistant tile is treated with an abrasive material to "rough up" the smooth surface for safety. Some tiles are rated for indoor or outdoor use only; others can be used in either application.

Floor tile is usually ½ inch to ¾ inch thick, manufactured in squares measuring 4 inches by 4 inches up to 24 inches by 24 inches. Other shapes, such as octagonal and hexagonal are available. (Wall tile is thinner and comes in squares from 3 inches by 3 inches up to 6 inches by 6 inches.)

Mosaic tiles are 2 inches square or smaller and can be installed individually. Mosaic tiles are also available in premounted paper or fabric mesh sheets.

Firing. The hardness of tile is affected by the firing process. Usually, the longer and hotter the firing, the harder the tile will be. The raw tile material, called **bisque,** is either single-fired or double-fired.

- For **single-fired** tiles, the glaze is applied to the raw material and baked once in a kiln.
- **Double-fired** tiles are thicker. Raw material is baked a second time after additional color or decoration is added.

Tile Ratings

All tile feels hard, but some types of tile are actually harder than others. Tile is rated by a series of standardized tests. The tests evaluate a tile's relative hardness (the Moh scale), its ability to stand up to wear, and the percentage of water absorbed. The Porcelain Enamel Institute hardness ratings are:

- **Group I Light Traffic:** Residential bathroom floors where bare or stockinged feet are the norm.
- **Group II Medium Traffic:** Home interiors where little abrasion occurs. Don't use in kitchens or entries.
- **Group III Medium-Heavy Traffic:** Any home interior.
- **Group IV Heavy Traffic:** Homes or light-to-medium commercial areas.
- **Group V Extra-Heavy Traffic:** Use it anywhere.

These ratings are important, but don't get too bogged down in analysis—they serve to help you find the right tile for your application.

Porosity

Pay closer attention to the ratings test that measures the percentage of water absorbed, or porosity. A tile's porosity is critical especially when choosing tile for kitchens and baths because these areas need moisture-proof flooring. Porous tile should not be used outdoors where cold weather produces freeze/thaw cycles. The classifications for the porosity of tile are: **Impervious** (least absorbent), **Vitreous, Semi-vitreous** and **Non-vitreous** (most absorbent).

Installing Tile

On the installation scale, installing tile ranges from easy to challenging. Tiles usually require some cutting to fit. They're applied with mortar or other adhesives, followed by a final application of grout.

As with all types of tile, areas that require precision cuts may be more difficult. Flooring presents its own set of concerns. Because tile is not a resilient material, it requires a very stable sub-surface. Subfloors frequently have to be built up to the thickness required for tile flooring. See the table below for some common (and some less-common) floor tile.

Types of Floor Tile

Brick	Brick tiles are a good floor choice for informal or rustic décor. Available in several earth-tone colors, brick tiles should be treated with a stain-resistant sealer. Floor brick is normally used in outdoor settings (such as patios) and can be arranged in interesting geometric patterns.
Cement	Cement-bodied tiles are poured into molds, then fired or dried naturally. Color may be added. Sealing is required after installation for moisture and stain resistance.
Ceramic	Ceramic tile is made from clay or other minerals. The extruded material is shaped and heat-treated (fired) in a kiln. Clay tiles are then further treated in one of two ways: **Glazed.** Color is added to the tile after firing. The glasslike surface is bonded to the tile. Glazing allows brighter colors to be used and adds stain resistance. Because of their slick, glassy surface, glazed tiles are used mostly on walls or countertops. Glazed tile offers more color choices than unglazed. **Unglazed** (also called quarry tiles). The pigment or natural color is present during firing and is part of the tile itself. Unglazed tile needs sealing for stain resistance.
Mosaic	Porcelain or ceramic mosaic tiles are 2 inches square or smaller. They can be installed individually or can be found premounted on mesh or paper sheets. Mosaics may be glazed or unglazed.
Pavers	Pavers resemble brick but are thinner. Shale-based pavers are used for patios as well as interior floors. Like quarry tile, pavers need sealing for moisture and stain proofing.
Porcelain	The material is fired at a high temperature, making a dense tile. The density makes porcelain tile more resistant to moisture.
Quarry	Quarry tile is unglazed and requires sealing in wet areas. Clay-based quarry tile is used extensively in commercial settings. Because it's a durable and relatively inexpensive material, it's becoming more acceptable in homes. The predominant colors are earth shades of red and orange.
Saltillo	Saltillo, or Mexican, tile is air dried rather than kiln dried. Drying outdoors in the sun makes this tile a little softer and less durable. The exposure to the elements also gives the tile a look that is unique. When used indoors, a sealer is required.
Terra-cotta	Terra-cotta is the same material in construction and appearance as clay garden pots. Tiles are absorbent and need to be treated for indoor use.
Terrazzo	Stone or marble chips embedded in cement make up a terrazzo floor. The polished surface makes a durable floor material.

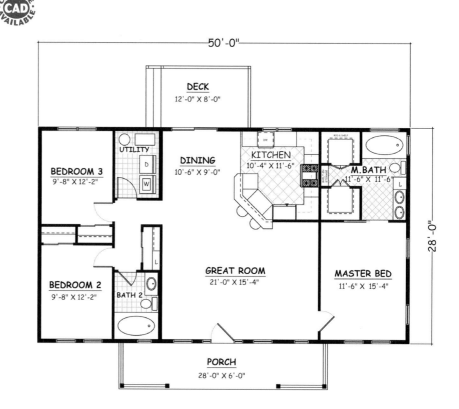

Images provided by designer/architect.

Plan # 731061

Dimensions: 50' W x 28' D

Levels: 1

Heated Square Footage: 1,200

Bedrooms: 3

Bathrooms: 2

Foundation: Crawl space, slab, or basement

Material Take-off Included: Yes

Price Category: B

Details such as oval windows and side-lights enhance the exterior of this home.

Features:

- Great Room: This great room is the ideal space for entertaining. It is generous in its size and open to both the kitchen and the dining room, creating continuity throughout the home.

- Kitchen: While this kitchen design offers you plenty of counter and cabinet are for preparing meals, an angled snack bar open to the great room is the perfect place for a quick bite to eat.

Front View

Rear Elevation

Left Elevation

Right Elevation

- Master Suite: Situated apart from the other bedrooms in the house is this beautiful master suite. With such amenities as a private bathroom that features a sunlit whirlpool tub, dual-sink vanity, as well as his and her walk-in closets, this space will surely be the ideal place to retreat to after a long day.

- Secondary Bedrooms: An additional two bedrooms and a full bathroom complete this home.

Images provided by designer/architect.

Plan # 731080

Dimensions: 51'8" W x 60' D

Levels: 1

Heated Square Footage: 1,260

Bedrooms: 3

Bathrooms: 2½

Foundation: Crawl space, slab, or basement

Material Take-off Included: Yes

Price Category: B

The splendid design of this ranch home will please the homeowner with its wonderful layout and amenities.

Features:

- Foyer: Featuring tiled flooring and a coat closet for convenience, this cozy foyer welcomes you into the home.

- Kitchen: Ample counter space, an abundance of cabinets, and a pantry in this kitchen will be sure to delight the family chef.

- Family Room: From the foyer you enter into this gracious family room. Ample in its size, this room will surely be the place the family will congregate most often.

- Master Suite: After a long day, you will look forward to some rest and relaxation in this beautiful master suite. The suite has a walk-in closet and a private bathroom with such amenities as an oversized tub, a separate shower, and a dual-sink vanity. At the rear of the room is a French door that leads you out to an expansive rear deck.

Copyright by designer/architect.

Plan # 731045

Dimensions: 61'3" W x 31' D

Levels: 1

Heated Square Footage: 1,268

Bedrooms: 3

Bathrooms: 2

Foundation: Crawl space, slab, or basement

Material Take-off Included: Yes

Price Category: B

Images provided by designer/architect.

Front and rear porches give this charming ranch home a country feel.

Features:

- Family Room: This room is not only generous in its size but also open to both the kitchen and dining room, certain to make it the central gathering place for all.

- Dining Room: Open to the kitchen and the family room, this dining room also includes a sliding glass door leading to the rear porch, making dining indoors or outdoors easily accessible.

- Master Suite: A large walk-in closet and private bathroom help to add both privacy and comfort to this already lovely master suite.

- Bedrooms: Rounding out the home are an additional two bedrooms and full bathroom.

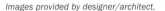

Copyright by designer/architect.

Rear View

Plan # 731050

Dimensions: 51'4" W x 41'2" D

Levels: 1

Heated Square Footage: 1,295

Bedrooms: 3

Bathrooms: 2

Foundation: Crawl space, slab, or basement

Material Take-off Included: Yes

Price Category: B

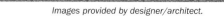
Images provided by designer/architect.

Multiple gables and a brick facade add character and charm to this lovely ranch home.

Features:

- Entry: This simple foyer welcomes you home and guides you to the heart of the home—the great room.

- Great Room: Just steps from the foyer and connected to the dining room, this great room will become the central gathering spot for all. Enhanced with sliding glass doors leading to a rear deck, this spacious room offers you a wonderful place for entertaining or just relaxing as a family.

Copyright by designer/architect.

Rear Elevation

Left Elevation

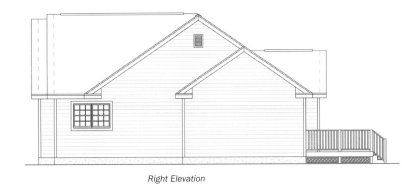

Right Elevation

- **Dining Room:** This lovely dining room, adjacent to the kitchen, is perfectly suited for family meals as well as formal dinner parties

- **Kitchen:** Designed with efficiency in mind, this kitchen will make mealtime tasks simple and enjoyable. A step away is a utility room that houses the washer and dryer, giving busy families a way to multitask.

- **Master Suite:** With a private bathroom and a walk-in closet, this master suite will provide you with a place to relax your body and renew your attitude after a long day.

Plan # 731055

Dimensions: 26' W x 50' D

Levels: 1

Heated Square Footage: 1,300

Bedrooms: 3

Bathrooms: 2

Foundation: Crawl space, slab, or basement

Material Take-off Included: Yes

Price Category: B

Images provided by designer/architect.

This home's charming front porch welcomes you inside.

CAD FILE AVAILABLE

Features:

- Foyer: This generously sized foyer welcomes you into the home and brings you through to the family room.

- Family Room: Step directly from the foyer into the heart of the home. With its gracious size and central location, this family room will certainly be the spot for all of the family to gather.

- Kitchen: Efficient organization is easy in this L-shaped kitchen that features a large pantry. Abundant counter and cabinet space will make mealtime prep a snap.

- Master Suite: This large master suite with a walk-in closet and private bathroom will offer you a place to relax after a long day.

- Secondary Bedrooms: Steps away from a centrally located full bathroom are two additional moderately sized bedrooms.

Copyright by designer/architect.

Images provided by designer/architect.

Plan # 731043

Dimensions: 40' W x 48'9" D

Levels: 1

Heated Square Footage: 1,311

Bedrooms: 3

Bathrooms: 2

Foundation: Crawl space, slab, or basement

Material Take-off Included: Yes

Price Category: B

This cottage-style home uses simple clean lines, making it attractive and charming.

Features:

- Front Porch: Turned columns add a touch of grace to this lovely front porch.

- Kitchen: This tidy kitchen features a snack bar for simple family meals and after-school snacks.

- Family Room: Open to the kitchen, this family room is both bright and airy, making it sure to be the central gatherng place for all. Sliding glass doors open to the rear porch, which spans the entire width of the house.

- Bedrooms: A spacious master bedroom with a private bathroom, two additional bedrooms, and a centrally located bathroom help to complete this home.

COVERED PORCH
40'-0" X 5'-0"

MASTER BEDROOM
14'-8" X 14'-0"

M. BATH

FAMILY ROOM
17'-10" X 16'-6"

BEDROOM 3
14'-0" X 8'-2"

KITCHEN
10'-0" X 11'-0"

LAUNDRY
9'-4" X 5'-0"

BATH 2
10'-4" X 5'-0"

BEDROOM 2
14'-0" X 8'-0"

FOYER

GARAGE
19'-6" X 20'-0"

COVERED PORCH
20'-0" X 5'-0"

40'-0"

48'-9"

Copyright by designer/architect.

Plan # 731051

Dimensions: 70'6" W x 27'4" D

Levels: 1

Heated Square Footage: 1,324

Bedrooms: 3

Bathrooms: 2

Foundation: Crawl space, slab, or basement

Material Take-off Included: Yes

Price Category: B

Images provided by designer/architect.

Designed for the young family, this home has a good balance between private and public spaces.

Features:

- Great Room: From the front porch, enter immediately into this great room, the heart of the home. This delightfully open space is adjacent to the dining room and the kitchen, making it the gathering spot for all.

- Dining Room: Open to the kitchen and the great room, family meals as well as formal dinner parties will be a delight in this lovely dining room. Step through a set of sliding doors leading to a gracious rear deck for easy outdoor dining.

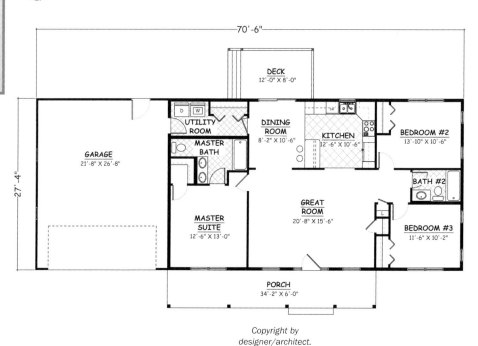

Copyright by designer/architect.

Rear Elevation

Left Elevation

Right Elevation

- Kitchen: A stand-alone island with countertop seating separating this kitchen and the dining room enables the cook to interact with others while preparing meals.

- Master Suite: This master suite is set apart from the secondary bedrooms in the home and features a private bathroom, giving the lovely suite a bit of privacy.

- Secondary Bedrooms: Moderately sized, these rooms are located just off the great room and include a separate hallway as well as a centrally located bathroom.

Plan # 731073

Dimensions: 31' W x 42'5" D

Levels: 1

Heated Square Footage: 1,315

Bedrooms: 3

Bathrooms: 2

Foundation: Crawl space, slab, or basement

Material Take-off Included: Yes

Price Category: B

This long ranch home features a lovely front porch, wonderful for relaxing on at the end of the day.

CAD FILE AVAILABLE

Features:

- Front Porch: Spacious enough for the placement of a small sitting area, this front porch will be the perfect spot to sit on a warm summer evening.

- Kitchen: Wonderfully designed with ample counter space and a plethora of cabinets, this kitchen will surely please the family cook. It also features a utility closet housing the washer and dryer, making multitasking much easier.

- Breakfast Nook: Located directly off of the kitchen is this cozy breakfast nook. The French door at the rear of the room leads you out to a generously sized rear deck, a perfect spot for summer meals.

- Master Suite: At the rear of the home is this delightful master suite, which features a large walk-in closet, a private bathroom, and a French door leading to the rear deck.

Copyright by designer/architect.

Images provided by designer/architect.

Plan # 731100

Dimensions: 62' W x 32' D

Levels: 1

Heated Square Footage: 1,344

Bedrooms: 2

Bathrooms: 2

Foundation: Crawl space, slab, or basement

Material Take-off Included: Yes

Price Category: B

This lovely ranch-style home features an open floor plan that is perfect for both entertaining and relaxing.

Features:

- Foyer: Step from the front porch, and be immediately welcomed into the home in this spacious foyer.

- Living Room: This lovely living room is the perfect spot for entertaining. The open floor plan, along with multiple windows, makes this room bright and inviting.

- Deck: A sliding glass door in the dining room leads out to this rear deck, which expands the indoor living space to the beautiful outdoors.

- Kitchen: Open to the dining room, this U-shaped kitchen offers many modern conveniences. The family cook will surely be pleased with the abundance of cabinet and counter space.

- Master Suite: Two walk-in closets, multiple windows, and a private bathroom that features a dual-sink vanity, an oversize tub, and a separate shower make this master suite a welcoming retreat after a long day.

Plan # 731087

Dimensions: 71'3" W x 27'6" D

Levels: 1

Heated Square Footage: 1,345

Bedrooms: 3

Bathrooms: 2

Foundation: Crawl space, slab, or basement

Material Take-off Included: Yes

Price Category: B

Images provided by designer/architect.

Copyright by designer/architect.

Rear View

Plan # 731078

Dimensions: 70' W x 39' D

Levels: 1

Heated Square Footage: 1,358

Bedrooms: 3

Bathrooms: 2

Foundation: Crawl space, slab, or basement

Material Take-off Included: Yes

Price Category: B

Images provided by designer/architect.

Copyright by designer/architect.

Plan # 731097

Dimensions: 78'4" W x 31' D

Levels: 1

Heated Square Footage: 1,366

Bedrooms: 3

Bathrooms: 1

Foundation: Crawl space, slab, or basement

Material Take-off Included: Yes

Price Category: B

Images provided by designer/architect.

CAD FILE AVAILABLE

Copyright by designer/architect.

Plan # 731062

Dimensions: 76'10" W x 31'4" D

Levels: 1

Heated Square Footage: 1,370

Bedrooms: 3

Bathrooms: 2

Foundation: Crawl space, slab, or basement

Material Take-off Included: Yes

Price Category: B

Images provided by designer/architect.

CAD FILE AVAILABLE

Copyright by designer/architect.

Plan # 731079

Dimensions: 68' W x 36' D

Levels: 1

Heated Square Footage: 1,372

Bedrooms: 3

Bathrooms: 2

Foundation: Crawl space, slab, or basement

Material Take-off Included: Yes

Price Category: B

Images provided by designer/architect.

CAD FILE AVAILABLE

Copyright by designer/architect.

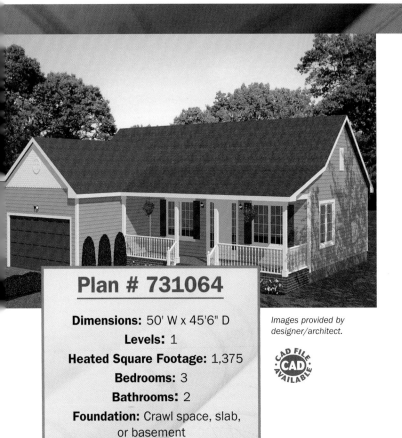

Plan # 731064

Dimensions: 50' W x 45'6" D

Levels: 1

Heated Square Footage: 1,375

Bedrooms: 3

Bathrooms: 2

Foundation: Crawl space, slab, or basement

Material Take-off Included: Yes

Price Category: B

Images provided by designer/architect.

CAD FILE AVAILABLE

Copyright by designer/architect.

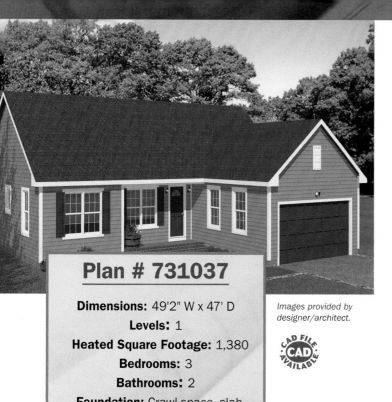

Images provided by designer/architect.

Copyright by designer/architect.

Plan # 731037

Dimensions: 49'2" W x 47' D

Levels: 1

Heated Square Footage: 1,380

Bedrooms: 3

Bathrooms: 2

Foundation: Crawl space, slab, or basement

Material Take-off Included: Yes

Price Category: B

Images provided by designer/architect.

Copyright by designer/architect.

Plan # 731058

Dimensions: 50'4" W x 27'6" D

Levels: 1

Heated Square Footage: 1,381

Bedrooms: 3

Bathrooms: 2

Foundation: Crawl space, slab, or basement

Material Take-off Included: Yes

Price Category: B

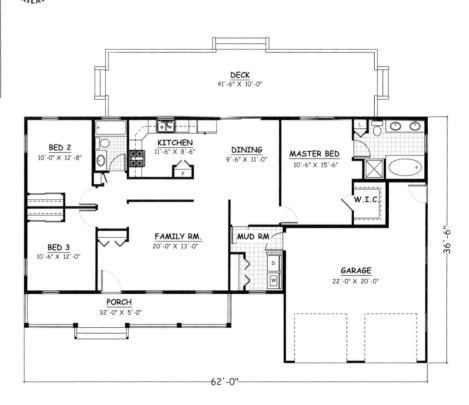

Images provided by designer/architect.

Plan # 731054

Dimensions: 62' W x 36'6" D

Levels: 1

Heated Square Footage: 1,360

Bedrooms: 3

Bathrooms: 2

Foundation: Crawl space, slab, or basement

Material Take-off Included: Yes

Price Category: B

For the family that enjoys outdoor living, this home features a charming front porch and expansive rear deck.

Features:

- Front Porch: This lovely front porch is deep enough to accommodate a small seating area.

- Family Room: Located directly off the main entrance is this gracious family room. Centrally located, this room is sure to be a place that the family will gather.

- Dining Room: Open to the kitchen, this lovely dining room features a sliding glass door leading to the expansive rear deck, ensuring many meals enjoyed outdoors.

DECK
41'-6" X 10'-0"

BED 2
10'-0" X 12'-8"

KITCHEN
11'-6" X 8'-6"

DINING
9'-6" X 11'-0"

MASTER BED
10'-6" X 15'-6"

W.I.C.

FAMILY RM.
20'-0" X 13'-0"

MUD RM

BED 3
10'-6" X 12'-0"

GARAGE
22'-0" X 20'-0"

PORCH
32'-0" X 5'-0"

36'-6"

62'-0"

Front View

Rear Elevation

Left Elevation   *Right Elevation*

- Kitchen: The family cook will certainly be pleased with the ample counter and cabinet space in this well-designed kitchen.

- Master Suite: Comfort and privacy are the main focus in this master suite, which features a large walk-in closet and a private bathroom. The bathroom boasts an oversized tub, a separate shower, and a dual-sink vanity.

- Secondary Bedrooms: Two additional nicely sized bedrooms and a full bath room round out the private areas of this home.

Garage Doors, Storm Doors & More

A garage door is a big—but necessary—investment, adding both style and interest to a home. The style, color, and condition of the door have a great influence on the overall appearance and curb appeal of the home. When shopping for a garage door you should also consider how your clients will use their garages. If it also serves as a workshop, utility room or play area, then you'll need a door with good insulating properties. Here are a few tips to help you make the right decision.

Garage Door Sizes

The first thing you must do when selecting a garage door is to determine what size door you need. Garage doors are available to fit virtually any opening. Just measure the opening, and take the measurements to your local Lowe's to get the door you need.

Garage Door Styles

Because garage doors make up such a large portion of a home's exterior, the style you choose should complement the rest of the home's exterior. Start the style selection by choosing a panel design. There are four main panel designs from which to choose:

- **Flush panels** are flat, slightly textured panels that can be used to complement the surrounding wall area without drawing too much attention to the door itself.
- **Long-raised panels** give depth and distinction to the door, while adding to the home's overall appearance.

- **Short-raised panels** also lend depth to the door. They are excellent additions to Victorian-style homes with intricately detailed trim, the symmetrical facades of colonial-style homes, or the strong architectural lines of a Tudor home.
- **Painted panels** add more pizzazz to plain, raised panels when the sloped portion of the panel is painted in a contrasting color.

Windows and window panels are another way to add style and a personal touch to a garage door. Double-paned windows allow natural light in but keep extreme seasonal temperatures out.

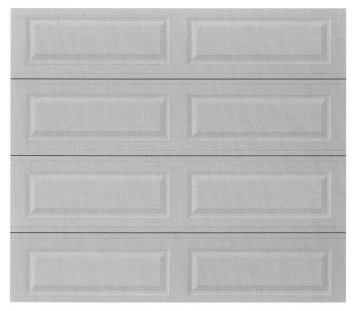

Long-raised panels

Short-raised panels

Garage-Door Construction Materials

Most garage doors are made of either wood or steel.

- **Wood doors** offer a wide variety of options. You can find anything from standard, raised-panel designs to doors that mimic the ornate styles commonly used on the carriage houses of the eighteenth and nineteenth centuries. Wood doors are also available in several species, either paint or stain grade.

- **Steel doors** are usually more economical than wood doors and are the most common type of garage door. Most manufacturers offer several colors out of the box. You can also paint the door to match the home. There are three distinct types of steel doors:

  - **Single-layer doors** are stamped from a single sheet of galvanized steel. These are usually the most economical of all steel doors.

  - **Double-layer steel doors** have a galvanized steel skin on the outside, with a thick layer of either polystyrene or polyurethane as a backer. The backer provides soundproofing and additional insulating value to the door.

  - **Triple-layer doors** are constructed of the same materials as double-layer doors, with the addition of a galvanized skin on the inside to protect the polystyrene or polyurethane from damage. The additional layer of steel makes triple-layer doors the strongest, most secure, and most soundproof of all garage doors. These are also available with thicker insulation for greater R-value (a measure of thermal resistance).

Workshop or Living Space

More and more homeowners are using their garages as extensions of their living space: as children's play areas, workshops, hobby areas, laundry rooms, and more. As the activity in the garage increases, so does the need to maintain a constant, comfortable temperature in this space.

For the attic, walls, and crawl space, you can use standard insulation techniques to increase the comfort level in your extended living space. But there is one more, often overlooked, space in a garage where you can increase insulation value and energy efficiency — the garage door. Below are some tips for choosing the right garage door if the space will be used for more than parking cars.

- **Good insulating qualities.** Look for a door with an R-value of at least 3 in moderate to temperate climates. In harsher climates, go up to an R-value of 10.

- **Weather seals between the sections.** The seal may be designed into the mating surfaces of the panels, or it may be in the form of gasket material that compresses when the door is closed.

- **A bottom seal / threshold.** If the door doesn't come with a bottom seal standard, you can always add one to keep drafts and rain out.

For a garage-workshop application, get the highest R-value you can in the door to make heating and cooling the work space easier.

Garage Storage Systems

As people spend more time in their garages, whether using them as workshops or expanded playrooms for children, the need to organize this space grows ... almost as quickly as the clutter. We can show you how to help your clients keep clutter down and even make enough room in the garage for the family car. All they will need are the right storage solutions and a little motivation.

Shelving Units

Garage shelving makes use of the space in the vertical plane and helps get stored items off the floor. Storing items vertically can save a lot of valuable floor space, increase the garage's overall storage capacity, and provide a safer, more productive work area. Garage shelving has come a long way in the past several years. Homeowners can still build their own shelves from dimensional lumber and plywood, but now they also have many other options from which to choose:

■ **Wall-mounted shelving:** Wall-mounted, heavy-duty wire shelving is now designed especially for the garage. Most wall-mounted shelves are designed to hold up to 100 pounds per linear foot of shelf. Some systems have a plastic coating that protects the shelving from the sometimes harsh garage environment and prevents rust and corrosion. The open wire construction of the shelves allows air to circulate around the stored items and helps decrease mold and mildew in moist climates. Another option: metal shelving brackets that support lumber, MDF, or plywood shelves.

■ **Freestanding shelving:** Available in wood, wire and resin, these units give the flexibility of having the shelves well away from walls. A strategically placed set of freestanding shelving units can even serve to separate a part of the garage dedicated to laundry or shop activities from other areas. Some of these shelving units are even available with locking-caster wheels that allow moving the entire unit with ease and then locking it securely in place.

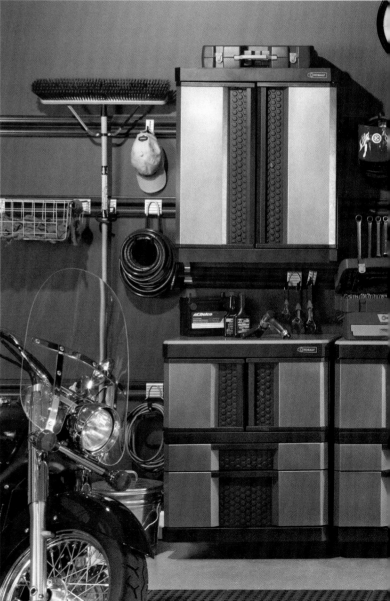

Utility Cabinets

Utility cabinets are available in resin, metal, and wood/wood composite materials. They are a convenient way to store items behind doors and out of sight. Some even offer lockable doors to keep curious little ones from accessing sharp tools or dangerous household chemicals.

Peg Hooks

Peg hooks are a time-tested and versatile method of storing items in shops and garages because they are portable. The homeowner can easily move the hooks around and adjust them as your storage needs change.

Wall-and-Rafter Hangers

There are many types of hooks and hangers available. Simply secure the hook to a wall stud or ceiling rafter and provide storage for anything from ladders and hoses to bicycles, depending on the type of hanger installed.

Storm-Door Basics

A storm door protects the exterior door from bad weather and provides ventilation. Most door manufacturers sell pre-hung doors in kits, so installation is easy. The kits include all the hardware you need to install the door, such as hinges, pneumatic closers, and latches. Choose a door based on specific requirements and the size and style of the house.

Storm doors come with varying combinations of screen and glass panels. Many have removable panels that can be changed depending on the season. Along the bottom, most doors have a sweep—one or more flexible strips designed to keep moisture, dirt, and outside air from entering your home.

If security is a concern, look for a model with protective grilles and dead-bolt locks. Certain brands of storm doors have more security features than others. Two things to look for are laminated security glass and a multipoint locking system.

Before you buy a storm door, though, be sure to check its components in the store. Open and close the door to make sure the hinges and latches operate smoothly. For long life, the components should be of the highest quality you can afford.

Fitting a Storm Door

Most storm-door units can be adjusted slightly to fit into a door frame. The parameters for this adjustment vary by manufacturer, so ask a millwork associate at your local Lowe's for help in determining the best size door for you.

Measure the height and width of your door frame care-

fully before you visit the store so you will have the information needed to find the correct door size. Measure the space between the exterior brick-mold trim pieces, not the inner doorjamb.

If the opening is too big for a standard door, you can install a Z-bar extender—a device that fills in the extra space between the door and frame. Some homeowners find the look unappealing. An alternative is to order custom doors, which can be made to fit any size.

Before installing the door, inspect the wood jamb and trim around the door opening to make sure it is secure and will support the weight of the storm door. Use a level to make sure the door frame is square. If it is not, use shims—pieces of wood or aluminum—to ensure a correct fit. A Z-bar extender can also be used to square an opening.

Storm-Door Screens and Panels

If the storm door is exposed to direct sun, the owner should change over to screens early in the spring and wait until the end of fall before putting the glass panels back on. The panels can act like a greenhouse, heating up the space between the two doors and causing weatherstripping to deteriorate quickly. In extreme cases, the heat could warp metal house doors.

When choosing metal replacement screens, check with your dealer about the compatibility of the metal screens you want to buy with the metal of the door. In some cases, different metals in contact with each other will hasten corrosion.

- Screens made of **galvanized steel** are the least expensive and are highly resistant to holes and tears. But the galvanized coating can wear off. A spray of household lubricant once a year helps prevent rust.
- **Aluminum screens** resist corrosion, except in seaside areas, but are not as strong as galvanized steel. In areas with a lot of smog, aluminum tends to darken. Aluminum screens can be protected with commercial spray products.
- **Bronze screens** are the most durable but also the most expensive. Use a thin coat of varnish to protect the screen against corrosion. Renew the coating every few years by painting or spraying with thinned varnish.
- **Fiberglass screens** resist corrosion and are easy to install, making them a practical replacement screen if a metal screen deteriorates.

Storm-Door Closers and Door Stops

Most storm doors come with either a door closer or a door stop—both devices control how far your door will open.

- A **door stop,** also called a snubber, uses a chain attached to a spring to control the door. It is easy to install and adjust.
- A **pneumatic closer** not only prevents a door from opening too fast or too far but also closes the door slowly and firmly. A sliding washer can hold the door open—a handy feature when you are carrying packages. Most doors have one pneumatic closer, but some have two for extra protection against high winds. You can add a second closer if necessary.

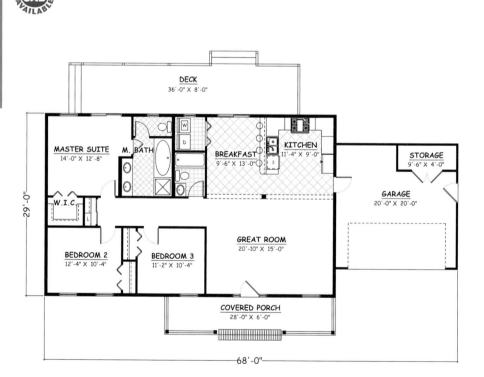

Plan # 731048

Dimensions: 68' W x 29' D

Levels: 1

Heated Square Footage: 1,392

Bedrooms: 3

Bathrooms: 2

Foundation: Crawl space, slab, or basement

Material Take-off Included: Yes

Price Category: B

CAD FILE AVAILABLE · CAD ·

Thoughtful design will ensure comfortable family living in this spacious country-style home.

Features:

- Front Porch: This delightful front porch invites you to sit and enjoy a beautiful summer evening.

- Great Room: Generous in its size, this great room is the perfect place for the family to gather.

- Kitchen: Connected to the breakfast room by a snack bar and located directly off the great room, this kitchen is ideal for family meals or festive dinner parties.

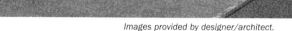

DECK
36'-0" X 8'-0"

MASTER SUITE
14'-0" X 12'-8"

M. BATH

BREAKFAST
9'-6" X 13'-0"

KITCHEN
11'-4" X 9'-0"

STORAGE
9'-6" X 4'-0"

GARAGE
20'-0" X 20'-0"

W.I.C.

29'-0"

BEDROOM 2
12'-4" X 10'-4"

BEDROOM 3
11'-2" X 10'-4"

GREAT ROOM
20'-10" X 15'-0"

COVERED PORCH
28'-0" X 6'-0"

68'-0"

Copyright by designer/architect.

Front View

Rear Elevation

Left Elevation

Right Elevation

- Rear Deck: Outdoor entertaining will surely occur quite frequently with this expansive rear deck, which can be reached through patio doors leading from the master bedroom or the breakfast room.

- Master Suite: A comfortable retreat, this master suite features such amenities as a large walk-in closet, a spalike master bathroom, and a

beautiful patio door that connects to the rear deck. The private bathroom features a whirlpool tub, a separate shower, and a private toilet room.

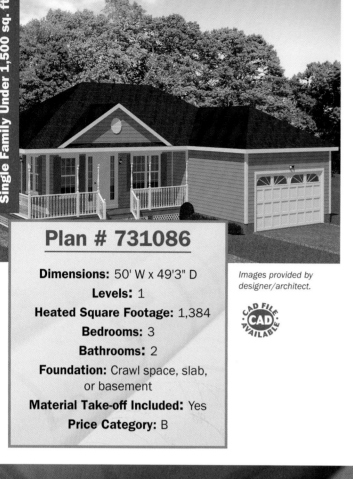

Plan # 731086

Dimensions: 50' W x 49'3" D

Levels: 1

Heated Square Footage: 1,384

Bedrooms: 3

Bathrooms: 2

Foundation: Crawl space, slab, or basement

Material Take-off Included: Yes

Price Category: B

Images provided by designer/architect.

CAD FILE AVAILABLE

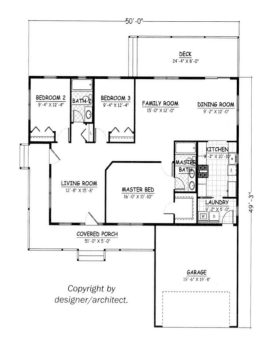

Copyright by designer/architect.

Plan # 731005

Dimensions: 67'5" W x 38'3" D

Levels: 1

Heated Square Footage: 1,396

Bedrooms: 3

Bathrooms: 2½

Foundation: Crawl space, slab, or basement

Material Take-off Included: Yes

Price Category: B

Images provided by designer/architect.

CAD FILE AVAILABLE

Copyright by designer/architect.

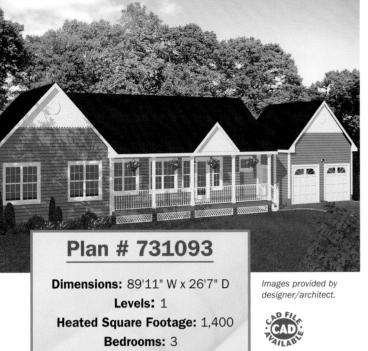

Plan # 731093

Dimensions: 89'11" W x 26'7" D

Levels: 1

Heated Square Footage: 1,400

Bedrooms: 3

Bathrooms: 2½

Foundation: Crawl space, slab, or basement

Material Take-off Included: Yes

Price Category: B

Images provided by designer/architect.

Copyright by designer/architect.

Plan # 731065

Dimensions: 51' W x 47' D

Levels: 1

Heated Square Footage: 1,419

Bedrooms: 3

Bathrooms: 2½

Foundation: Crawl space, slab, or basement

Material Take-off Included: Yes

Price Category: B

Images provided by designer/architect.

Copyright by designer/architect.

Plan # 731023

Dimensions: 59'5" W x 52' D

Levels: 1

Heated Square Footage: 1,430

Bedrooms: 3

Bathrooms: 2

Foundation: Crawl space, slab, or basement

Material Take-off Included: Yes

Price Category: B

Images provided by designer/architect.

Copyright by designer/architect.

Plan # 731049

Dimensions: 47'7" W x 35'4" D

Levels: 1

Heated Square Footage: 1,438

Bedrooms: 3

Bathrooms: 2

Foundation: Crawl space, slab, or basement

Material Take-off Included: Yes

Price Category: B

Images provided by designer/architect.

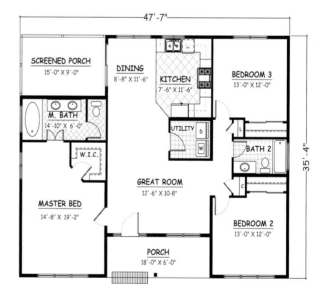

Copyright by designer/architect.

Images provided by designer/architect.

Copyright by designer/architect.

Plan # 731009

Dimensions: 57'6" W x 28' D

Levels: 1

Heated Square Footage: 1,452

Bedrooms: 3

Bathrooms: 2

Foundation: Crawl space, slab, or basement

Material Take-off Included: Yes

Price Category: B

Plan # 731084

Dimensions: 53'8" W x 53'4" D

Levels: 1

Heated Square Footage: 1,498

Bedrooms: 3

Bathrooms: 2

Foundation: Crawl space, slab, or basement

Material Take-off Included: Yes

Price Category: B

Images provided by designer/architect.

Copyright by designer/architect.

Plan # 731077

Dimensions: 56' W x 43'6" D

Levels: 1

Heated Square Footage: 1,386

Bedrooms: 3

Bathrooms: 2

Foundation: Crawl space, slab, or basement

Material Take-off Included: Yes

Price Category: B

This lovely ranch home is designed with plenty of open space for entertaining or relaxing.

CAD FILE AVAILABLE

Features:

- Entry Porch: A small entry porch is the perfect spot to welcome guests into the home.

- Living Room: From the entry door, step into this lovely living room, which is open to the dining room and welcomes both friends and family inside.

- Dining Room: Open to the living room and the kitchen, and featuring a sliding glass door leading to a moderately sized deck, this dining room is sure to be the host to family dinners as well as festive parties.

Images provided by designer/architect.

- Kitchen: Open to the dining room, this tidy kitchen features a large pantry for additional appliance and food storage.

- Master Suite: Set apart from secondary bedrooms in the home is this grand master suite, which features a private bathroom.

Rear View

Copyright by designer/architect.

Images provided by designer/architect.

Plan # 731056

Dimensions: 60'8" W x 36' D

Levels: 1

Heated Square Footage: 1,480

Bedrooms: 3

Bathrooms: 2

Foundation: Crawl space, slab, or basement

Material Take-off Included: Yes

Price Category: B

This ranch-style home is designed with wonderful amenities that will surely be appreciated.

Features:

- Front Porch: This entry porch features turned columns adding grace and charm to the home.

- Living Room: From the entry porch, step into this open and airy living room. The room is centrally located and open to both the dining room and the kitchen—sure to make it the gathering spot for all.

- Kitchen: Featuring a large center island, this L-shaped kitchen is a cook's dream. It is open to both the living room and the dining room, allowing interaction between the cook and the family during mealtime preparations.

- Master Suite: Set apart from the additional bedrooms in the home is this spacious master suite. The suite features a walk-in closet and a private bathroom, providing additional comfort and privacy.

- Secondary Bedrooms: Finishing out the private areas of the home are two additional bedrooms and a full bathroom.

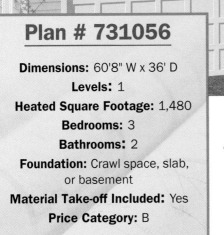

Copyright by designer/architect.

Images provided by designer/architect.

Plan # 731059

Dimensions: 64'5" W x 28' D

Levels: 1

Heated Square Footage: 1,392

Bedrooms: 3

Bathrooms: 2

Foundation: Crawl space, slab, or basement

Material Take-off Included: Yes

Price Category: B

Country charm is everywhere in this lovely ranch home.

CAD FILE AVAILABLE

Features:

- Front Porch: Spanning the length of the home is this beautiful front porch. The porch is wide enough to allow for a seating area and planters, making it a wonderful spot to sit on a warm summer's night.

- Dining Room: Open to the kitchen and featuring a sliding glass door that opens to a large rear deck, this lovely dining room will make the decision to dine indoors or outdoors a tough one.

- Kitchen: Featuring a countertop eating area that will allow for interaction during the preparation of meals and a large pantry, this kitchen is certain to please the family chef.

- Master Suite: With features such as a large closet and a private bathroom, this master suite will provide you with the perfect place to relax after a long day. The bathroom features a full-size tub and dual vanities, adding to the privacy and comfort of the suite.

- Secondary Bedrooms: Two secondary bedrooms and a full bathroom round out the home. One of the secondary bedrooms features a set of sliding glass doors leading onto the rear deck, providing abundant natural light.

Copyright by designer/architect.

Images provided by designer/architect.

Plan # 731057

Dimensions: 59'7" W x 31'2" D

Levels: 1

Heated Square Footage: 1,453

Bedrooms: 3

Bathrooms: 2

Foundation: Crawl space, slab, or basement

Material Take-off Included: Yes

Price Category: B

With its fluid design, this modestly sized ranch home includes a front porch and rear deck.

CAD FILE AVAILABLE

Features:

- Front Porch: This entry porch features turned columns that give the home a country feel.

- Living Room: Open to the dining area, this spacious living room will be the place that family will congregate and guests will gather.

- Kitchen: This kitchen is open to the living room and dining room, which will allow family members and guests to interact with the family chef during meal preparations.

- Master Suite: : A large walk-in closet and a private bathroom help to make this gracious master suite a welcome retreat after a long day. The bathroom features such amenities as a dual-sink vanity, an oversized tub, a separate shower, and a private toilet room.

- Secondary Bedrooms: Private areas of the home are made complete with two additional bedrooms and a full bathroom.

Copyright by designer/architect.

Images provided by designer/architect.

Plan # 731015

Dimensions: 42'8" W x 42'1" D

Levels: 1

Heated Square Footage: 1,500

Bedrooms: 3

Bathrooms: 2

Foundation: Crawl space, slab, or basement

Material Take-off Included: Yes

Price Category: C

This ranch home features front and rear covered patios, ensuring many afternoons and evenings will be spent outdoors. The simple lines and thoughtful design of this home make it affordable to build.

Features:

- Kitchen: This galley-style kitchen features an abundance of counter and cabinet space. A utility room containing the washer and dryer connects to the kitchen.

- Breakfast Nook: This breakfast nook is a cozy space to enjoy everyday family meals. It is open to the kitchen and the living room and opens into the back porch.

- Master Suite: Privacy and comfort are ensured in this lovely master suite, which features a large walk-in closet and a private bathroom.

- Secondary Bedrooms: Rounding out the home are two more moderately sized bedrooms and a full bathroom.

Copyright by designer/architect.

Images provided by designer/architect.

Plan # 731019

Dimensions: 47'8" W x 50' D

Levels: 1

Heated Square Footage: 1,520

Bedrooms: 3

Bathrooms: 2

Foundation: Crawl space, slab, or basement

Material Take-off Included: Yes

Price Category: C

An entry porch and an expansive rear deck are some of the features this home has to offer. The home is thoughtfully designed so that spans used will be simple, making the cost to build highly manageable.

Features:

- Covered Porch: This simple covered entry porch provides a lovely transition from the outside.

- Family Room: Step from the foyer into this family room. The room is located at the center of the home—sure to make it the main family gathering space.

- Kitchen: The L-shaped layout of this kitchen keeps the traffic flowing. An abundance of counter space makes meal prep easy and more enjoyable.

- Master Suite: This spacious master suite features a walk-in closet and private bath. The bath helps to provide comfort and a bit of privacy.

- Secondary Bedrooms: The home is made complete with full bathroom and an additional two bedrooms.

Copyright by designer/architect.

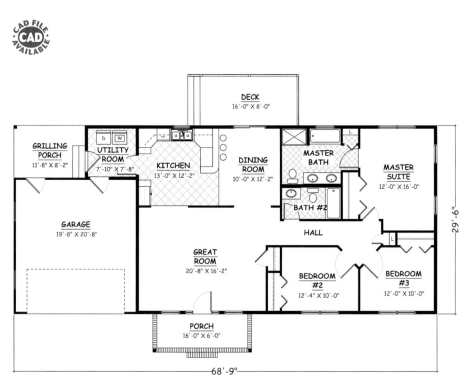

Images provided by designer/architect.

Plan # 731052

Dimensions: 68'9" W x 29'6" D

Levels: 1

Heated Square Footage: 1,508

Bedrooms: 3

Bathrooms: 2

Foundation: Crawl space, slab, or basement

Material Take-off Included: Yes

Price Category: C

The roof line of this gracious home gives it a welcoming and traditional feel.

Features:

- Dining Room: This dining room is open to the kitchen and great room, and features a sliding glass door leading to a large rear deck, giving it a more formal atmosphere.

- Kitchen: This kitchen will surely please the family cook with its open feel and abundance of counter space. Weekday breakfast or afternoon snacks can be enjoyed at the countertop seating area.

Copyright by designer/architect.

DECK
16'-0" X 8'-0"

GRILLING PORCH
11'-8" X 8'-2"

UTILITY ROOM
7'-10" X 7'-8"

KITCHEN
13'-0" X 12'-2"

DINING ROOM
10'-0" X 12'-2"

MASTER BATH

MASTER SUITE
12'-0" X 16'-0"

BATH #2

GARAGE
19'-8" X 20'-8"

GREAT ROOM
20'-8" X 16'-2"

HALL

BEDROOM #2
12'-4" X 10'-0"

BEDROOM #3
12'-0" X 10'-0"

PORCH
16'-0" X 6'-0"

29'-6"

68'-9"

Rear Elevation

Left Elevation

Right Elevation

- Utility Room: The multitasking that is often required with today's active family lifestyle is made much easier with this utility room, which is located directly off of the kitchen.

- Grilling Porch/Rear Deck: Dining outdoors will be a common occurrence, with this covered grilling porch located off the kitchen area and the expansive rear deck connected to the dining room.

- Master Suite: This master suite features its own bathroom, which houses a tub, a separate shower, and a dual-sink vanity, adding additional comfort to an already delightful space.

Plan # 731007

Dimensions: 50'6" W x 35'4" D

Levels: 1

Heated Square Footage: 1,526

Bedrooms: 3

Bathrooms: 2

Foundation: Crawl space, slab, or basement

Material Take-off Included: Yes

Price Category: C

This traditional-design home exhibits style and versatility packed into a simple, affordable design.

Features:

- Front Porch: Brick accents and stately columns grace this lovely front entry porch. The porch is wide enough to fit a small sitting area or perhaps some planters, providing additional charm to the home.

- Great Room: Step through the front door into this spacious and grand great room. Centrally located, the great room is sure to be the perfect area for the family to gather.

- Kitchen: Cooking will be a pleasure for all in this wonderfully designed U-shaped kitchen, which is open to the dining room.

Images provided by designer/architect.

Copyright by designer/architect.

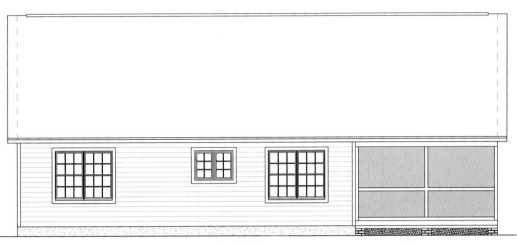

Rear Elevation

Left Elevation

Right Elevation

- Screened Porch: Step through sliding glass doors from the dining room into this generously sized screened porch. The porch provides you with a beautiful place to dine and relax on a warm summer night.

- Master Suite: Relaxation and privacy abound in this lovely master suite. The room features a triple-window unit, providing lots of natural light, a large walk-in closet, and a private bath. The bath houses a sunlit whirlpool tub, dual vanity, and separate toilet room.

- Secondary Bedrooms: Rounding out the home are two additional bedrooms and a second full bathroom.

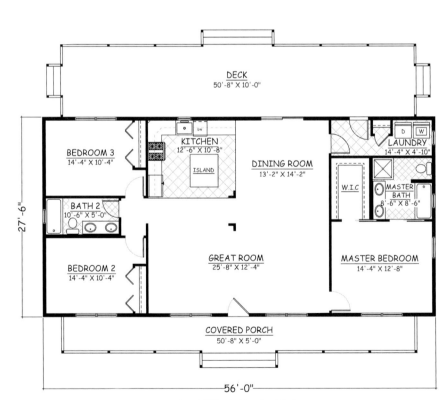

Plan # 731033

Dimensions: 56' W x 27'6" D

Levels: 1

Heated Square Footage: 1,538

Bedrooms: 3

Bathrooms: 2

Foundation: Crawl space, slab, or basement

Material Take-off Included: Yes

Price Category: C

Images provided by designer/architect.

With a front porch and dormers, this ranch home is given a bit of country charm.

CAD FILE AVAILABLE · CAD

Features:

- **Front Porch:** This delightful front porch with turned posts and a decorative railing is the perfect spot to sit on a warm summer evening.

- **Great Room:** From the front porch, step directly into this grand great room. The room is open to both the kitchen and the dining room, allowing for a seamless transition from one area to the next.

DECK
50'-8" X 10'-0"

BEDROOM 3
14'-4" X 10'-4"

KITCHEN
12'-6" X 10'-8"

ISLAND

DINING ROOM
13'-2" X 14'-2"

LAUNDRY
14'-4" X 4'-10"

W.I.C

MASTER BATH
8'-6" X 8'-6"

BATH 2
10'-6" X 5'-0"

BEDROOM 2
14'-4" X 10'-4"

GREAT ROOM
25'-8" X 12'-4"

MASTER BEDROOM
14'-4" X 12'-8"

COVERED PORCH
50'-8" X 5'-0"

27'-6"

56'-0"

Copyright by designer/architect.

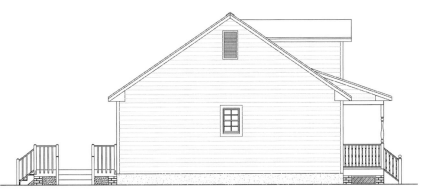

Rear Elevation

Left Elevation

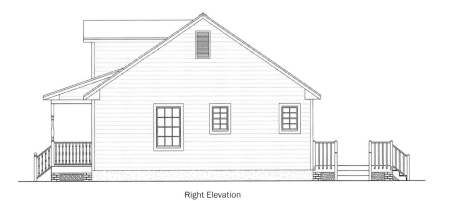

Right Elevation

- Kitchen: Equipped with modern conveniences and a center island, preparing meals in this lovely kitchen is sure to be a joy. The room is open to both the great room and the dining room, providing for interaction between the chef and family members.

- Master Suite: Tucked away from the secondary bedrooms in the home is this generously sized master suite. The suite features a large walk-in closet and a private bathroom, thus providing you with the perfect place to relax after a long day. The bathroom features a

tub, a separate shower, and dual vanities, adding to the privacy and comfort of the suite.

- Secondary Bedrooms: Along with a full bathroom there are two additional bedrooms in the home.

Images provided by designer/architect.

CAD FILE AVAILABLE

Plan # 731003

Dimensions: 44'10" W x 42'6" D

Levels: 1

Heated Square Footage: 1,540

Bedrooms: 3

Bathrooms: 2

Foundation: Crawl space, slab, or basement

Material Take-off Included: Yes

Price Category: C

Copyright by designer/architect.

Images provided by designer/architect.

CAD FILE AVAILABLE

Plan # 731072

Dimensions: 65' W x 40' D

Levels: 1

Heated Square Footage: 1,554

Bedrooms: 3

Bathrooms: 2

Foundation: Crawl space, slab, or basement

Material Take-off Included: Yes

Price Category: C

Copyright by designer/architect.

Plan # 731017

Dimensions: 66'11" W x 36'6" D

Levels: 1

Heated Square Footage: 1,564

Bedrooms: 3

Bathrooms: 2

Foundation: Crawl space, slab, or basement

Material Take-off Included: Yes

Price Category: C

Images provided by designer/architect.

CAD FILE AVAILABLE

Copyright by designer/architect.

Plan # 731013

Dimensions: 73'10" W x 44' D

Levels: 1

Heated Square Footage: 1,593

Bedrooms: 3

Bathrooms: 2½

Foundation: Crawl space, slab, or basement

Material Take-off Included: Yes

Price Category: C

Images provided by designer/architect.

CAD FILE AVAILABLE

Copyright by designer/architect.

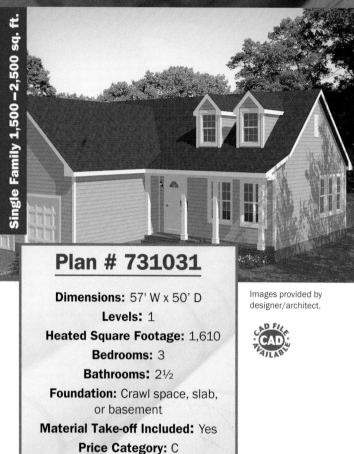

Plan # 731031

Dimensions: 57' W x 50' D

Levels: 1

Heated Square Footage: 1,610

Bedrooms: 3

Bathrooms: 2½

Foundation: Crawl space, slab, or basement

Material Take-off Included: Yes

Price Category: C

Images provided by designer/architect.

CAD FILE AVAILABLE

Copyright by designer/architect.

Plan # 731025

Dimensions: 57'1" W x 47' D

Levels: 1

Heated Square Footage: 1,614

Bedrooms: 3

Bathrooms: 2

Foundation: Crawl space, slab, or basement

Material Take-off Included: Yes

Price Category: C

Images provided by designer/architect.

CAD FILE AVAILABLE

Copyright by designer/architect.

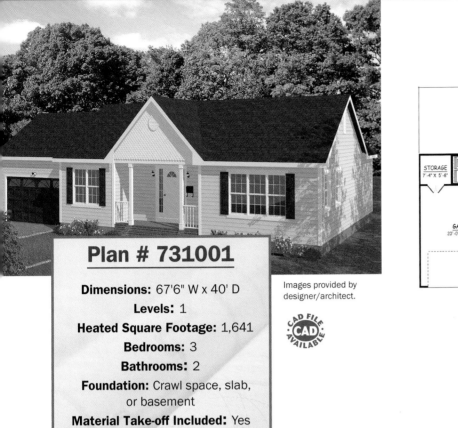

Images provided by designer/architect.

Copyright by designer/architect.

Plan # 731001

Dimensions: 67'6" W x 40' D

Levels: 1

Heated Square Footage: 1,641

Bedrooms: 3

Bathrooms: 2

Foundation: Crawl space, slab, or basement

Material Take-off Included: Yes

Price Category: C

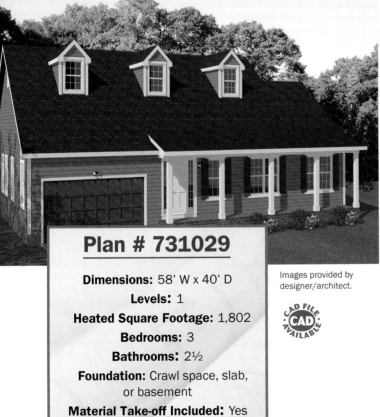

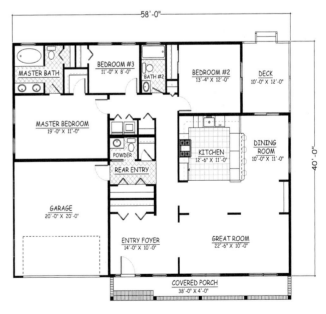

Images provided by designer/architect.

Copyright by designer/architect.

Plan # 731029

Dimensions: 58' W x 40' D

Levels: 1

Heated Square Footage: 1,802

Bedrooms: 3

Bathrooms: 2½

Foundation: Crawl space, slab, or basement

Material Take-off Included: Yes

Price Category: D

Plan # 731038

Dimensions: 62' W x 39' D

Levels: 1

Heated Square Footage: 1,704

Bedrooms: 3

Bathrooms: 2½

Foundation: Crawl space, slab, or basement

Material Take-off Included: Yes

Price Category: C

Images provided by designer/architect.

A wraparound porch and small gabled dormers give this home all of the charm of an old-fashioned country farmhouse.

CAD FILE AVAILABLE

Features:

- Front Porch: This expansive wraparound porch gives added charm to the home while providing a relaxing place to sit and enjoy the outdoors. French doors off the porch lead to two of the bedrooms.

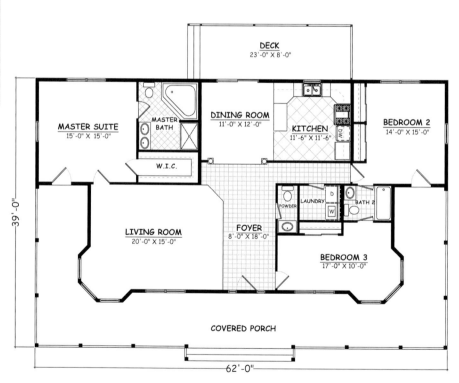

Copyright by designer/architect.

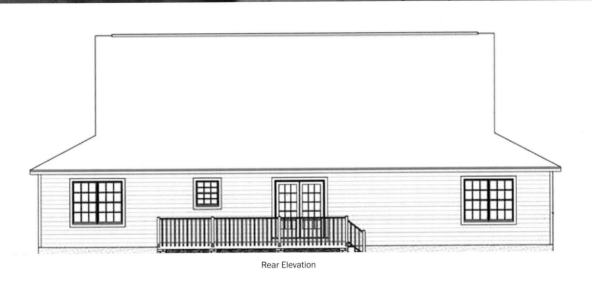

Rear Elevation

Left Elevation

Right Elevation

- Living Room: A bay-window area bathes this room in natural light. An open floor plan and generous dimensions will make this room a gathering place for the entire family.

- Kitchen: Cooking will be a pleasure in this well-designed kitchen, which features a snack bar for informal meals.

- Master Suite: This stylish master suite features a large walk-in closet and a private bathroom with a corner whirlpool tub. A French door leads out to the porch, inviting the outdoors inside.

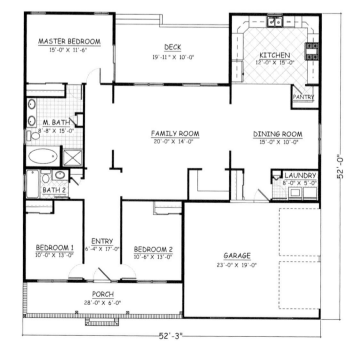

Images provided by designer/architect.

Plan # 731021

Dimensions: 52'3" W x 52' D

Levels: 1

Heated Square Footage: 1,840

Bedrooms: 3

Bathrooms: 2

Foundation: Crawl space, slab, or basement

Material Take-off Included: Yes

Price Category: D

This home's front porch and rear deck create plentiful outdoor living space.

Features:

- **Front Porch:** The turned columns and decorative porch railing provide added charm to this front entry porch.

- **Family Room:** All will flock to this grand family room, which is open to the dining room and kitchen and features a set of sliding glass doors leading to an expansive rear deck.

- **Dining Room:** The whole family will enjoy both formal and informal meals in this lovely dining room, which is open to both the kitchen and the family room.

- **Kitchen:** This U-shaped kitchen features an abundance of counter space

and numerous cabinets certain to please the family chef. A good-size pantry offers you more space for food storage.

- **Master Suite:** Situated apart from the other bedrooms in the home is this generously sized master suite. The

room features sliding glass doors leading to the outdoor deck, as well as a private bathroom. The bathroom houses an oversize tub, a separate shower, and a private toilet room, providing additional comfort.

Copyright by designer/architect.

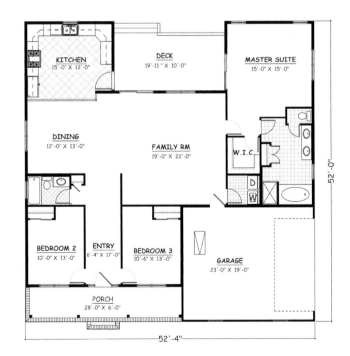

Images provided by designer/architect.

Plan # 731040

Dimensions: 52'4" W x 52' D

Levels: 1

Heated Square Footage: 1,840

Bedrooms: 3

Bathrooms: 2

Foundation: Crawl space, slab, or basement

Material Take-off Included: Yes

Price Category: D

This home features numerous amenities sure to make a homeowner happy.

Features:

- Front Porch: Turned columns and a decorative rail add charm to the entry porch, welcoming all home.

- Dining Room: A set of double windows gives this generously sized dining room an open and airy feeling.

- Kitchen: Meal prep will be made easy in this kitchen featuring expansive countertops and numerous cabinets. Step through the hinged French door and onto a large deck for outdoor dining.

- Family Room: This wonderfully sized family room has large windows and patio door, making it a central gathering spot for all.

- Master Suite: Generous in its size, this master suite features sliding glass doors leading to the outdoor deck, as well as a private bathroom. The bathroom houses an oversize tub, a separate shower, and a toilet room, adding comfort and privacy.

Plan # 731067

Dimensions: 56' W x 32' D

Levels: 2

Heated Square Footage: 1,841

Main Level Sq. Ft.: 1,050

Upper Level Sq. Ft.: 791

Bedrooms: 4

Bathrooms: 3

Foundation: Crawl space, slab, or basement

Material Take-off Included: Yes

Price Category: D

Images provided by designer/architect.

This home has such lovely features as a wraparound porch, multiple gables, and a half-circle-topped window.

CAD FILE AVAILABLE

Features:

- Porch: This wraparound covered porch graces the front of the home and is sure to become one of the family's favorite spots to gather on warm summer evenings.

- Dining Room: Enjoy family Sunday dinner or a formal dinner party in this warm and inviting dining room, which is open to both the foyer and living room.

- Kitchen: This wonderfully large kitchen provides the family chef with lots of cabinet and counter space, making cooking a joy. Open to the living room,

the kitchen also features a snack bar, which is perfect for informal meals or an after-school snack.

- Guest Bedroom: This moderately sized guest bedroom gives your friends and family a private place all to their own during while visiting.

- Master Suite: Luxury abounds in this master suite, which houses its own

bathroom, sitting area and large walk-in closet. The bathroom features a private toilet room, dual-sink vanities, and a whirlpool tub.

- Upper Level: Along with the master suite, the upper level of this home features an additional two bedrooms and full bathroom.

Upper Level Floor Plan

Main Level Floor Plan

Copyright by designer/architect.

Images provided by designer/architect.

Plan # 731070

Dimensions: 54' W x 48' D

Levels: 1

Heated Square Footage: 1,870

Bedrooms: 3

Bathrooms: 2

Foundation: Crawl space, slab, or basement

Material Take-off Included: Yes

Price Category: D

This home is filled with amenities that everyone in the family will love.

Features:

- Great Room: Step through the front entry door and directly into the heart of the home. This expansive great room brings you straight through the home from front to back, where a sliding glass door leads you to the backyard.

- Kitchen: A center island provides this L-shaped kitchen with additional counter space. Located adjacent to this spacious kitchen is a bright and airy breakfast nook.

- Rear Porch: Perfect for outdoor entertaining, this moderately sized rear covered porch is easily reached through the sliding glass door in the great room.

- Master Suite: Escape the everyday in this grand master suite. With his and her walk-in closets and a private bathroom with large tub, separate shower, and dual-sink vanity, this suite will provide all the respite you need after a long day. Added details such as a tray ceiling only continue to enhance this wonderful space.

- Secondary Bedrooms: An additional two modestly sized bedrooms along with a full bathroom help to round out the house.

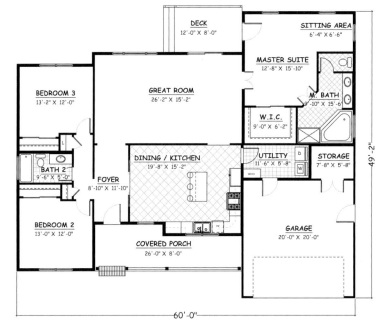

Images provided by designer/architect.

Plan # 731066

Dimensions: 60 W x 49'2" D

Levels: 1

Heated Square Footage: 1,878

Bedrooms: 3

Bathrooms: 2

Foundation: Crawl space, slab, or basement

Material Take-off Included: Yes

Price Category: D

This comfortable home is thoughtfully designed with plenty of both social and private areas.

Features:

- **Front Porch:** This expansive front-entry porch will not only offer you shelter from the elements but also provide you with an area to relax after dinner.

- **Kitchen:** This thoughtfully designed kitchen, open to the dining room, has plenty of cabinet and counter space, which is sure to delight the family cook. The dual sink will make cleanup even easier.

- **Master Suite:** After a long day, you can unwind in this lovely master suite, which features a large walk-in closet and a private bathroom. The bath boasts a whirlpool tub and a dual-sink vanity, adding both comfort and privacy.

- **Secondary Bedrooms:** Flanking the spacious foyer are an additional two bedrooms and a full bathroom.

Copyright by designer/architect.

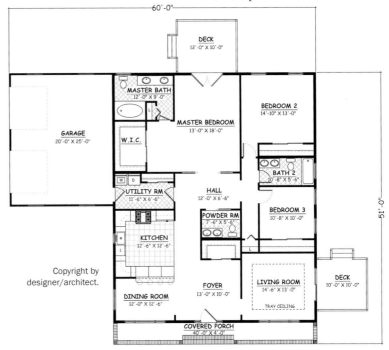

Images provided by designer/architect.

Plan # 731092

Dimensions: 60' W x 47' D

Levels: 1

Heated Square Footage: 1,880

Bedrooms: 3

Bathrooms: 2½

Foundation: Crawl space, slab, or basement

Material Take-off Included: Yes

Price Category: D

A large front porch with stately columns welcomes family and friends to this home.

Features:

- Foyer: From the front porch, step into this open foyer, which connects you to both the living room and the dining room.

- Living Room: This beautiful living room is a wonderful space for entertaining guests. The room has a large picture window, providing lots of natural light, and a tray ceiling, giving the room a touch of elegance. Enhancing the space even more is a sliding glass door that leads to the rear deck, perfect for enjoying a warm summer's evening.

- Kitchen: This kitchen features numerous cabinets, as well as ample counter space, sure to please the family cook. This spacious kitchen is also connected to the dining room by a counter-top seating area, encouraging extra family time during meal preparations.

- Master Suite: You will feel immediately relaxed when you step through the dual pocket doors into this grand master suite. The suite features amenities such as a private bathroom, a large walk-in closet, and French doors that open onto a private deck.

Copyright by designer/architect.

DECK 12'-0" X 10'-0"

MASTER BATH 12'-0" X 9'-0"

GARAGE 20'-0" X 25'-0"

W.I.C.

MASTER BEDROOM 13'-0" X 18'-0"

BEDROOM 2 14'-10" X 13'-0"

UTILITY RM 11'-6" X 6'-6"

HALL 12'-0" X 6'-6"

BATH 2 10'-8" X 5'-6"

POWDER RM 7'-6" X 5'-6"

BEDROOM 3 10'-8" X 10'-0"

KITCHEN 12'-6" X 12'-6"

FOYER 13'-0" X 10'-0"

LIVING ROOM 14'-6" X 13'-0"

TRAY CEILING

DECK 10'-0" X 10'-0"

DINING ROOM 12'-0" X 12'-6"

COVERED PORCH 40'-0" X 4'-0"

60'-0"

51'-0"

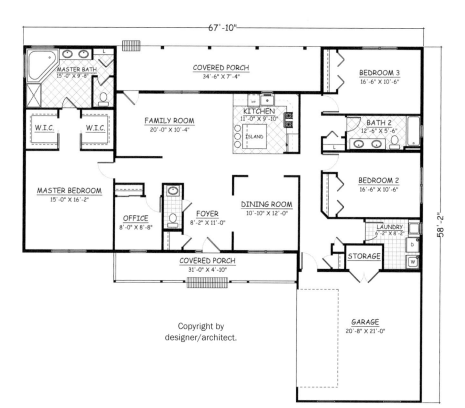

Images provided by designer/architect.

Plan # 731044

Dimensions: 67'10" W x 58'2" D

Levels: 1

Heated Square Footage: 1,975

Bedrooms: 3

Bathrooms: 2½

Foundation: Crawl space, slab, or basement

Material Take-off Included: Yes

Price Category: D

This thoughtfully designed ranch home, with a country-style front porch, welcomes friends and family.

Features:

- **Entry Foyer:** This spacious foyer, open to the formal dining room, immediately makes you feel welcome.

- **Formal Dining Room:** Directly off the foyer and located across from the kitchen, this lovely formal dining room will surely host many family gatherings.

Copyright by designer/architect.

Rear Elevation

Left Elevation

Right Elevation

- Kitchen: This kitchen features a center island that adds not only additional counter space but also an area for informal eating, making it a delight for any chef.

- Master Suite: This master suite features two walk-in closets, as well as a private bathroom. The private bathroom includes a separate shower, a private toilet room, a dual-sink vanity, and a luxurious soaking tub. The master suite is also set apart from the secondary bedrooms in the home giving it an sdditional feeling of privacy.

- Office: Located just off foyer, this office provides quiet and privacy for doing household finances or home work.

Kitchen Cabinet Buying Guide

Creating the kitchen is one of the biggest and most exciting projects a builder can undertake. The choices and decisions may seem endless, but the possibilities and the payoff are immense. The new family will love cooking and eating together in a new space. And best of all, kitchen installation offers one of the highest return-on-investment results of any project. Start the kitchen planning with this buying guide to get an idea of what choices await you.

Kitchen Cabinets

The starting point for every kitchen, the bone structure of the room, is its cabinetry. Kitchen cabinets can be arranged to meet specific needs, whether you're building for a wine collector, a pastry chef, or a family of nine. Numerous specialty cabinets and accessories are available to fit just about any specific situation.

The first decision to make about cabinetry is which type will work best for this project. Kitchen cabinets are available in three levels of specialization and price:

Stock cabinets come in standard sizes and shapes, and they are usually available to take home from the store the same day or just a few days later. Sizes and styles are limited with stock cabinetry, but the price is right for builders on a budget.

Semicustom cabinets are built after your order is placed, so you can choose from certain sizes and styles. That flexibility makes it easier to design a kitchen that fits your particular requirements. Semicustom cabinetry usually requires a longer lead time for delivery than stock. They are more expensive than stock cabinets.

Custom cabinets are made by hand to fit almost any standard you require. An odd-sized or irregular-shaped space in the kitchen might not accommodate a stock or semicustom piece, but a custom cabinetmaker starting from scratch can build nearly anything you need. Custom cabinets are the most expensive of the three types; the exact price varies widely because of size, materials, and options. The time it takes to receive a custom-cabinet order depends on the cabinetmaker's schedule.

The starting point for every kitchen is its cabinetry.

Cabinet Hardware

Cabinet hardware provides the visual punch to dress up the look of the kitchen after you've chosen the new cabinets. The hardware is stylish and functional, and it's easy to find something to match almost any desired look. You can choose everything from the finish of the hardware to the style that suits the kitchen design.

Some cabinet hardware is made specifically to work with the principles of universal design, which aims to make living and working spaces more accessible to people with limited physical abilities.

Countertops

Once you make all the cabinetry decisions, select a countertop to complete the look of the kitchen. Countertops are available in various materials and price ranges, and the best configuration for the kitchen may involve more than one type of countertop material.

Select cabinet hardware to match the cabinet style.

Cabinet Hardware Finishes

When choosing the finish for hardware, you may be tempted to select the latest trend. Before making your decision, think about what style will look best in this home.

If the style is **traditional,** brushed finishes, polished brass, nickel or pewter will complement the decor. If the decor is more **contemporary,** choose finishes with an enameled or choose high-gloss-metal shine or theme hardware to blend with the overall look of the kitchen. Knobs, pulls, and hinges are available in various colors, metals, and finishes:

- Antique copper
- Polished chrome
- Polished, sterling, or antique brass
- Nickel
- Aged bronze
- Ceramics (knobs and pulls only)
- Iron

GOOD IDEA: select good-quality hardware to give the kitchen an upscale look.

Cabinet Knobs and Pulls

You've picked the perfect cabinets and now you're ready to choose cabinet hardware. Many decorative styles of hinges, knobs, and pulls are available, and choosing can be a tough task. Here is all the information you need to make the right decision.

Knobs and pulls are available in various finishes. They are the most visible of cabinet hardware and can help define the look of cabinets.

- **Knobs** are handles mounted to doors or drawers with a single screw and bolt. Some knobs have screws built in and are easier to install than ones with separate screws. Knobs can be combined with a backplate or used alone. Knobs range from ¾ inch to 2 inches in diameter.
- **Pulls** serve the same function as knobs but occupy more space. Therefore, pulls greatly impact the appearance of a cabinet. Pulls can be combined with a backplate or used alone and are usually attached using two screws.

Determine the size needed by measuring from hole to hole on the pull, not by the length of the pull.

Cabinet Backplates

A backplate is placed between the door or drawer surface and the knob or pull. The backplate may be used:

- **To protect the cabinet surface**
- **To enhance the decorative hardware**

Cabinet Construction

Before determining the type of hinge you need, you must first know the type of cabinet construction you are dealing with:

Frameless, or **European,** cabinets have flush or inset doors and concealed hinges.

- **Full-overlay door:** The door covers the cabinet end panel.
- **Half-overlay door:** The cabinet door covers approximately half of the cabinet end panel.
- **Inset door:** The cabinet door is inset or flush with the cabinet face.

Face-frame cabinets have a wooden frame on the face of the cabinet.

- **Flush door:** The door is completely flush with the face of the frame.
- **⅜-inch-inset (lipped) door:** The door overlays the face frame and has a rabbet cut on the back edge.
- **Overlay door:** The door overlays the face frame completely.

Hinges

Determining the number of hinges you need is important for door stability.

- For a door less than 40 inches high and less than 11 pounds, you need two hinges.
- For a door 40 inches to 60 inches high and 13 pounds to 20 pounds, you need three hinges.
- For a door 60 inches to 80 inches high and 29 pounds to 33 pounds, you need four hinges.
- For a door 80 inches to 85 inches high and 40 pounds to 48 pounds, you need five hinges.

Types of Hinges

- **Mortise hinges** are permanent installation hinges. The area of the cabinet door and frame is cut out for the hinges to attach.

Hinges: Visible or Invisible?

Hinges can be **fully concealed,** so you see only the surface of the door, or **semi-concealed,** so you see only the knuckle of the hinge. (Use semi-concealed hinges if you have inset doors.)

- **Non-mortise hinges** do not need to be set into the side of the door or cabinet. You simply fasten the hinges down with screws.

Most hinges come with a card template for drilling the screw holes. Technically, hinges are specified for use on left- or right-hand doors. Hinges come in different sizes to support different door weights. Some hinges are made specifically for framed or frameless cabinets.

European Hinges

European, or Frameless, Hinges: These are the most popular hinges for full-overlay and inset doors due to ease of installation and the ability to handle heavy doors. European hinges can be adjusted to align and level cabinet doors. They can also be used on face-frame cabinets. These are self-closing hinges.

European Overlay Hinges: These are for frameless cabinet doors with half-overlay doors. European overlay hinges can also be used for face-frame cabinets with doors that overlap the frame. These are self-closing hinges.

Face-Frame Hinges

Variable Overlay Hinges: These are for face-frame cabinets with doors that completely overlay the frame and do not have a rabbet on the back edge.

⅜-inch-Inset Hinges: The door overlays the face-frame and has a rabbet cut on the back edge. These are self-closing hinges.

Partial Wraparound Hinges: These are face-frame hinges with a large surface area that improves stability. Use on flush, inset, or overlay doors. These are self-closing hinges.

H-Style Hinges: They look like the letter "H" with one side attaching to the frame and one side attaching to the door and are used with flush doors. These hinges do not self-close.

⅜-inch-Offset H-Hinges: These provide support and smooth operation for offset doors. These hinges do not self-close.

Butterfly Hinges: For flush doors, both wings of the hinges are mounted to the outside surfaces of the cabinet door and frame. These hinges do not self-close.

T-Style Hinges: These look like the letter "T" with the vertical piece attaching to the door frame and the horizontal piece attaching to the door. These hinges do not self-close.

Full-Inset Pin Hinges (Butt Hinges): They are for doors completely flush with the face of the cabinet. Can be recessed or surface mounted on face-frame cabinets. These hinges do not self-close.

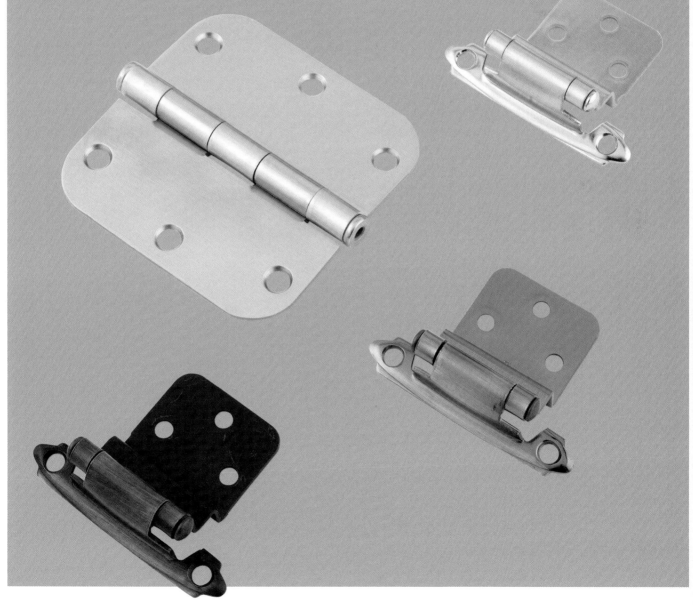

Cabinet Door Catches

Catches are used on doors that do not have self-closing hinges.

Magnetic Catches

- Metal plate mounts on the door with the magnetic part mounted on the frame.
- They are the most widely used of all catches.
- Magnetic-touch latches open and close with a light push on the door.
- Magnetic catches are often used on glass doors.

Spring-Roller Touch Catches

- They have one or two rollers set close together and mounted on the cabinet frame, and a catch that mounts to the door.
- These close when the rollers hook on the strike plate.
- They provide a quiet alternative to the clicking sound of magnetic catches.

Friction Catches

- They have male and female parts that work with spring tension similar to the roller type.
- These provide a secure grasp of the door.
- Their catch is invisible on an inset door.

Drawer Slides

The first thing to make note of is the weight capacity required for the drawer. Drawer slides have load ratings of light, medium, or heavy.

- Side-mount hardware is always more durable than single-center mono-rail or center-bottom-mount slides.
- Options such as ball-bearing or nylon rollers, partial or full drawer extension, drawer stop (to prevent the drawer from coming out), and self-closing design are available.
- Full-extension slides are perfect for providing access to every inch of a drawer.
- You must know the slide length and drawer length required before choosing slides.

Mini ball-bearing drawer slides may require a ¼-inch mortise in the drawer side for installation. Drawer stops are available.

Center-mount drawer slide for face-frame cabinets. No hardware is visible on drawer sides.

European-style self-closing side-mount drawer slide also has a stop to prevent it from sliding out completely.

Full-extension, self-closing drawer slide uses the maximum length of your drawer. Drawer stops are available.

Basic side-mount drawer slide uses surface installation on face-frame cabinets.

Selecting a Kitchen Countertop

Finding the perfect countertop for the most active room in the home can be a challenge. In addition to being durable and stain-resistant, the countertop you choose must be easy to clean and attractive. Think it's an impossible mission? Here's a rundown (below) on the types of countertops, with pros and cons of each.

Combining Surfaces

The ideal kitchen would have a mixture of the various countertop surfaces discussed below.

- Some form of stone or solid-surface material would be installed near the range area for placement of hot pots and pans.
- A solid-surface or plastic laminate would be placed around the sink and in the remaining areas for easy cleaning and good looks—at less cost if you choose laminate.

Choosing a Countertop

COUNTERTOP MATERIAL	PROS	CONS
Natural Quartz	• Smooth, durable • Requires little or no maintenance • Resists heat, scratching, bacteria, stains • Deep, consistent colors • Less-visible seams	• More expensive than some other choices • Odd/large sizes have visible seams
Stone	• Smooth, durable • Resists heat and water • Rich texture • Great for baking preparations	• Expensive • Odd/large sizes have visible seams • Scratches are hard to remove
Solid Surface	• Smooth, durable • No visible seams • Resists heat and water • Scratches can be sanded out	• Can be expensive • Color options are limited
Ceramic Tile	• Durable, heat-resistant • Easy to install • Lots of colors, design flexibility	• Leaves an uneven countertop • Grout lines may be hard to clean • Can crack or chip
Plastic Laminate	• Durable • Inexpensive • Easy to install • Lots of color/style options	• Won't tolerate direct heat • Thin surface color can fade • Noticeable seams and edges

Images provided by designer/architect.

Plan # 731039

Dimensions: 98' W x 35' D

Levels: 1

Heated Square Footage: 2,114

Bedrooms: 3

Bathrooms: 2½

Foundation: Crawl space, slab, or basement

Material Take-off Included: Yes

Price Category: D

This home is designed to include amenities sure to please the homeowner.

Features:

- Front Porch: Turned columns add charm to this lovely front porch. The porch is wide enough to allow for the placement of chairs and planters, creating a welcoming entry to the home.

Copyright by designer/architect.

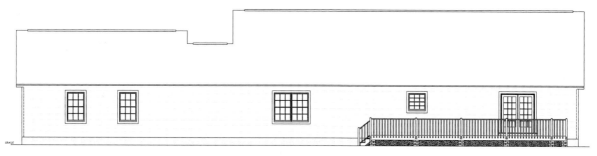

Rear Elevation

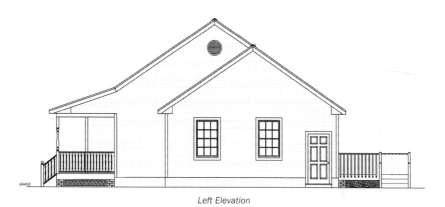

Left Elevation

Right Elevation

- Kitchen: This spacious kitchen features a large pantry, ample counter space, and lots of cabinet space, making it easy to organize. A window above the sink, along with cased openings leading to both the dining room and the central hallway, give this space a bright and airy feeling.

- Master Suite: With a private bathroom featuring an oversized tub and dual vanity, as well as a large walk-in closet, this master suite will offer you a place to relax after a long day.

- Secondary Rooms: Two additional comfortably sized bedrooms have private entrances to the hall bathroom.

Images provided by designer/architect.

Plan # 731089

Dimensions: 70' W x 25' D

Levels: 2

Heated Square Footage: 1,900

Main Level Sq. Ft.: 1,150

Upper Level Sq. Ft.: 750

Bedrooms: 4

Bathrooms: 3

Foundation: Crawl space, slab, or basement

Material Take-off Included: Yes

Price Category: D

This country-style two-story home offers plenty of living space, both indoors and outdoors.

CAD FILE AVAILABLE

Features:

- Foyer: All will feel welcome when they step from the charming porch directly into this spacious foyer.

- Kitchen: This cozy kitchen keeps efficiency in mind. The kitchen is adjacent to the laundry room, allowing for multitasking.

- Office: A moderately sized office is placed toward the rear of the home. Its location provides a quiet area to complete homework or manage household finances.

- Master Suite: At the day's end, relax in this lovely master suite. This suite is set apart from the secondary bedrooms in the home and houses a private bathroom, providing additional comfort and privacy.

- Upper Level: While the main level features a full bathroom and one secondary bedroom, this upper level includes an additional full bathroom, two secondary bedrooms, and a generously sized family room.

Main Level Floor Plan

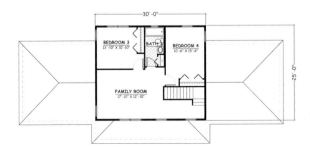

Copyright by designer/architect.

Upper Level Floor Plan

Plan # 731027

Dimensions: 84'6" W x 31' D

Levels: 1

Heated Square Footage: 1,904

Bedrooms: 3

Bathrooms: 2½

Foundation: Crawl space, slab, or basement

Material Take-off Included: Yes

Price Category: D

Images provided by designer/architect.

A grand front porch creates an inviting entry to this spacious ranch home.

Features:

- **Dining Room:** This lovely dining room is open to the great room. It features a large cased opening through to the kitchen and has a set of sliding glass doors that open onto an expansive rear deck. The open and airy feel of this room will cause many to linger after meals to enjoy pleasant conversation.

- **Kitchen:** Organization will be made easy in this spacious kitchen, which features a large pantry, ample counter space, and a plethora of cabinet space. The kitchen is also large enough to accommodate a small table and chairs, a great place for breakfast or a quick snack.

- **Master Suite:** Find some peace and quiet at the end of the day in this gracious master suite, which features a large walk-in closet and a private bathroom. The bathroom features an oversize tub and a dual vanity, providing additional comfort.

- **Secondary Rooms:** Rounding out the home are an additional two bedrooms, which have private entrances to a full bathroom. This home also features a powder room located off of the great room for both family and guests and a utility room housing the washer and dryer, within close proximity to all of the bedrooms.

Copyright by designer/architect.

Plan # 731035

Dimensions: 67'10" W x 53'2" D

Levels: 1

Heated Square Footage: 1,957

Bedrooms: 3

Bathrooms: 2½

Foundation: Crawl space, slab, or basement

Material Take-off Included: Yes

Price Category: D

Images provided by designer/architect.

A lovely ranch home is given additional curb appeal with a front porch that spans the width of the home.

CAD FILE AVAILABLE

Features:

- Entry Porch: Enjoy warm summer evenings on this front porch, which is wide enough for a small sitting area or a few planters.

- Great Room: This great room is a large and airy room that will make everyone feel at home. It is open to the kitchen and has a set of French doors that lead onto an expansive rear deck.

- Kitchen: Open to the great room and steps from the dining room is this wonderfully designed L-shaped kitchen. The center island provides additional counter space for preparing meals.

- Master Suite: Situated apart from the secondary bedrooms in the home is this lovely master suite, which features two large walk-in closets and a private bath. The bathroom contains a corner whirlpool tub, a separate shower, a separate toilet room, and a dual vanity.

- Secondary bedrooms: Two moderately sized secondary bedrooms flank a full bathroom, helping to complete the private areas of the home.

Copyright by designer/architect.

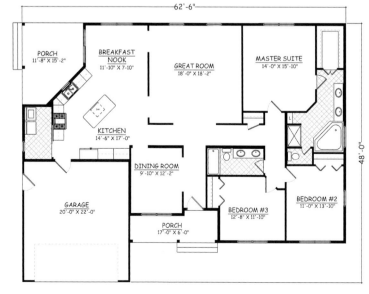

Images provided by designer/architect.

Plan # 731011

Dimensions: 62'6" W x 48' D

Levels: 1

Heated Square Footage: 1,996

Bedrooms: 3

Bathrooms: 2

Foundation: Crawl space, slab, or basement

Material Take-off Included: Yes

Price Category: D

This expansive home uses clever design to provide a smart mix of public areas and private quarters that are sure to please every member of the family.

Features:

- Covered Porch: Simple and under stated, this entry porch provides an elegant entry into the home.

- Great Room: The foyer draws you straight back to this grand great room. Connected to the kitchen, breakfast room, and main entry hall, the great room is certainly the place where friends and family will gather for some quality time.

- Kitchen: This kitchen is well designed, mixing and efficient use of space with modern styling. A center island provides additional counter space and houses the dishwasher. In addition, the kitchen flows into the breakfast nook, which features sliding glass doors that open to the rear covered porch.

- Dining Room: Located off the foyer and steps away from the kitchen, this room is perfect for the formal dining experience.

- Master Suite: Decompress at the end of the day in this bright and spacious master suite. The room features a large walk-in closet and a private bath, which boasts a corner bathtub, a separate shower, a private toilet room, and a dual-lav vanity.

- Secondary Bedrooms: An additional two bedrooms and a full bathroom complete the private areas of this home.

Copyright by designer/architect.

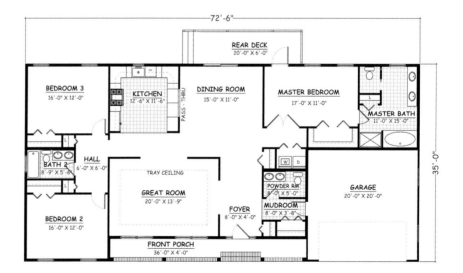

Images provided by designer/architect.

Plan # 731091

Dimensions: 72'6" W x 35' D

Levels: 1

Heated Square Footage: 1,996

Bedrooms: 3

Bathrooms: 2½

Foundation: Crawl space, slab, or basement

Material Take-off Included: Yes

Price Category: D

This beautiful ranch-style home features lovely touches you and your guests will appreciate.

Features:

- Foyer: Step from the entry porch directly into this welcoming foyer. The foyer leads you to the great room and the dining room and features a small coat closet, and is located just steps from a powder room.

- Great Room: Certain to be the main gathering spot for all is this grand great room. This room features large cased openings and a tray ceiling, giving the space a touch of elegance.

- Kitchen: With large countertop work spaces and numerous cabinets, this kitchen is easy to organize and an ideal place to cook. A pass-through to the dining room makes getting dinner on the table effortless.

- Master Suite: Step through a set of double doors into this gracious master suite where comfort and privacy abound. The suite features a private bathroom, a walk-in closet, and a single French door that leads to the rear deck.

The bathroom houses a dual-sink vanity, a large tub, a separate shower, and a private toilet room, adding to the comfort of the entire suite.

Copyright by designer/architect.

Images provided by designer/architect.

Plan # 731090

Dimensions: 50' W x 49'3" D

Levels: 2

Heated Square Footage: 2,032

Main Level Sq. Ft.: 1,384

Upper Level Sq. Ft.: 648

Bedrooms: 4

Bathrooms: 3

Foundation: Crawl space, slab, or basement

Material Take-off Included: Yes

Price Category: D

A wraparound porch with turned columns provides this home with added curb appeal.

CAD FILE AVAILABLE

Features:

- **Living Room:** This gracious living room, perfect for entertaining or just relaxing, can be entered from the charming porch at two locations.

- **Family Room:** This spacious family room is certain to be the main gathering spot for all. The room is open to the dining room and is adjacent to the kitchen, providing seamless transitions between rooms.

- **Kitchen:** This galley-style kitchen was designed while keeping efficiency in mind. The ample counter space will certainly please the family cook.

- **Master Suite:** This generously sized master suite features a private bathroom and a large walk-in closet and will provide you all the comfort and privacy you seek.

- **Upper Level:** This upper level is home to an additional secondary bedroom, full bathroom, a spacious office area, and a storage room. The office offers privacy for the completion of homework or for working on the household finances, while the storage room is a great spot for stowing seasonal items in a location that is easily accessible.

Main Level Floor Plan

Copyright by designer/architect.

Upper Level Floor Plan

Images provided by designer/architect.

Plan # 731041

Dimensions: 51' W x 47' D

Levels: 2

Heated Square Footage: 2,128

Main Level Sq. Ft.: 1,419

Upper Level Sq. Ft.: 709

Bedrooms: 4

Bathrooms: 3

Foundation: Crawl space, slab, or basement

Material Take-off Included: Yes

Price Category: D

This two-story design has multiple gables and a front porch for pleasing curb appeal.

Features:

- Front Porch: This charming front porch graces the entry to the home.

- Living Room: This expansive living room will certainly be a central gathering spot. It features a built-in media-storage area and has a large cased opening, adding a touch of elegance.

Main Level Floor Plan

Upper Level Floor Plan

Copyright by designer/architect.

Rear Elevation

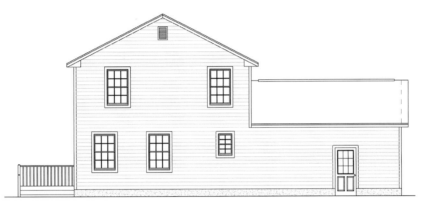

Left Elevation

Right Elevation

- Kitchen: With an angled snack bar, a pantry, and plenty of counter space, this kitchen will certainly please the family chef. The nearby dining room can be used for daily meals as well as formal dinner parties, and it has a French door that leads to the rear deck.

- Master Suite: Set apart from the other bedrooms in the home is this private retreat. This master suite boasts a generously sized master bathroom, which includes a whirlpool tub, a dual-sink vanity, and a walk-in closet.

- Upper Level: Two additional bedrooms along with a shared bathroom, a family room, and a computer room complete the upper floor. The shared bathroom is open to the hallway and to one of the bedrooms and features a separate dual-sink vanity area.

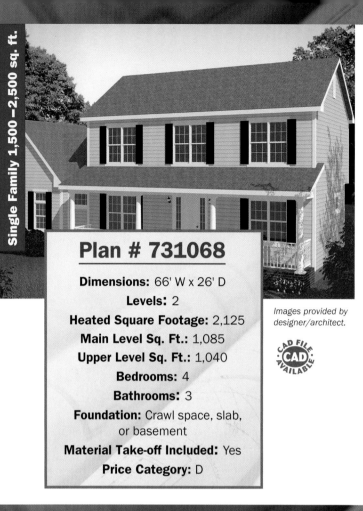

Plan # 731068

Dimensions: 66' W x 26' D

Levels: 2

Heated Square Footage: 2,125

Main Level Sq. Ft.: 1,085

Upper Level Sq. Ft.: 1,040

Bedrooms: 4

Bathrooms: 3

Foundation: Crawl space, slab, or basement

Material Take-off Included: Yes

Price Category: D

Images provided by designer/architect.

Main Level Floor Plan

Copyright by designer/architect.

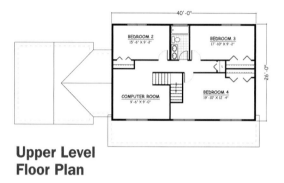

Upper Level Floor Plan

Plan # 731069

Dimensions: 50' W x 28' D

Levels: 2

Heated Square Footage: 2,240

Main Level Sq. Ft.: 1,400

Upper Level Sq. Ft.: 840

Bedrooms: 3

Bathrooms: 2

Foundation: Crawl space, slab, or basement

Material Take-off Included: Yes

Price Category: E

Images provided by designer/architect.

Main Level Floor Plan

Copyright by designer/architect.

Upper Level Floor Plan

Main Level Floor Plan

Copyright by designer/architect.

Upper Level Floor Plan

Plan # 731006

Dimensions: 67'5" W x 38'3" D

Levels: 2

Heated Square Footage: 2,261

Main Level Sq. Ft.: 1,396

Upper Level Sq. Ft.: 865

Bedrooms: 5

Bathrooms: 4½

Foundation: Crawl space, slab, or basement

Material Take-off Included: Yes

Price Category: E

Images provided by designer/architect.

CAD FILE AVAILABLE

Main Level Floor Plan

Upper Level Floor Plan

Copyright by designer/architect.

Plan # 731034

Dimensions: 56' W x 27'6" D

Levels: 2

Heated Square Footage: 2,269

Main Level Sq. Ft.: 1,538

Upper Level Sq. Ft.: 731

Bedrooms: 5

Bathrooms: 3

Foundation: Crawl space, slab, or basement

Material Take-off Included: Yes

Price Category: E

Images provided by designer/architect.

CAD FILE AVAILABLE

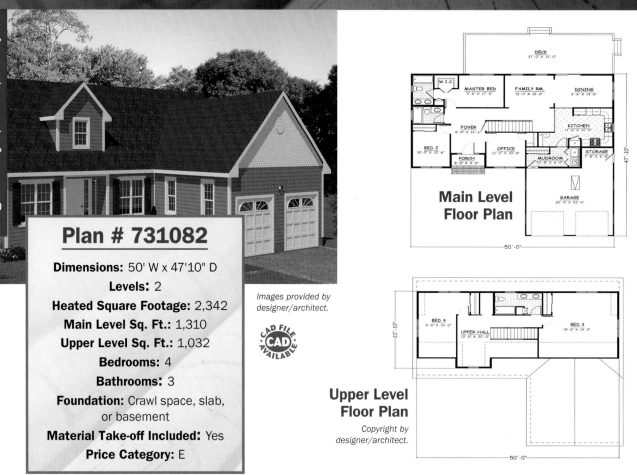

Plan # 731082

Dimensions: 50' W x 47'10" D

Levels: 2

Heated Square Footage: 2,342

Main Level Sq. Ft.: 1,310

Upper Level Sq. Ft.: 1,032

Bedrooms: 4

Bathrooms: 3

Foundation: Crawl space, slab, or basement

Material Take-off Included: Yes

Price Category: E

Images provided by designer/architect.

Main Level Floor Plan

Upper Level Floor Plan

Copyright by designer/architect.

Plan # 731076

Dimensions: 59' W x 39'1" D

Levels: 2

Heated Square Footage: 2,344

Main Level Sq. Ft.: 1,244

Upper Level Sq. Ft.: 1,100

Bedrooms: 5

Bathrooms: 4

Foundation: Crawl space, slab, or basement

Material Take-off Included: Yes

Price Category: E

Images provided by designer/architect.

Main Level Floor Plan

Upper Level Floor Plan

Copyright by designer/architect.

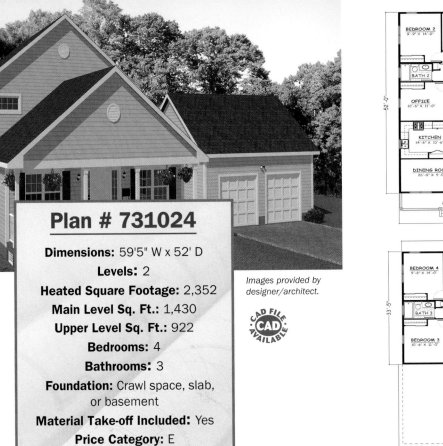

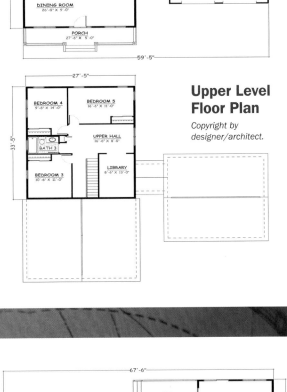

Main Level Floor Plan

Upper Level Floor Plan

Copyright by designer/architect.

Plan # 731024

Dimensions: 59'5" W x 52' D

Levels: 2

Heated Square Footage: 2,352

Main Level Sq. Ft.: 1,430

Upper Level Sq. Ft.: 922

Bedrooms: 4

Bathrooms: 3

Foundation: Crawl space, slab, or basement

Material Take-off Included: Yes

Price Category: E

Images provided by designer/architect.

Main Level Floor Plan

Copyright by designer/architect.

Upper Level Floor Plan

Plan # 731002

Dimensions: 67'6" W x 40' D

Levels: 2

Heated Square Footage: 2,394

Main Level Sq. Ft.: 1,641

Upper Level Sq. Ft.: 753

Bedrooms: 4

Bathrooms: 3

Foundation: Crawl space, slab, or basement

Material Take-off Included: Yes

Price Category: E

Images provided by designer/architect.

Plan # 731099

Dimensions: 78'4" W x 31' D

Levels: 2

Heated Square Footage: 2,446

Main Level Sq. Ft.: 1,366

Upper Level Sq. Ft.: 1,080

Bedrooms: 4

Bathrooms: 2

Foundation: Crawl space, slab, or basement

Material Take-off Included: Yes

Price Category: E

Images provided by designer/architect.

This moderately sized home has the perfect blend of private and public spaces for every member of the family.

CAD FILE AVAILABLE

Features:

- Living Room: Generous in its size, this living room features a large picture window to fill the space with natural light while a large cased opening provides an elegant entrance into the dining room.

- Kitchen: This efficiently designed kitchen features a cooktop, a wall oven, and a snack bar that is perfect for grabbing a quick meal.

- Master Bedroom: At the end of the day, escape to this spacious master bedroom, which features a large walk-in closet and multiple window units, bathing the room in plenty of natural light.

- Upper Level: At the top of the stairs, step into a large playroom. This upper level also boasts three additional bedrooms with large closets and a full-size bathroom.

Main Level Floor Plan

Upper Level Floor Plan

Copyright by designer/architect.

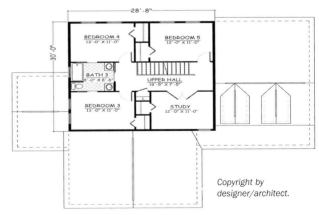

Images provided by designer/architect.

Plan # 731032

Dimensions: 57' W x 50' D

Levels: 2

Heated Square Footage: 2,470

Main Level Sq. Ft.: 1,610

Upper Level Sq. Ft.: 860

Bedrooms: 5

Bathrooms: 3½

Foundation: Crawl space, slab, or basement

Material Take-off Included: Yes

Price Category: E

This cottage-style two-story home is filled with amenities you will love.

Features:

- **Foyer:** This cozy foyer ushers you gently into the home.

- **Great Room:** Step through one of three cased openings into this spacious great room. Its central location is sure to be the gathering spot for all.

- **Kitchen:** A center island provides additional counter space in this already spacious kitchen. It is open on one side to the dining room, encouraging interaction between family members and the chef during mealtime prep.

- **Master Bedroom:** This lovely master suite, set apart from the secondary bedrooms in the home, will provide you with a quiet place to relax after a long day. The room features a large walk-in closet, houses a private bathroom, and has a set of sliding glass doors leading out to a private rear deck.

- **Upper Floor:** In addition to one secondary bedroom on the main floor, the upper floor contains three additional bedrooms, a full bathroom, and a moderately sized study.

Main Level Floor Plan

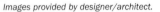

Copyright by designer/architect.

Upper Level Floor Plan

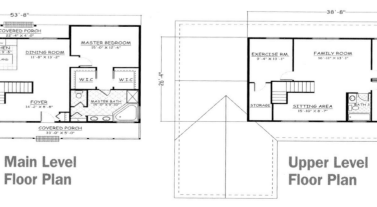

Images provided by designer/architect.

Plan # 731088

Dimensions: 53'8" W x 53'4" D

Levels: 2

Heated Square Footage: 2,517

Main Level Sq. Ft.: 1,498

Upper Level Sq. Ft.: 1,019

Bedrooms: 4

Bathrooms: 3

Foundation: Crawl space, slab, or basement

Material Take-off Included: Yes

Price Category: E

This country-style two-story home has many amenities the whole family will love.

Features:

- Foyer: This foyer is bound to make a statement with its grand staircase. Step from the front porch into the foyer, which has a small coat closet for convenience, and feel immediately welcome.

- Dining Room: Step from the foyer into this centrally located dining room. This room is open to the kitchen, allowing for interaction between the chef and the family during the preparation of meals. With a sliding glass door leading to a rear porch, the family is sure to be dining outdoors on many occasions.

- Kitchen: Getting dinner to the table will seem effortless in this thoughtfully designed kitchen, which features a center island.

- Master Suite: Offering you refuge from daily life is this wonderful master suite. The suite is located on the main floor apart from the secondary bedrooms in the home and features a private bath room and two large walk-in closets. The spa-like bathroom houses a dual-sink vanity, a private toilet room, a separate shower, and a large soaking tub that will surely leave you feeling refreshed.

- Secondary Room: An office, full bath-room, and a good sized bedroom help to complete the main floor living areas, while the upper floor boasts an additional two bedrooms, a full bathroom, an exercise room with large storage closet, a family room, and a cozy sitting area.

Copyright by
designer/architect.

**Main Level
Floor Plan**

**Upper Level
Floor Plan**

Plan # 731018

Dimensions: 66'11" W x 36'6" D

Levels: 2

Heated Square Footage: 2,526

Main Level Sq. Ft.: 1,564

Upper Level Sq. Ft.: 962

Bedrooms: 4

Bathrooms: 3

Foundation: Crawl space, slab, or basement

Material Take-off Included: Yes

Price Category: E

This home features a wonderfully spacious rear deck and a charming front covered porch, making it perfect for the family that enjoys outdoor living.

Images provided by designer/architect.

Features:

- **Entry Porch:** With room for a seating area or a few planters filled with flowers this covered porch welcomes all home.

- **Family Room:** Step from the entry porch into this spacious family room. Its central location is sure to make it the place that family and friends will gather.

- **Kitchen:** Cabinet and counter space abounds in this well-designed kitchen, which is open on one side to the dining room.

- **Dining Room:** Open to the kitchen, this moderately sized dining room features a sliding glass door to the expansive rear deck, ensuring that many meals will be enjoyed outdoors.

- **Master Suite:** A spacious master suite featuring a walk-in closet and a private bath is given a touch more privacy, as it is set apart from other bedrooms in the home. The bath features an oversize tub, a separate shower, and a dual-sink vanity adding to the suite's comfort.

- **Upper Level:** The upper level offers an additional two bedrooms, a full bathroom, and an open area for relaxing.

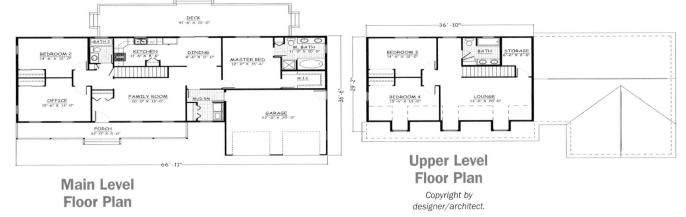

Main Level Floor Plan

Upper Level Floor Plan

Copyright by designer/architect.

Images provided by designer/architect.

Plan # 731098

Dimensions: 40' W x 44' D

Levels: 2

Heated Square Footage: 2,558

Main Level Sq. Ft.: 1,198

Upper Level Sq. Ft.: 1,360

Bedrooms: 4

Bathrooms: 3

Foundation: Crawl space, slab, or basement

Material Take-off Included: Yes

Price Category: E

CAD FILE AVAILABLE

This moderately sized traditional home features amenities that the entire family will appreciate.

Features:

- Front Porch: This expansive front porch offers you shelter from the elements and is wide enough to fit a small seating area, the perfect spot for relaxing after dinner.

- Living Room: This open and airy living room is a wonderful spot for entertaining. It is connected to the dining room and the kitchen, making it a spot where all will gather.

- Kitchen: This spacious kitchen with features such as a double-sink and snack bar is sure to please the family cook. Open to the dining room for more formal meals, the snack bar is the perfect place for an afternoon snack or an informal meal.

- Master Suite: Relax at the end of the day in this lovely master suite. The suite is set apart from the secondary bedrooms in the home and has a private bathroom that adds to its comfort and privacy. Amenities such as a whirlpool tub and a dual-sink vanity are sure to leave you feeling refreshed.

- Upper Level: With three secondary bedrooms, a full bathroom, and a generously sized game room that has its own kitchenette, this upper level is sure to please each and every member of the family.

Main Level Floor Plan

Upper Level Floor Plan

Copyright by designer/architect.

Plan # 731008

Dimensions: 50'6" W x 35'4" D

Levels: 2

Heated Square Footage: 2,567

Main Level Sq. Ft.: 1,526

Upper Level Sq. Ft.: 1,041

Bedrooms: 4

Bathrooms: 4

Foundation: Crawl space, slab, or basement

Material Take-off Included: Yes

Price Category: E

The straightforward design of this traditionally styled two-story home keeps it affordable to build while offering a multitude of versatility.

Images provided by designer/architect.

Features:

- **Great Room:** Upon entering the home you are immediately welcomed into this grand great room. The spacious room is centrally located, sure to make it the place the family will most gather.

- **Kitchen:** Open to the dining room is this wonderful kitchen. The U-shaped design provides the family chef with plenty of counter space for preparing of meals.

- **Screened Porch:** A beautiful place to dine and relax on a warm summer night, this generously sized screened room has sliding glass doors that connect it to the dining room.

- **Master Suite:** With a triple-window unit providing lots of natural light, a large walk-in closet, and a private bath-room, this master suite is sure to leave you feeling rejuvenated at the day's end. The bath houses a sunlit whirl pool tub, a dual vanity, and a separate toilet room.

- **Upper Level:** This upper floor contains an additional three bedrooms, two full bathrooms, and a beautiful library with built-in bookcases.

Main Level Floor Plan

Upper Level Floor Plan

Copyright by designer/architect.

Plan # 731074

Dimensions: 70'6" W x 27'4" D

Levels: 2

Heated Square Footage: 2,648

Main Level Sq. Ft.: 1,324

Upper Level Sq. Ft.: 1,324

Bedrooms: 5

Bathrooms: 4

Foundation: Crawl space, slab, or basement

Material Take-off Included: Yes

Price Category: F

Images provided by designer/architect.

Main Level Floor Plan

Upper Level Floor Plan

Plan # 731083

Dimensions: 30' W x 51' D

Levels: 2

Heated Square Footage: 2,682

Main Level Sq. Ft.: 1,422

Upper Level Sq. Ft.: 1,260

Bedrooms: 5

Bathrooms: 3

Foundation: Crawl space, slab, or basement

Material Take-off Included: Yes

Price Category: F

Images provided by designer/architect.

Main Level Floor Plan

Upper Level Floor Plan

Copyright by designer/architect.

Main Level Floor Plan

DECK
12'-0" X 8'-0"

BREAKFAST
10'-10" X 17'-0"

KITCHEN
12'-10" X 11'-0"

W.I.C.

M. BATH

MASTER BED
12'-10" X 14'-0"

D W

UTILITY

BATH 2

LIVING ROOM
23'-6" X 15'-4"

OFFICE
12'-6" X 14'-0"

DINING
10'-4" X 11'-0"

PORCH
18'-6" X 6'-0"

42'-6"

44'-10"

Plan # 731004

Dimensions: 44'10" W x 42'6" D

Levels: 2

Heated Square Footage: 2,684

Main Level Sq. Ft.: 1,540

Upper Level Sq. Ft.: 1,144

Bedrooms: 5

Bathrooms: 4

Foundation: Crawl space, slab, or basement

Material Take-off Included: Yes

Price Category: F

Images provided by designer/architect.

44'-10"

BEDROOM 4
14'-2" X 9'-6"

BATH 4

BEDROOM 2
15'-6" X 9'-4"

BATH 3

BEDROOM 3
14'-2" X 9'-4"

LOFT
9'-6" X 10'-2"

STUDY/GUEST
17'-8" X 9'-6"

25'-6"

Upper Level Floor Plan

Copyright by designer/architect.

Plan # 731075

Dimensions: 53' W x 30' D

Levels: 2

Heated Square Footage: 2,745

Main Level Sq. Ft.: 1,420

Upper Level Sq. Ft.: 1,325

Bedrooms: 5

Bathrooms: 4

Foundation: Crawl space, slab, or basement

Material Take-off Included: Yes

Price Category: F

Images provided by designer/architect.

Main Level Floor Plan

DECK
18'-0" X 8'-0"

MASTER BATH
12'-6" X 10'-0"

BEDROOM #2
11'-0" X 10'-0"

BREAKFAST NOOK
8'-4" X 10'-0"

KITCHEN
11'-0" X 10'-0"

HALL

MASTER SUITE
12'-6" X 18'-10"

STUDY
11'-10" X 10'-0"

LIVING ROOM
19'-4" X 13'-10"

W.I.C.

PORCH
34'-0" X 5'-0"

30'-0"

53'-0"

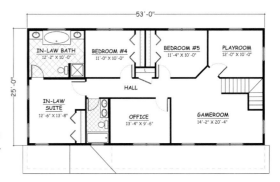

53'-0"

IN-LAW BATH
12'-2" X 10'-0"

BEDROOM #4
11'-0" X 10'-0"

BEDROOM #5
11'-4" X 10'-0"

PLAYROOM
12'-0" X 10'-0"

HALL

IN-LAW SUITE
12'-6" X 13'-8"

OFFICE
13'-4" X 9'-6"

GAMEROOM
14'-2" X 20'-4"

25'-0"

Upper Level Floor Plan

Copyright by designer/architect.

Main Level Floor Plan

DECK
10'-0" X 12'-0"

KITCHEN
12'-8" X 12'-0"

DINING ROOM
13'-0" X 12'-0"

MASTER SUITE
13'-6" X 14'-0"

LIVING ROOM
12'-9" X 14'-8"

ENTRY
8'-6" X 15'-0"

BEDROOM #3
11'-8" X 9'-4"

BEDROOM #2
10'-0" X 12'-10"

PORCH
28'-0" X 6'-0"

57'-6"

28'-0"

Plan # 731010

Dimensions: 57'6" W x 28' D

Levels: 2

Heated Square Footage: 2,768

Main Level Sq. Ft.: 1,452

Upper Level Sq. Ft.: 1,316

Bedrooms: 5

Bathrooms: 4

Foundation: Crawl space, slab, or basement

Material Take-off Included: Yes

Price Category: F

Images provided by designer/architect.

CAD FILE AVAILABLE

47'-0"

BEDROOM #3
12'-8" X 13'-6"

BATH #3
11'-4" X 8'-0"

BEDROOM #4
12'-6" X 11'-4"

HALL
24'-6" X 4'-6"

PLAYROOM
19'-8" X 13'-4"

BATH #4
8'-4" X 13'-4"

IN LAW SUITE
15'-2" X 13'-4"

28'-0"

Copyright by designer/architect.

Upper Level Floor Plan

42'-8"

MASTER SUITE
14'-0" X 11'-8"

PORCH
13'-10" X 5'-0"

BREAKFAST NOOK
8'-10" X 12'-4"

W.I.C.

LIVING ROOM
14'-2" X 18'-0"

42'-1"

BATH #2

MASTER BATH

KITCHEN
8'-10" X 11'-2"

UTILITY

BEDROOM #3
10'-0" X 10'-4"

BEDROOM #2
15'-6" X 10'-0"

PORCH
13'-10" X 5'-0"

Main Level Floor Plan

Plan # 731016

Dimensions: 42'8" W x 42'1" D

Levels: 2

Heated Square Footage: 2,784

Main Level Sq. Ft.: 1,500

Upper Level Sq. Ft.: 1,284

Bedrooms: 5

Bathrooms: 4

Foundation: Crawl space, slab, or basement

Material Take-off Included: Yes

Price Category: F

Images provided by designer/architect.

CAD FILE AVAILABLE

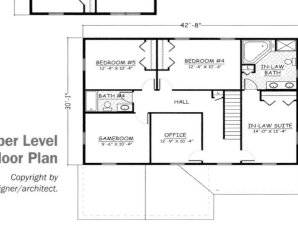

42'-8"

BEDROOM #5
12'-4" X 10'-4"

BEDROOM #4
12'-4" X 10'-4"

IN-LAW BATH

BATH #4

HALL

30'-1"

GAMEROOM
9'-6" X 10'-4"

OFFICE
12'-9" X 10'-4"

IN-LAW SUITE
14'-0" X 13'-4"

Upper Level Floor Plan

Copyright by designer/architect.

Main Level Floor Plan

MASTER BEDROOM 15'-0" X 11'-6"
DECK 19'-11" X 10'-0"
KITCHEN 12'-0" X 15'-0"
M. BATH 8'-8" X 15'-0"
PANTRY
FAMILY ROOM 20'-0" X 14'-0"
DINING ROOM 15'-0" X 10'-0"
BATH 2
LAUNDRY 8'-0" X 5'-0"
BEDROOM 1 10'-0" X 13'-0"
ENTRY 6'-4" X 17'-0"
BEDROOM 2 10'-6" X 13'-0"
GARAGE 23'-0" X 19'-0"
PORCH 28'-0" X 6'-0"
52'-3"
52'-0"

Plan # 731022

Dimensions: 52'3"W x 52' D

Levels: 2

Heated Square Footage: 2,808

Main Level Sq. Ft.: 1,840

Upper Level Sq. Ft.: 968

Bedrooms: 5

Bathrooms: 3

Foundation: Crawl space, slab, or basement

Material Take-off Included: Yes

Price Category: F

Images provided by designer/architect.

CAD FILE AVAILABLE

Upper Level Floor Plan

Copyright by designer/architect.

28'-5"
34'-0"
BEDROOM 4 10'-0" X 14'-0"
STORAGE
BEDROOM 3 16'-0" X 14'-0"
BATH 3
BEDROOM 5 10'-0" X 13'-0"
SITTING 6'-4" X 14'-0"
CRAFT 10'-6" X 13'-0"

Main Level Floor Plan

DECK 26'-0" X 9'-0"
BEDROOM 3 9'-6" X 13'-4"
KITCHEN 8'-6" X 15'-0"
BATH 2
MUD ROOM 8'-0" X 9'-4"
LAUNDRY 7'-0" X 9'-4"
BEDROOM 2 9'-6" X 10'-2"
M BATH
FAMILY ROOM 15'-0" X 15'-0"
GARAGE 22'-0" X 20'-0"
GUEST BEDROOM 17'-6" X 10'-4"
ENTRY 7'-6" X 10'-4"
PORCH 10'-0" X 6'-0"
50'-0"
47'-8"

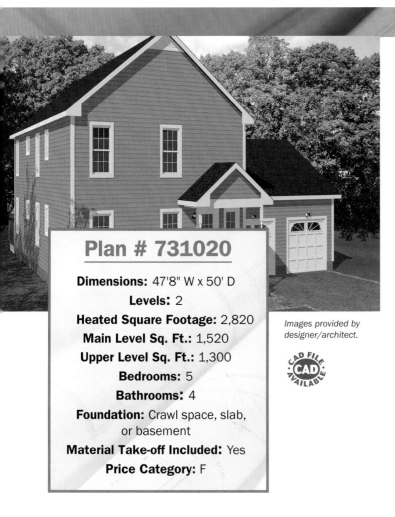

Plan # 731020

Dimensions: 47'8" W x 50' D

Levels: 2

Heated Square Footage: 2,820

Main Level Sq. Ft.: 1,520

Upper Level Sq. Ft.: 1,300

Bedrooms: 5

Bathrooms: 4

Foundation: Crawl space, slab, or basement

Material Take-off Included: Yes

Price Category: F

Images provided by designer/architect.

CAD FILE AVAILABLE

Upper Level Floor Plan

Copyright by designer/architect.

47'-8"
50'-0"
BEDROOM 4 9'-6" X 13'-4"
BEDROOM 5 9'-6" X 13'-4"
BATH 3
BEDROOM 6 9'-6" X 10'-6"
STORAGE 7'-6" X 9'-0"
M BATH
SITTING ROOM
MASTER SUITE 17'-6" X 10'-4"
W.I.C.

Appliance Buying Guide

I f your customers are like other families, the appliances they use get a real workout. The newest refrigerators, ranges, clothes washers and dryers, and dishwashers provide a number of labor- and money-saving features.

Refrigerators

Refrigerators come in four basic configurations. Before you decide which type is for your project, think about how much room you have for the fridge. Then, consider all of the features and options that are available.

You can find a refrigerator to fit any layout.

- Plenty of space? Chances are you're free to choose any configuration you like, including a French-door refrigerator.
- Limited by side walls or other obstacles? Top-freezer and bottom-freezer models have reversible doors, so doors can swing left or right.
- Dealing with a narrow galley kitchen? A side-by-side refrigerator can be ideal because its narrower doors require less swing space.
- Want a built-in look? A counter-depth refrigerator is a stylish option that sits flush with cabinet fronts, providing a built-in look without a built-in price.

What does it all mean, anyway?

- **Bottom Mount:** The refrigerator compartment is on top with the freezer below. This allows for easier accessibility to the fresh foods compartments and main refrigerator area than the more common top-mount-style refrigerators.
- **Top Mount:** The freezer compartment is on top, with the much larger refrigerator section on the bottom. This is the most common refrigerator type on the market.
- **Side by Side:** The refrigerator and freezer are adjacent and equal in size. This is the best bet for a kitchen with limited space, as it takes up the least room with the doors open. It isn't always the best for capacity. Fortunately, some models make up for this by offering adjustable shelves.
- **Compact:** A scaled-down version often used in dorm rooms, basements, or family rooms. There is usually little to no freezer space.

The Basics

Before you start shopping, carefully measure the layout for where the new fridge will go. The most common reason for refrigerator returns is the inability to fit the new fridge into an existing space. Measure the height, width, and depth of the space the new refrigerator will occupy. Also, make sure the one you choose will fit through doorways for delivery.

After you measure, you can start thinking about the good stuff — new features you can telegraph to your customers.

Cleanability

- When it comes to the fridge, spills are inevitable. Spill-proof shelving is useful for capturing the mess and preventing it from leaking all over the refrigerator.
- Also consider glass shelves with sealed edges. They can help contain spills and make cleanup quick and easy—while providing a clear view of what's inside the refrigerator.

Flexibility

- Shelves can be removed, retracted, and adjusted to different levels. Decide how flexible your shelving needs to be, and prioritize this feature accordingly.
- If more space is needed for frozen foods, consider a side-by-side model. Traditional ice makers take up freezer space, and this model moves the ice maker and bin to the refrigerator door. Depending on the manufacturer and model, these in-door ice systems can free up to 30 percent more freezer space. On some models, the ice bucket can even tilt out or be removed with one hand.

Organization

- Keep items within easy reach with gallon-size door bins. They're great for placing milk, juice, and soda right where someone can grab them. Gallon-plus door bins offer an enhancement to gallon-size door bins by allowing more than one gallon jug in the door, plus allowing enough room for cans and small jars.
- For a place to keep appetizers and deli trays fresh, consider bottom-freezer refrigerators. They come equipped with full-width pantry drawers. Some models are even temperature-controlled, so the homeowner can set the ideal temperature based on what's inside the drawer.
- To please or provide a handy spot for snacks, consider a refrigerator drawer that pulls open from the outside. It eliminates opening the fridge for popular items, as well as letting out all the cold air.

Extra Options

- **LED Lights:** They are brighter and more energy efficient, and they provide a more natural light than incandescent bulbs. They illuminate the entire refrigerator compartment while eliminating shadows.

- **Clean, Filtered Water:** Refrigerator water dispensers can filter contaminants—such as minerals, chemicals, metals, and microorganisms—from drinking water. Available on top- or bottom-freezer refrigerators, there are different options available, such as internal and through-the-door water dispensing.

ENERGY SAVINGS

Choose an ENERGY STAR®-approved refrigerator, and it will use a minimum of 20 percent less energy than non-rated models,* saving money on utility bills. Local rebates from municipalities may also be available when buying ENERGY STAR models. This rating is earned by meeting energy-efficiency requirements established by the Environmental Protection Agency. A new ENERGY STAR-qualified refrigerator uses less energy than a 60-watt lightbulb.

*Environmental Protection Agency

Ranges and Cooktops

To make sure your clients get the maximum cooking performance, pay careful attention to several features when buying a kitchen range or cooktop. Size and style can vary, as well as whether the unit uses electricity or gas. Before you buy, make sure you know what the best fit is for the kitchen.

Three styles of ranges are available. To select a range, think about the kitchen's design first:

- Freestanding ranges have finished sides and a backsplash. They can go between cabinets, at the end of a cabinet run, or stand alone. The electric ones have controls on the backsplash, while gas ranges have controls in the front.
- Slide-in ranges have a seamless built-in look with no backsplash. The controls are on the front. The sides are not finished or enclosed, so they require a cabinet on both sides.
- Drop-in ranges look similar to slide-ins, but they may require cabinet modification for a tight fit. You can tell slide-ins by the strip of cabinetry under their ovens. Their controls are on the front.

Types of Power

Most cooks agree that gas elements are more responsive to temperature adjustments than electric elements. Those who bake often will enjoy the even and consistent heat of an electric oven. A dual-fuel range combines an easy-to-control gas cooking surface with an even-heat, electric convection oven. Most dual-fuel ranges require a 240-volt circuit in addition to a gas hookup.

Electric Cooking Appliances

Electric ranges are available in coil-element and smooth-top designs. Sizes of ranges and cooktops range from 20 to 36 inches or more.

- **Coil-Element (radiant surface) Range:** This radiant element plugs in and can be easily removed for cleaning. The drip pans also lift out for cleaning. Coil elements provide even heat distribution when cooking. The more rings a coil has the more even the distribution.
- **Smooth-Top (radiant surface) Range:** This radiant element heats quickly and is sometimes adjustable in size. It can accommodate large or small pans with an adjustable element, and it can heat a large griddle or casserole dish with a connector element. The ceramic-glass cooking surface is uninterrupted for exceptionally easy cleanup.
- **Ceramic-Glass Cooktop:** Easy to keep clean, and it offers flexibility for dual elements and simmer burners.
- **Induction Cooktop:** It's the most efficient cooking method and provides accurate temperature control. Induction uses the power of electromagnetic waves to quickly turn the bottom of the pot into an active heating surface, rather than the cooktop surface itself, to provide a cooler surface temperature.

Gas Cooking Appliances

You must have access to natural gas from your home to use a gas range. A gas range or cooktop is available in open and sealed burners and works the best for even cooking. Some gas ranges have continuous interlocking grates that allow a pot to easily be moved between burners. Sizes vary from 20 to 40 inches. Also, gas ranges and cooktops work during power outages.

- **Open Burner:** Includes large openings in the range or cooktop surface for the burner. The cooking surface lifts to clean spills that drain into the opening, and drip pans can be easily cleaned in the sink.
- **Sealed-Surface Burner:** The burner is recessed below the surface of the countertop, and a sealed burner is attached directly to the cooking surface. Spills and spatters are contained on the cooking surface for easy cleanup.

Dual-Fuel Ranges

Want the best of both worlds? Try dual fuel. It combines the accuracy of gas surface cooking with the even and consistent heating of an electric oven. These ranges have the best features of gas and electric ranges.

After you measure, you can start thinking about the good stuff — new features for your clients.

Convection

In addition to the standard bake and broil elements, there is a third oven-heating element around the fan in the rear of the oven.

- Convection cooking uses a fan in the back of the oven to circulate air over, under, and around foods to cook approximately 30 percent faster than conventional baking.
- Convection ovens allow the cook to choose between conventional baking and roasting or convection baking and roasting.
- By circulating hot air around the oven, convection cooking can eliminate hot and cool spots for more even cooking. A turkey roasted in a convection oven will brown all over, rather than just on top.

Selecting an Oven Size

Before you choose a range, measure the available space. Use the simple table below to determine the oven size best suited for the kitchen.

SIZE OF FAMILY	OVEN CAVITY SIZE
1-2 people	2-3 cubic feet
3-4 people (small family)	3-4 cubic feet
4 or more people (large family)	4+ cubic feet

Other Features

- Cooks can manage the mess with a recessed cooking surface. It's flush with the countertop—sitting at the same level as the countertop —because the grates can sit lower. This helps to contain spills, making it much easier to clean.
- For a gas cooktops and ranges, consider full-surface grates to form a continuous usable surface, allowing the cook to shift a full pot from one burner to the next without lifting it—or risking a spill.

Safety

- Some ranges have programs available that automatically turn the oven on and off
- Many cooktops and ranges include hot-surface indicator lights to remind the cook that the grates are still hot.
- Cooktop and range controls may include safety knobs that must be pushed in to turn on.

Heat Options

- Look for a cooktop or range with a power burner to quickly bring foods to a rolling boil. A gas unit typically has a 15,000-BTU power burner. An electric unit's power burner has at least 3,200 watts of power.
- Certain dishes require excellent low-heat control. A simmer burner aids in preparing delicate sauces or melting chocolate with low, even heat. The simmer burner on a gas unit typically has 5,000 BTUs. On an electric unit, it has 1,200 watts to 1,500 watts. Simmer burners are good for cooking small quantities of rice, holding an emulsion without it breaking, and keeping a finished meal warm without it overcooking.

Controls

For the most accurate temperature adjustment, go with a digital or touch-activated screen control. This control is simple to use, and its flat surface is great for fast and easy cleaning. This style is available on electric cooktops and ranges.

Washers

The washing machine is one of the longest-lasting appliances in the home, and it can have the biggest cost difference when trying to reduce utility bills. Before you buy, think about the space constraints. There are a lot of options from which to choose, and with so many models available, you are sure to find the right machine for your project.

Why Your Clients Will Love a Top Loader

If there is a large, open area to arrange the appliances or the space is flexible, top loaders are a good option.

- No bending or kneeling necessary
- They use any kind of detergent
- Offers the most budget-friendly models
- Provides a traditional look

Why Your Clients Will Love a Front Loader

Is your laundry area a confined space like a closet? With space at a premium, consider going vertical by stacking a convenient front-load pair.

- Stack them, and free up floor space; or put side-by-side under a counter
- Less wear and tear on the laundry
- Offers the highest-efficiency and energy-saving models
- They prefer a modern look

The Basics

Capacity

- Even smaller families can find themselves washing larger loads consistently. A large-capacity washer can lessen the burden of doing laundry.
- Washer tubs are measured in cubic feet. In washer language, there's about five towels per cubic foot.

ENERGY SAVINGS

Saving Energy and Water Saves Homeowners Money

ENERGY STAR

Homeowners may pay a little more up front for washers with these ratings, but the units make up for the cost by saving energy and water—some up to 7,000 gallons a year (enough water to take 3,000 showers).

ENERGY STAR® or High-Efficiency?

- **ENERGY STAR®** washers meet government standards to conserve resources. They can save about 30 percent on energy use without sacrificing features or style.
- **High-Efficiency** washers are not only ENERGY STAR® qualified but also have higher spin speeds to remove more water from laundry, saving drying time, too.

Cycles

- **Delicates:** Washing takes its toll on clothing, especially lightweight garments and loosely woven fabrics. A cycle that uses colder water and mild agitation to gently clean fabrics that need special care makes delicates last longer.
- **Wash Now, Dry Later:** There's no need to rewash a load that was left in the washer with this feature. It uses a fan to vent fresh air into the washer while tumbling clothes intermittently. No more musty smelling clothes, even if they sit in the washer for hours.
- **Add-a-Garment:** When front-load washers first entered laundry rooms, they could not be opened during a cycle because water would spill out onto the floor. Today, most front-load washers offer an add-a-garment feature that stops the machine to add that dirty sock, dirty towel, and anything else—at any time.
- **Quick Wash:** Many washer brands offer cycles that wash and dry a small load in about a half hour. It's perfect for getting a uniform ready for a game or quickly washing a favorite outfit.

Cleaning

Of course, everyone wants a washer that cleans clothes thoroughly. But some people have specific cleaning needs, and new models do a good job of addressing them.

- **Sanitization:** For babies or pets in the home, there are models that can sanitize clothing and eliminate bacteria and allergens.
- **Steam:** For tough-to-remove stains, a steam feature will eliminate the need to pretreat laundry.
- **Cleaning Additives:** Many washers have advanced cleaning technology that eliminates the need to pretreat stains. You can also find models that release oxygen-based cleaners into the wash water at just the right time, to brighten clothes without bleach.

Noise

New innovations make washers quieter. For laundry rooms near a living area or bedroom, consider a washer that provides more peace and quiet.

Dryers

Because a dryer can affect clothing's appearance and life span, the one your client buys is important. Remember to consider the features available, and think about what's best for your project and your client.

All dryers use an electric motor to tumble clothes and an electric fan to distribute heated air. The difference is how heat is generated—either with natural gas or electricity. The decision to purchase gas versus electric depends on whether there is a gas line in the laundry area. If you want to change the dryer's fuel source, you may need the help of a plumber or electrician.

- **Electric:** Generally, they're slightly more expensive to operate than gas dryers and use twice the strength of an ordinary household electric current. Most run on a 240-volt current to heat up coils and require a 240-volt outlet in the laundry area.
- **Gas:** The initial cost of gas can be slightly higher than that of an electric dryer, but it's typically less expensive to operate. It usually takes only a year or two to make up the purchase-price difference due to energy savings.

The Basics

When you're ready to shop for a new dryer, remember the 3 Cs: Capacity, Controls, and Cycles.

Capacity

The more one can dry in a single load, the less time and money spend doing laundry. Also, clothes tend to wrinkle less in larger drums because there's more tumbling room. You should look for a model with about twice the capacity of the selected washer—it will dry more in less time—and it can keep up with the pace of the washer.

Controls

As with washers, controls on dryers are more sophisticated and easier to use. Digital displays and one-touch selections can be programmed and preset to meet numerous drying needs. For a more traditional look, choose dial or push-button controls.

Cycles

- **Sensor Dry:** A moisture sensor knows how wet the laundry is and adjusts the drying time accordingly. This not only saves time and money on energy costs, but can also prevent over-drying (which can cause shrinkage) and extend the life of the clothes. A moisture sensor adjusts the unit for the the desired level of dryness—whether that's damp or completely dry.
- **Eco-cycle:** Dryers with an eco-cycle use significantly less energy than normal cycles by accurately monitoring the dryness of clothes, saving money on energy bills, and helping clothes last longer. Some models even have a monitor on the console that displays the energy use and efficiency of different drying cycles.

- **Steam:** Steam is one of the newest dryer innovations that makes doing laundry easier. A steam cycle can refresh an outfit, relaxing wrinkles and removing odors. During this cycle, a small amount of water is sprayed into the dryer drum after several minutes of tumbling with heat. It can also be set to periodically tumble, rearrange, and fluff the load to help keep wrinkles from forming.
- **Delicate:** Many dryers have a delicate cycle that uses an ultralow temperature to safely and gently dry lightweight garments and loosely woven fabrics. Clothes will last longer and keep their color if dried using the correct temperatures.
- **Wrinkle:** Wrinkles can set in to clothes that sit in the dryer for too long after a cycle, especially if they're warm. A wrinkle-prevention option is great if clothes sit in the dryer for some time. It continues to tumble clothes without heat to avoid creating set-in wrinkles.
- **Sanitization:** Bacteria and germs can easily find their way into fabrics. A dryer with a sanitizing cycle can help provide some relief to children and adults with allergies by using high heat or steam to sanitize items that cannot be easily washed. A sanitization cycle eliminates up to 99.9 percent of common household bacteria.

ENERGY SAVINGS

According to ENERGY STAR®, clothes dryers are not rated in the government program because there is little difference in the energy use between models. To reduce energy in other ways, buy units with the moisture sensor cycle in the dryer or a high-spin cycle in the washing machine. Both will reduce the amount of drying time needed and ultimately use less energy.

Dishwashers

Dishwashers are great time-saving devices, but they also save water and energy over hand-washing the dishes. Hand-washing uses more water than you might think, as does pre-rinsing before loading the dishwasher. Do a little research before buying your next dishwasher — your customers will thank you.

Built-in dishwashers are the traditional 24-inch models that most people own, installed below the kitchen counter.

Double-drawer dishwashers can be installed in the space of a traditional built-in. They offer extra flexibility when washing large and small loads.

Single-drawer and **compact** dishwashers are perfect for popular areas, like a media room, wet bar, or butler's pantry.

Portable dishwashers are convenient and great for smaller living spaces.

The Basics

Water Temperature

The key to getting dishes clean is using very hot water. Some dishwashers have a device that raises the temperature of the water coming out of the water heater.

ENERGY SAVINGS

Some dishwashers use sensor technology to detect how dirty the dishes are and then adjust the cycle accordingly. You can start the washer with a touch of a button, and this feature prevents water from being wasted. A delay-start timer also will start your dishwasher when the energy rates are lower.

Go with an ENERGY STAR® approved dishwasher to get your dishes clean while using less water and energy. You also may be eligible for local rebates from your city when buying ENERGY STAR-approved models. This rating is earned by meeting energy-efficiency requirements established by the Environmental Protection Agency.

- The energy saved every year by purchasing a new ENERGY STAR qualified dishwasher over a new non-qualifying model is enough to brew nearly 9,000 cups of coffee.
- Washing dishes by hand uses up to 27 gallons of water versus the 5 gallons of water used by many ENERGY STAR dishwashers. That's a savings of more than 4,700 gallons of water a year.
- According to the EPA and DOE, choosing an ENERGY STAR qualified dishwasher can save up to 10 percent in energy operating costs per year.

Tub Material

Interior tubs come in different finishes. Stainless steel resists stains and odors, and it transfers heat better for faster drying. Gray or slate-colored tubs resist rust and minimize the appearance of stains. Plastic tubs, which are often found on more affordable dishwashers, are also very durable.

Noise Level

The amount of insulation around the dishwasher tub reduces the noise, so check to see how thick the insulation is. Another factor to consider is the decibel level of the dishwasher. A decibel level of 41 to 52 is virtually silent, while a decibel level of 60 or more may disrupt conversation in the kitchen.

Cleanability

Another feature is a built-in food disposer. Also, check the size of the spray holes on the wash arms. The smaller the holes, the more scrubbing power they provide to the dishwasher.

Cycles

From pots and pans to fine china and crystal, there's a cycle for just about anything.

- Rinse-and-hold cycle to prevent buildup when dishes are washed once every two or three days.
- The quick-wash cycle can finish a load of lightly soiled dishes in 30 minutes.
- A sanitizing rinse option kills 99.9 percent of bacteria. This is great for households with young children or sick family members.
- Some dishwashers offer a cycle that combines steam with a high-temperature rinse to safely remove spots. The high temperature of steam also kills bacteria and sanitizes dishes.

Flexibility

Some dishwashers feature fold-down shelving.

- Make room in the bottom rack for oversize dishes and pans with adjustable upper racks.
- Put dinner plates in the top rack. Some adjustable racks can be lowered enough to provide room.
- Load the lower rack with large items, such as stock pots and oven racks with a removable upper rack.

The True Cost of an Appliance

When buying an appliance, remember that it has two price tags: the cost to take it home and the cost of the energy and/or water to use it.

To know the yearly cost of running an appliance, start by looking at the yellow and black Federal Trade Commission's EnergyGuide label. Manufactures are required to display the label on many appliances including refrigerators, washing machines, dishwashers, air conditioners, and water heaters.

The label provides information on how much energy the appliance uses, compares energy use of similar products, and lists approximate annual operating costs. Exact costs will depend on local utility rates and the source of your energy. Looking at the EnergyGuide label can be a key factor in helping you make a decision on an appliance. For example, a refrigerator with a yearly operating cost of $50 may be more expensive to buy than a refrigerator with a yearly operating cost of $70. However, if you take into account a $20 annual savings over an appliance's lifetime, the purchaser might save more money in the long run by investing up front in an energy-efficient appliance. In addition, an EnergyGuide label usually states whether an appliance is ENERGY STAR qualified. The ENERGY STAR logo ensures that the appliance meets or exceeds the ENERGY STAR performance level. Because an ENERGY STAR qualified appliance uses 10 percent to 66 percent less water and / or energy than standard models, the homeowners can save money in addition to resources.

New Ways to Save

Homeowners can save even more money through energy rebate programs from local utilities and energy-efficiency groups. More than 28 million people in the United States and Canada are eligible for a rebate or tax credit for purchasing an ENERGY STAR-qualified appliance. Some areas offer as much as $200.

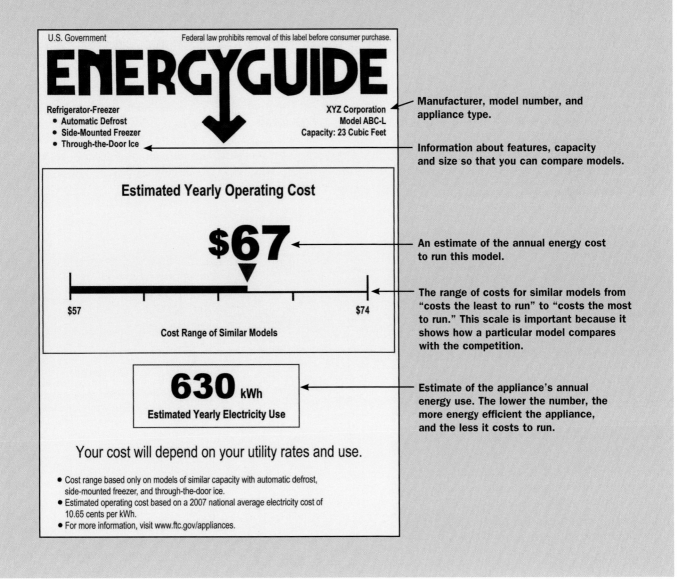

U.S. Government — Federal law prohibits removal of this label before consumer purchase.

ENERGYGUIDE

Refrigerator-Freezer
- Automatic Defrost
- Side-Mounted Freezer
- Through-the-Door Ice

XYZ Corporation
Model ABC-L
Capacity: 23 Cubic Feet

— Manufacturer, model number, and appliance type.

— Information about features, capacity and size so that you can compare models.

Estimated Yearly Operating Cost

$67

— An estimate of the annual energy cost to run this model.

$57 $74

Cost Range of Similar Models

— The range of costs for similar models from "costs the least to run" to "costs the most to run." This scale is important because it shows how a particular model compares with the competition.

630 kWh
Estimated Yearly Electricity Use

— Estimate of the appliance's annual energy use. The lower the number, the more energy efficient the appliance, and the less it costs to run.

Your cost will depend on your utility rates and use.

- Cost range based only on models of similar capacity with automatic defrost, side-mounted freezer, and through-the-door ice.
- Estimated operating cost based on a 2007 national average electricity cost of 10.65 cents per kWh.
- For more information, visit www.ftc.gov/appliances.

Images provided by designer/architect.

Plan # 731042

Dimensions: 85' W x 35' D

Levels: 2

Heated Square Footage: 3,123

Main Level Sq. Ft.: 2,038

Upper Level Sq. Ft.: 1,085

Bedrooms: 4

Bathrooms: 4

Foundation: Crawl space, slab, or basement

Material Take-off Included: Yes

Price Category: G

This two-story home has an abundance of living space—something to suit any need.

Features:

- **Front Porch:** The front porch is wide enough to sit in a rocking chair and enjoy an afternoon breeze.

- **Living Room:** A large front picture window makes this living room a bright and inviting space. It is a place to either entertain friends or just relax with the family.

- **Kitchen:** A snack bar at the center island invites the family to spend time together while the meals are being prepared. A nice-size pantry provides additional storage for dry goods, while the adjoining dining room features a door leading to the rear deck, adding to the spaciousness.

- **Mudroom/Utility Room:** This mudroom/utility room features access from the garage and the front yard and is located just steps away from the kitchen. Today's busy families will certainly make use out of this room, which houses a washer and dryer, a storage cabinet, a closet, and a built-in bench.

- **Master Suite:** A perfect place for relaxing, this spacious master suite features a luxurious bath with a corner whirlpool tub, a separate shower, and a dual-sink vanity.

Main Level Floor Plan

Copyright by designer/architect.

Upper Level Floor Plan

Images provided by designer/architect.

Plan # 731094

Dimensions: 72'6" W x 35' D

Levels: 2

Heated Square Footage: 3,150

Main Level Sq. Ft.: 1,996

Upper Level Sq. Ft.: 1,154

Bedrooms: 4

Bathrooms: 4½

Foundation: Crawl space, slab, or basement

Material Take-off Included: Yes

Price Category: G

Stately columns gracing the front of this home, and many more elegant features and details within, add to this home's character.

Features:

- Front Porch: Wide enough for a small sitting area, this large front porch provides an elegant entrance into the home.

- Dining Room: Located adjacent to the kitchen, this spacious dining room is the perfect place for the everyday family meal or a festive gathering with friends and family. A sliding glass door at the rear of the room leads to a large deck, making the decision to dine indoors or outdoors a difficult one.

- Kitchen: Large countertop workspaces and numerous cabinets that provide plenty of storage make this kitchen

perfect for the family chef. Getting dinner on the table will be made even easier with a large pass-through to the dining room.

- Master Suite: Set apart from the secondary bedrooms in the home is this grand master suite. A set of double

doors grants you entrance to the space, which includes a private bathroom, a walk-in closet, and a single French door that leads to the rear deck. The bathroom houses a dual-sink vanity, a large tub, a separate shower, and a private toilet room.

Main Level Floor Plan

Copyright by designer/architect.

Upper Level Floor Plan

Images provided by designer/architect.

Plan # 731026

Dimensions: 57'1" W x 47' D

Levels: 2

Heated Square Footage: 3,156

Main Level Sq. Ft.: 1,614

Upper Level Sq. Ft.: 1,542

Bedrooms: 5

Bathrooms: 4

Foundation: Crawl space, slab, or basement

Material Take-off Included: Yes

Price Category: G

A generously sized two-story home includes plenty of public and private spaces for the entire family.

CAD FILE AVAILABLE

Features:

- Front Porch: This front porch with brick accents will not only shelter you from the elements but also provide additional curb appeal to an already lovely home.

- Kitchen: Cased openings to the living room and dining room give this kitchen a touch of elegance, while amenities such as a double sink and a wall oven will certainly please the family cook.

- Dining Room: This dining room is open to both the living room and kitchen, giving it an open and airy feeling. At the rear of the room is a French door that leads to the backyard.

- Secondary Rooms: There are five bedrooms in the home, two located on the main floor and three on the upper floor. There are three full bathrooms in this home, providing accommodations for every member of a large family. On the upper level, one of the bedrooms features a private bathroom that would make it an ideal guest room.

- Upper Level: In addition to the bedrooms and bathrooms, this level is home to an office and a loft like family room. This space can easily accommodate either work or play.

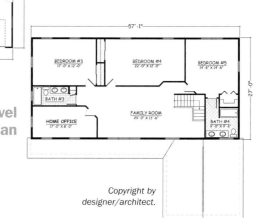

Main Level Floor Plan

Upper Level Floor Plan

Copyright by designer/architect.

Images provided by designer/architect.

Plan # 731014

Dimensions: 73'10" W x 32' D

Levels: 2

Heated Square Footage: 3,186

Main Level Sq. Ft.: 1,593

Upper Level Sq. Ft.: 1,593

Bedrooms: 5

Bathrooms: 4½

Foundation: Crawl space, slab, or basement

Material Take-off Included: Yes

Price Category: G

With front and rear covered porches this two-story expanded ranch home has room for the entire family.

Features:

- Great Room: Feel immediately welcome when you step from the covered entry porch into this expansive great room. The room is located at the center of the home and is open to both kitchen and breakfast area, ensuring that this is the spot the family will gather the most.

- Kitchen/Breakfast Nook: Mealtime prep is made easy in this kitchen that has plenty of counter space. The sink is located in a wraparound countertop seating area that will be the perfect place for the kids to sit for an after school snack. Sliding glass doors grace the rear of this lovely breakfast nook and connect it to a covered porch.

- Master Suite: Placed toward the rear of the home is this lovely master suite. The room has a large walk-in closet and private bath. The bath features a full-size tub, as well as a separate shower and a dual vanity providing you comfort and privacy.

- Upper Level: This upper level provides the home with an additional two bedrooms, a full bathroom, a media room, game room, and a spacious in-law suite. The suite has its own private bathroom, providing your extended family privacy during their visit.

Main Level Floor Plan

Copyright by designer/architect.

Upper Level Floor Plan

Images provided by designer/architect.

Plan # 731030

Dimensions: 58' W x 40' D

Levels: 2

Heated Square Footage: 3,208

Main Level Sq. Ft.: 1,802

Upper Level Sq. Ft.: 1,406

Bedrooms: 4

Bathrooms: 5½

Foundation: Crawl space, slab, or basement

Material Take-off Included: Yes

Price Category: G

This farmhouse-style two-story home has plenty of features to keep the entire family happy.

Features:

- Great Room: Sure to be the central gathering spot for all is this grand great room that features large windows and multiple cased openings.

- Kitchen: A countertop seating area provides this already spacious kitchen with additional counter space for preparing meals. The seating area connects the kitchen to the dining room and allows for interaction during meal prep.

- Dining Room: This lovely dining room is open to the kitchen, just steps from the great room, and features sliding glass doors to a rear deck, encouraging outdoor dining.

- Guest Suite: Your guests will surely feel welcome in this lovely guest suite. The suite features a private bathroom and is separated from the other bedrooms, giving your guests privacy during their stay.

- Master Suite: Relax at the end of the day in this amazing master suite.

With a private sitting room, a large walk-in closet, and a luxurious bath room, the suite will provide you with all the comfort you deserve. The bath room features a large tub, separate shower, dual vanity, and separate toilet room.

Main Level Floor Plan

Upper Level Floor Plan

Copyright by designer/architect.

Images provided by designer/architect.

Plan # 731036

Dimensions: 67'10" W x 53'2" D
Levels: 2
Heated Square Footage: 3,310
Main Level Sq. Ft.: 1,957
Upper Level Sq. Ft.: 1,353
Bedrooms: 5
Bathrooms: 3
Foundation: Crawl space, slab, or basement
Material Take-off Included: Yes
Price Category: G

This moderately sized two-story home has amenities that are sure to please each and every member of the family.

CAD FILE AVAILABLE

Features:

- Entry Porch: Spanning the length of the home is this lovely entry porch. The porch has turned columns and decorative railings, giving it a country feel.

- Great Room: Everyone will feel at home in this large and airy great room. At the rear of the room is a set of French doors leading to an expansive rear deck for outdoor entertaining.

- Kitchen: This L-shaped kitchen has an abundance of cabinet and counter space sure to please the family cook. A center island provides even more counter space for preparing meals.

- Master Suite: This lovely master suite provides a welcome retreat at the end of the day and features two walk-in closets and private bath. The bathroom contains a whirlpool tub, a separate shower, and a separate toilet room.

- Additional Bedrooms: In addition to a single secondary bedroom, full bathroom, and office on the main floor, the upper floor boasts an additional three bedrooms, a full bathroom, a sitting room, and a media room.

Copyright by designer/architect.

Main Level Floor Plan

Upper Level Floor Plan

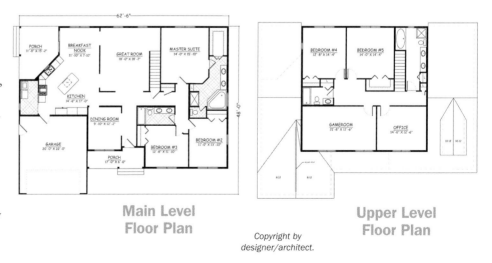

Images provided by designer/architect.

Plan # 731012

Dimensions: 62'6" W x 48' D

Levels: 2

Heated Square Footage: 3,330

Main Level Sq. Ft.: 1,996

Upper Level Sq. Ft.: 1,334

Bedrooms: 5

Bathrooms: 4

Foundation: Crawl space, slab, or basement

Material Take-off Included: Yes

Price Category: G

Every member of the family is sure to be pleased with the design of this two-story home, which features a smart mix of public and private spaces.

CAD FILE AVAILABLE CAD

Features:

- Covered Porch: Welcoming you to the home is small covered entry porch, which makes a big statement with its stately columns and decorative railing.

- Great Room: The entry foyer draws you straight back to this immense great room. The cased openings give the room a bit of elegance, while its central location will certainly make this the place where friends and family will gather.

- Kitchen: Modern styling mixes with efficient design in this kitchen, which features a center island for additional

counter space. The room is adjacent to the breakfast nook, which features sliding glass doors that open to a covered rear porch that is perfect for outdoor dining.

- Master Suite: With a private bath, which features a corner whirlpool tub, a separate shower, a private toilet room, a dual-sink vanity, and a walk-

in closet, this bright and spacious room is the perfect place to relax at the end of the day.

- Upper Level: This upper level houses another two bedrooms, two full bathrooms, office space, and a large game room, providing plenty of space for the entire family.

Main Level Floor Plan

Upper Level Floor Plan

Copyright by designer/architect.

Images provided by designer/architect.

Plan # 731028

Dimensions: 84'6" W x 35' D

Levels: 2

Heated Square Footage: 3,552

Main Level Sq. Ft.: 1,904

Upper Level Sq. Ft.: 1,648

Bedrooms: 5

Bathrooms: 3½

Foundation: Crawl space, slab, or basement

Material Take-off Included: Yes

Price Category: H

CAD FILE AVAILABLE

A generously sized two-story home is thoughtfully designed with plenty of public and private spaces for the entire family.

Features:

- Great Room: From the front entry porch, step directly into this gracious great room. Its spaciousness, combined with the open floor plan leading back to the dining room, makes it a wonderful spot for entertaining and the perfect place for family to gather for an evening of fun.

- Dining Room: Open to the great room and kitchen, this dining room gains an open and airy feeling from a sliding glass door leading out to an expansive rear deck. The rear deck will provide the family a place to dine in warmer weather.

- Kitchen: A large pantry, ample counter space, and plenty of cabinet space will surely please the family chef. This kitchen is also large enough to accommodate a small table and chairs, creating a space for breakfast or a quick snack.

- Master Suite: Comfort and privacy abound in this gracious master suite, which features a large walk-in closet and a private bathroom. The bathroom features an oversize tub and a dual vanity.

- Secondary Bedrooms: There are four additional bedrooms in this home, ensuring comfort and privacy for all. The single bedroom on the main floor has a private entrance to the hall bathroom, while the three upper-floor bedrooms share a hall bathroom that has a dual vanity and separate tub/shower area.

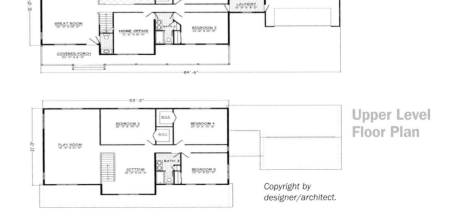

Main Level Floor Plan

Upper Level Floor Plan

Copyright by designer/architect.

Plan # 731095

Dimensions: 60' W x 51' D

Levels: 2

Heated Square Footage: 3,760

Main Level Sq. Ft.: 1,880

Upper Level Sq. Ft.: 1,880

Bedrooms: 4

Bathrooms: 4½

Foundation: Crawl space, slab, or basement

Material Take-off Included: Yes

Price Category: H

Images provided by designer/architect.

Spanning the width of this traditionally styled two-story home is a large and welcoming front porch.

CAD FILE AVAILABLE

Features:

- Living Room: Lots of sunlight will be brought into this wonderful living room through a large picture window and sliding glass door. Its tray ceiling and generously sized adjacent deck make this a place your guests will certainly enjoy.

- Kitchen: Large prep areas and a counter-top seating area that connects this kitchen to the dining room encourages extra family time while dinner is being prepared.

- Family Room: The perfect place for game night is this spacious family room, which is located on the upper floor. This room features a large front window and has plenty of cabinet space for storage.

- Master Suite: This master suite envelops you in comfort. The suite features a private sitting room, a private bathroom, and large closets. The bathroom includes a dual-sink vanity, a private toilet room, a large soaking tub, and a separate shower.

Main Level Floor Plan

Upper Level Floor Plan

Copyright by designer/architect.

Images provided by designer/architect.

Plan # 731081

Dimensions: 74' W x 44' D

Levels: 2

Heated Square Footage: 4,536

Main Level Sq. Ft.: 2,268

Upper Level Sq. Ft.: 2,268

Bedrooms: 6

Bathrooms: 3

Foundation: Crawl space, slab, or basement

Material Take-off Included: Yes

Price Category: I

Multiple gables and a gracious front porch give this ranch home a country feel.

CAD FILE AVAILABLE — **CAD**

Features:

- **Family Room:** Step directly from the foyer into this spacious family room through a cased opening. It will be a place where the family is sure to gather often. At the rear of the room, walk into the dining/kitchen area.

- **Dining Room:** Located directly across from the kitchen is this lovely dining room. At the rear of the room, step through a sliding glass doors leading onto an expansive rear deck, perfect for outdoor dining.

- **Kitchen:** With ample counter space and a large selection of cabinets, preparing family meals will be a snap in this kitchen.

- **Master Suite:** Set apart from the secondary bedrooms in the home is this lovely master suite, featuring a large walk-in closet and private bathroom, making it a perfect spot to retreat to after a long day.

- **Upper Floor:** With a library, a game room, four additional bedrooms, and a full bathroom, this home has plenty of space for all members of the family.

Main Level Floor Plan

Upper Level Floor Plan

Copyright by designer/architect.

Images provided by designer/architect.

Plan # 731163

Dimensions: 62' W x 44'6" D

Levels: 1

Heated Square Footage: 1,844

Bedrooms: 4

Bathrooms: 3

Foundation: Crawl space, slab, or basement

Material Take-off Included: Yes

Price Category: D

- Secondary Bedrooms: There are two moderately sized additional bedrooms and a full bathroom in the main house.

- Apartment: A porch at the side of the house grants you access to this cozy one-bedroom apartment.

The apartment features a combined kitchen and dining area, a den, a full bathroom, and a bedroom. This space will be perfect to use as a guest suite or as living space for the extended family.

With a spacious rear deck and a charming front covered porch, this three-bedroom ranch home also contains a one-bedroom apartment.

Features:

- Dining Room: Open to the kitchen and featuring a sliding glass door leading to the expansive rear deck, this dining room has an open and airy feeling.

- Kitchen: This well-designed kitchen offers plenty of cabinet and counter space that will please the family cook, while the pantry closet provides additional storage space.

- Master Suite: Situated away from the other bedrooms is this lovely master suite. The suite features a walk-in closet and a private bathroom. The bathroom contains an oversize tub, a separate shower, and a dual-sink vanity, adding both comfort and privacy.

Copyright by designer/architect.

Plan # 731159

Dimensions: 45'5" W x 56' D

Levels: 1

Heated Square Footage: 1,915

Bedrooms: 4

Bathrooms: 3

Foundation: Crawl space, slab, or basement

Material Take-off Included: Yes

Price Category: D

Images provided by designer/architect.

A front porch, reverse gable, and dormers provide this home with additional curb appeal.

Features:

- Kitchen: Connected to the living room, this efficiently designed kitchen has a pantry for extra storage, a countertop seating area, and at the rear a French door leading to the expansive rear deck.

- Master Suite: A luxurious space to retreat to at the end of the day, this master suite features a generous walk-in closet and a private bathroom. The bathroom houses a whirlpool tub, a separate shower, and a dual-sink vanity.

- Apartment: In addition to two secondary bedrooms and a full bathroom, the home also features a lovely one-bedroom apartment. The apartment has a kitchen, a dining room, a living room, a full bathroom, and a moderately sized bedroom. Both the bedroom and the living room have a French door that leads onto the rear deck. The apartment can be reached from the main house through a shared hallway, from the rear deck, or from an exterior door at the home's side elevation.

Copyright by designer/architect.

Images provided by designer/architect.

Plan # 731158

Dimensions: 50' W x 40' D

Levels: 1

Heated Square Footage: 1,936

Bedrooms: 4

Bathrooms: 3

Foundation: Crawl space, slab, or basement

Material Take-off Included: Yes

Price Category: D

This home is graced with a simple and elegant covered entry porch and an attached apartment.

CAD FILE AVAILABLE

Features:

- **Dining Room:** The open layout of this dining room combined with large front windows and a sliding glass door make this room bright and inviting. The sliding glass door connects this room to a generously sized deck, encouraging outdoor dining.

- **Kitchen:** This spacious kitchen is connected to the dining room via a countertop seating area, enabling interaction during the preparing of meals.

- **Master Suite:** Set toward the rear of the home is this spacious master suite, which features a walk-in closet and private bathroom. The bathroom features an oversize tub and dual-sink vanity adding comfort as well as privacy.

- **Apartment:** While the house has two secondary bedrooms, a full bathroom, and a laundry center, it also features a one-bedroom apartment. The apartment has an open floor plan for the great room and kitchen areas, a bedroom, and a full bathroom. It can be reached from an exterior side entry door or through a common mudroom area.

Images provided by designer/architect.

Plan # 731162

Dimensions: 56' W x 49'6" D

Levels: 1

Heated Square Footage: 1,948

Bedrooms: 4

Bathrooms: 3

Foundation: Crawl space, slab, or basement

Material Take-off Included: Yes

Price Category: D

Designed with clean lines and an open floor plan, this charming ranch home also features a spacious one-bedroom apartment.

CAD FILE AVAILABLE

Features:

- **Front Porch:** This front porch gives the entrance to the home an understated elegance while granting access to the main house and the apartment.

- **Living Room:** From the covered porch, step into this spacious living room. The room is the perfect place to relax with family and friends.

- **Kitchen:** Efficiently designed, this tidy kitchen is open on one side to the dining room and has a large pantry for extra storage.

- **Master Suite:** Set apart from the two secondary bedrooms in the home, this generously sized master suite features a private bathroom and a walk-in closet, providing additional comfort.

- **Apartment:** This apartment's living room, kitchen, and dining area are all open, mirroring the main house in design principles.

Copyright by designer/architect.

Plan # 731160

Dimensions: 70'6" W x 55'4" D

Levels: 1

Heated Square Footage: 1,961

Bedrooms: 4

Bathrooms: 3

Foundation: Crawl space, slab, or basement

Material Take-off Included: Yes

Price Category: D

Images provided by designer/architect.

A front porch and dormers add charm to this three-bedroom home, which features a private apartment.

Features:

- Great Room: Step from the covered porch into this generously sized great room, certain to be the main gathering spot for the entire family.

- Kitchen: Designed with efficiency in mind, this kitchen is open to the dining room and features a countertop eating area that will be perfect for an informal meal.

- Master Suite: After a long day, relax in this beautiful master bedroom, which features such amenities as a large walk-in closet and a private bathroom.

- Secondary Bedrooms: Two additional bedrooms and a full bathroom round out the private areas of the home, providing space for all.

- Apartment: Enter the spacious one-bedroom apartment through the garage, a shared utility space, or an exterior entrance at the side of the home. The apartment has a large living room, which is open to the kitchen, a full bathroom, and a moderately sized bedroom. The space is perfect for the extended family.

Copyright by designer/architect.

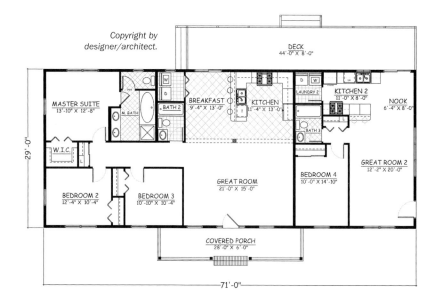

Plan # 731156

Dimensions: 71' W x 29' D

Levels: 1

Heated Square Footage: 2,059

Bedrooms: 4

Bathrooms: 3

Foundation: Crawl space, slab, or basement

Material Take-off Included: Yes

Price Category: D

Images provided by designer/architect.

A reverse front gable and dormers grace the front of this lovely three-bedroom home, which features a private apartment.

Features:

- Great Room: A perfect spot for gathering with the family, is this generously sized great room is open at the rear to both the kitchen and the breakfast room, creating a feeling of continuity.

- Kitchen: This U-shaped kitchen is perfectly located off the family room and connected to the breakfast room by a snack bar.

- Master Suite: After a long day, relax in this beautiful master suite, which features such amenities as a large walk-in closet, a spa-like master bathroom,

and a patio door that leads to an expansive rear deck. The bathroom features a whirlpool tub, a separate shower, and a private toilet room.

- Secondary Bedrooms: Two additional bedrooms and a full bathroom round out the private areas of the home, providing space for all.

- Apartment: A separate entrance at the side of the house leads you to a spacious apartment. The apartment has a large great room, a full bathroom, laundry facilities, and a galley-style kitchen with a countertop eating area. This space is perfect for the extended family.

Images provided by designer/architect.

Plan # 731169

Dimensions: 60' W x 49'2" D

Levels: 1

Heated Square Footage: 2,278

Bedrooms: 4

Bathrooms: 3

Foundation: Crawl space, slab, or basement

Material Take-off Included: Yes

Price Category: E

This home is ideal for any family, due to its spaciousness and versatility. Versatility is increased with the addition of a lovely one-bedroom apartment.

Features:

- Great Room: This splendid great room features a large picture window, a sliding patio door, and easy access to the kitchen, ensuring that it will be the main gathering spot for the entire family.

- Deck: Whether you need a quiet spot to enjoy your morning coffee or want to take advantage of the warm weather in the summer to entertain, this large deck connected to both the master suite and the great room is sure to fill the bill.

- Master Suite: At the rear of the home is this private retreat. This master suite features a sitting area, a large walk-in closet, a luxurious bathroom, and a French door leading to a rear deck.

- Apartment: While there are two additional bedrooms and a full bathroom in the main house, this lovely one-bedroom apartment features a cozy living room, a kitchen area, and a full bathroom, allowing you an extra private area for guests or extended family.

Copyright by designer/architect.

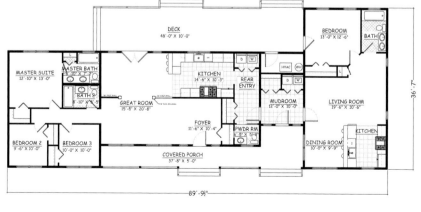

Plan # 731157

Dimensions: 89'9½" W x 36'7" D

Levels: 1

Heated Square Footage: 2,300

Bedrooms: 4

Bathrooms: 3½

Foundation: Crawl space, slab, or basement

Material Take-off Included: Yes

Price Category: E

This expanded three-bedroom ranch home features an attached one-bedroom apartment for extended family.

Features:

- **Front Porch:** Spanning the front of the home is this lovely front porch. It features stately columns, is wide enough for a few seating arrangements and planters, and grants you access to the main house, as well as the entrance to the shared mudroom space.

- **Great Room:** A wonderfully bright and airy space, this great room spans from the front of the home to the rear. In addition to being open to the kitchen, this room features a pair of elegant columns and a set of French doors that lead you to an expansive deck.

- **Kitchen:** Time spent in this kitchen will be a joy. It features a 48-in.-wide range, an abundance of cabinets, ample counter space, and a countertop seating area to encourage interaction between the chef and family members.

- **Secondary Bedrooms:** Two moderately sized bedrooms and a full bathroom help to complete the private areas of this home.

- **Apartment:** Through the shared mudroom space you can enter the main house or the lovely one-bedroom apartment. The apartment features a combined kitchen and dining area, a living room, a full bathroom, and a moderately sized bedroom. The apartment layout mimics that of the main house by keeping the public areas of the home open.

Images provided by designer/architect.

Plan # 731172

Dimensions: 60' W x 51' D

Levels: 1

Heated Square Footage: 2,380

Bedrooms: 4

Bathrooms: 3½

Foundation: Crawl space, slab, or basement

Material Take-off Included: Yes

Price Category: E

This spacious home features a covered entry porch, which spans the width of the home. Also included in this home is a cozy one-bedroom apartment, the perfect spot for a guest or perhaps extended family.

Features:

- Living Room: Large front windows, a tray ceiling, and a sliding glass door, leading to a generously sized deck, make this living room the perfect spot for entertaining.

- Kitchen: This U-shaped kitchen has plenty of counter and cabinet space for preparing of meals, while a countertop seating area connects the kitchen to the dining room, encouraging extra family time while dinner is being prepared.

- Dining Room: Large front windows make this dining room bright and inviting. It is open to the kitchen and foyer, creating continuity throughout the main living areas of the home.

- Master Suite: Through dual pocket doors you step into this luxurious master suite. The suite features a luxurious bathroom, a large closet, and hinged French doors that lead onto its own private deck.

- Additional rooms: There are two additional bedrooms, a full bathroom, and a powder room in the main house, while the private apartment houses a moderately sized bedroom, a full bathroom, and a kitchen/great room combination.

Copyright by designer/architect.

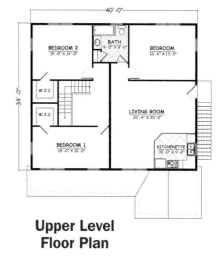

Images provided by designer/architect.

Plan # 731165

Dimensions: 40' W x 44' D

Levels: 2

Heated Square Footage: 2,558

Main Level Sq. Ft.: 1,198

Upper Level Sq. Ft.: 1,360

Bedrooms: 4

Bathrooms: 3

Foundation: Crawl space, slab, or basement

Material Take-off Included: Yes

Price Category: E

Busy families are sure to be pleased with all the amenities this home has to offer. The three-bedroom home also has a separate private apartment.

Features:

- Front Porch: An expansive front-entry porch offers you shelter from the elements. The space is also wide enough to fit a small seating area—a perfect spot for relaxing after dinner.

- Dining Room: Connected to the kitchen via the snack bar, this lovely dining room is open to the living room and has a sliding glass door that leads you into the backyard.

- Kitchen: This well-designed kitchen is sure to please the family cook with its abundance of cabinet and counter space as well as a double sink and snack bar. The snack bar is a perfect spot for informal meals.

- Master Suite: Relax at the end of the day in this lovely master suite, which features a large walk-in closet and a private bathroom. The bathroom has a luxurious feel, with such amenities as a whirlpool tub and dual-sink vanity, and it is sure to leave you feeling rejuvenated.

- Upper Level: This upper level houses two moderately sized bedrooms with walk-in closets, along with the private apartment. You can get access to the apartment from an exterior staircase located at the side of the house. The apartment includes a large living room, a kitchenette, a bedroom, and a full bathroom, the perfect space for extended family members.

Main Level Floor Plan

Copyright by designer/architect.

Upper Level Floor Plan

Plan # 731161

Dimensions: 53' W x 30' D

Levels: 2

Heated Square Footage: 2,745

Main Level Sq. Ft.: 1,420

Upper Level Sq. Ft.: 1,325

Bedrooms: 5

Bathrooms: 4

Foundation: Crawl space, slab, or basement

Material Take-off Included: Yes

Price Category: F

This welcoming two-story home houses a second-floor one-bedroom apartment.

Features:

- **Living Room:** From the front porch, step into this expansive great room, certain to be the main gathering spot for the entire family.

- **Kitchen:** This efficiently designed kitchen has plenty of counter and cabinet space to please the family chef. It is completely open to a cozy breakfast nook.

- **Master Suite:** After a long day, relax in this beautiful master suite, which features such amenities as a large walk-in closet and a private bathroom.

- **Upper Level:** In addition to the master suite and full bathroom on the first floor, this upper level has an additional two bedrooms, an office, a full bathroom, and the one-bedroom apartment.

- **Apartment:** Perfect for your extened family is this spacious one-bedroom apartment. You can get access to the apartment at the upper level from an exterior staircase or the upper hall of the main house. The apartment has its own kitchen, a moderately sized bedroom, a full bathroom, and an am ply sized living room.

Main Level Floor Plan

Copyright by designer/architect.

Upper Level Floor Plan

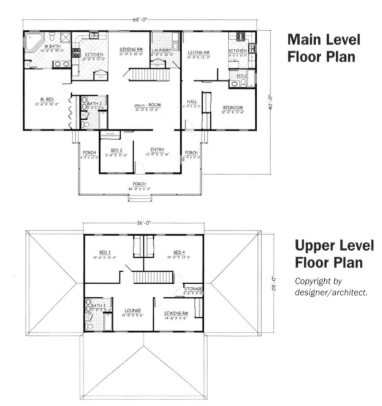

Images provided by designer/architect.

Plan # 731164

Dimensions: 68' W x 40' D

Levels: 2

Heated Square Footage: 3,056

Main Level Sq. Ft.: 2,192

Upper Level Sq. Ft.: 864

Bedrooms: 5

Bathrooms: 3

Foundation: Crawl space, slab, or basement

Material Take-off Included: Yes

Price Category: G

Its wraparound front porch gives this two-story home a country feel.

Features:

- Great Room: This wonderfully open and generously sized great room is centrally located and is certain to be the main gathering spot for the family.

- Kitchen: Efficiently designed, this kitchen provides the cook in the family with a generous amount of counter and cabinet space, making mealtime preparation much easier. It is open to the dining room, creating a seamless transition between rooms.

- Master Suite: Enjoy some alone time in this lovely master suite. Soak the cares of the day away in a distinctive corner bathtub.

- Upper Level: There are two bedrooms on the second floor that have multiple windows, making the rooms light and cheery. Both bedrooms are located close to the full bathroom.

- Apartment: With a private entrance off of the porch, this apartment is perfect for the extended family. It has a foyer with a closet, a living room, a kitchen, a bedroom, and a full bathroom.

Main Level Floor Plan

Upper Level Floor Plan

Copyright by designer/architect.

Buying a Faucet

 When you're selecting a faucet for a new kitchen, there is a lot to choose from and there are a few questions to ask before the water starts to flow.

Kitchen Faucet Buying Guide

How Many Holes Are in the Sink?

Be sure to choose a faucet that requires the same number of holes as the number of holes in the sink you've selected. One-piece faucets (with integrated handle and spout) need one hole for the handle/spout piece, and usually require a separate hole for a sprayer. Traditional faucets, with hot and cold taps, require three holes for the taps and spout and a fourth for a sprayer. Other options, such as integrated sprayers and soap dispensers, can create other requirements; make sure you are clear about your needs.

If you're starting from scratch with a new sink, you can select the sink to accommodate the faucet you want.

What Kind of Handles?

Typical kitchen faucets have either one handle that rotates directionally to choose a water temperature or two handles for mixing hot and cold water. One-piece faucets can have a handle that's attached to the faucet unit or a handle that sits to the side (in the same position a traditional sprayer would be).

Traditional faucets can feature the classic look of the rounded-X shaped tap, a more contemporary, cylindrical silhouette, or an easy-access lever shape. Lever taps are often easiest to manipulate. They fit in well with the concept of universal design, an attempt to make living spaces as accessible as possible to people of all levels of physical ability.

What Kind of Sprayer?

Some newer models have sprayers integrated right into the faucet itself.

What Goes in the Sink? If a large number of bulky pots and pans will be washed regularly, choose a faucet with a tall, curved neck. A pull-out sprayer can reach double- and triple-bowl sinks.

Is a Filter needed?

Many people choose to filter their tap water for drinking. There are a number of ways to install a filter, and some involve an attachment to the faucet itself. A few faucets come with the filtering mechanism built-in. If you choose to install a filter, think about the volume of water that will be used and maintenance requirements. (See page 156 for more.)

What Style and Finish Do You Want?

For a unified look, choose a style and finish for the new faucet that matches that of the kitchen cabinet hardware. Some faucets mount from the top of the sink, while others mount from the bottom. Most plumbers will be familiar with both types.

There are four main types of faucet mechanisms: ball valve, ceramic disk, compression valve, and cartridge. Which type the new faucet has won't make a big difference in day-to-day use, but some are easier to repair than others.

Choosing a Bathroom Faucet

A bathroom faucet can make a big difference in the look of the sink.

When selecting a faucet, match it to the hole-configuration of the sink. Faucets are available in a wide range of prices and styles. They range from very inexpensive, mostly plastic models, to high-quality brass units.

Bathroom Faucet Type

Not all faucet types work with every sink basin. Standard faucet drillings are widespread, center set, or single hole.

■ **Widespread faucet sets** have a spout with separate hot- and cold-water handles. All pieces appear to be separate. Widespread faucets are available from 6 to 16 inches drillings for three-hole predrilled installation basins.

■ **Center-set faucets** (mini-wide-spread) are made for 4-inch pre-drilled with three-hole installation basins. They combine a spout and valves on a single base unit. A center set faucet set may have a single handle mixing lever or two handles mounted onto a 6-inch plate.

■ **Wall-mounted faucets** are available for above-the-counter and free-standing basins that require a long spout for extended reach. Wall-mount faucets require a separate wall-mount valve and drain for installation. Make sure the spout is long enough for adequate basin clearance.

■ **Single-hole faucets** have a spout and a single-mixing handle all in one for single-handed control. Single-lever faucets require one-hole drill installation basins. Some brands of single-lever faucets have an optional 6-inch cover plate for pre-drilled 4-inch drill installations.

Faucet Color and Finish

The color/finish should coordinate with the rest of the fixtures and accessories in the bathroom. The following is a list of available colors/finishes:

- **Chrome (matte, brushed or polished)**
- **Brass (brushed or polished)**
- **Enamel-coated colors**
- **Ceramic**
- **Antique**
- **Pewter**
- **Nickel (brushed and pearl)**
- **Gold**
- **Platinum**
- **Bronze**

Some faucet sets come with a combination of finishes to draw more attention to their distinct styling. For example, a faucet with a brass-and-chrome combination finish creates a fresh but sophisticated look in any bathroom.

Faucet Handle Styles

Handle styles are available in various finishes to complement both sink and faucet. Before choosing a handle style, think about who will be using the bathroom. Choose from:

- **Lever handles:** the best universal design for children and older adults to grip and turn. Lever handles are available in many decorative styles.
- **Cross handles:** available in different finishes to coordinate with the room's décor.
- **Motion activated:** some brands have interchangeable colored temperature-control handles. These faucets are easy to use—adjust the temperature and place your hands under the spout to activate the water flow.

Faucet Construction

Every type of faucet has an inner valve that controls the flow of water through the spout. The valve quality, with or without a washer, determines the reliability and durability of the faucet. The best choices are faucets with solid-brass, brass-based-metal, or corrosion-resistant-metal workings.

Faucets with a Washer

- **Compression-valve faucets** are the most common types of faucets on the market. The faucet works by a stem that rises and falls to open and close the water's passageway.

Washerless Faucets

- **Cartridge faucets** use rubber O-rings inside a cylindrical cartridge to control the flow of water. These faucets are very reliable, especially if equipped with a brass cartridge.
- **Ball faucets** have a rotating metal/plastic ball that regulates the amount of incoming water. With only one moving part, the likelihood of a malfunction is greatly reduced. A plastic ball will eventually wear out, but a metal ball is designed to last a lifetime.
- **Ceramic-disc faucets,** are nearly maintenance-free. A ceramic-disc faucet has two ceramic discs that move against each other in a shearing action, blocking water or allowing it to pass through. The seal is watertight because the discs are nearly flat.

Choosing a Water Filter

Many people are looking to bottled water as an alternative to tap water. A number of home water filters allow homeowners to get freshly filtered water straight from the tap. They're easy to install and maintain, and may be just what's needed to improve the quality of the family's water.

Types of Water Contaminants

- **Taste- and odor-causing contaminants**
- **Rust/sediment**
- **Bacteria/parasites**
- **Lead**

The household water may, or may not, suffer from any of these contaminants. If you're concerned about the quality of the water, have it tested by an independent laboratory. The filtration system needed for the home depends upon the quality of the water supply. Water filters do require some occasional maintenance, and cartridges should be changed according to the manufacturer's recommendations.

Taste- and Odor-Causing Contaminants: If the water smells or tastes bad, there's little doubt that the house would benefit from a water filter. Municipal water often smells of chlorine, which is used to treat the water. Well water, which is dependent upon many local conditions affecting the water supply, also may

smell bad. Water filters often treat these conditions by using granular activated carbon (GAC), a substance that absorbs contaminants that would otherwise cause offensive tastes and odors.

Filters that use GAC may cause cloudy water for the first couple of weeks after a filter change. This is a harmless condition caused by the release of air from the GAC and can be reduced by running the water for several seconds before each use until the air is flushed out.

Rust and Sediment: You may notice visible particles in the water. Sediment can collect in the bottom of the dishwasher or commode, for example. Larger particles may collect behind the screens of a faucet aerator. Smaller particles may collect at the bottom of a glass of water that sits for a time. Rust and sediment are easily collected by particulate filters. Whole-house particulate filters are easy to install and protect not only the drinking water, but also your appliances such as dishwashers and ice makers.

Water filters aren't effective against clear-water iron, which can leave red stains in tubs and toilets. To treat this substance, a water softener is required.

Bacteria/Parasites: If the house relies on a well, the water is more likely to be contaminated by bacteria and parasites. Many bacteria and parasites occur naturally in clear-water supplies. Others are the result of water-supply contamination by sewage and wastes. Some bacteria and parasites affect the taste and smell of the water, but others don't. Cysts, such as Cryptosporidium and Giardia, are particularly hearty parasites and have been known to contaminate even chlorinated municipal water supplies. They can cause illness and are a serious hazard to the young, elderly, or those with immune deficiencies. Water filters are available with various filter cartridges that are effective against many of these contaminants.

Lead: Houses built before 1986 may have pipes joined with lead solder. The municipal water system also may be composed of components that contain or are soldered with lead. If you're concerned about the possibility of lead in the water supply, have the water tested by an independent laboratory.

Lead contained in water is tasteless and odorless but should be avoided as much as possible. It can be removed from drinking and cooking water by installing a lead filter directly under the sink in the kitchen. This filter placement ensures that even if there is lead in the pipes of the home, it'll be removed from the household drinking water.

Types of Home Water Filters

There are several types of water-filtration systems available. Anyone should be able to install the units described in this article simply by following the manufacturer's installation instructions. Choose the system that meets your needs based upon the contaminants you're trying to remove. Be aware that although the countertop and faucet-mounted filters are easiest to install initially, they're more bulky and less convenient than the hidden undersink filter. They're also less versatile if you're attempting to filter contaminants other than tastes, smells, and lead.

Whole-House Filters: Whole-house filters are available and easy to install. They're placed in the main water line entering the home and are designed to remove sediment and rust particles from all of the water entering the home. They can also benefit the other types of water filters by acting as a particulate prefilter.

Undersink Filters: Different varieties of undersink filters are available and should be chosen depending upon the home's individual needs. Some of these filters remove bad tastes and odors only. Others also may remove lead, bacteria, sediment, or any combination of the four. These units may have multiple cartridges, each designed to filter a particular type of contaminant.

Undersink filters are convenient because, once installed, no one will even know they are there. Turn on the water, and filtered water comes straight from the faucet. They're also efficient because they allow you to filter only the water going to a specific faucet, thereby reducing the demands on the filter cartridges. You don't need to filter bath water to remove a chlorine taste, for example, but you may want to remove it from drinking water. Undersink filters are also helpful if the plumbing is joined with lead solder. By being in line immediately before the faucet, undersink filters provide maximum filtration protection.

Faucet-Mounted Filters: These filters connect directly to the faucet and require no plumbing connections. Some models are designed simply to remove bad tastes and odors, while more sophisticated units now have lead- and cyst-filtering capabilities. Also, they filter the water at the point of use. But they are a highly visible attachment to the faucet.

Countertop or Canisters Filters: These are the simplest water filters available. They're countertop appliances, like toasters, and can filter drinking water for different contaminants. Unlike undersink filters, their use isn't transparent. Some of these filters must remain on the counter; some require connection to your spigot; and some require that water be poured through them, much like a drip coffee maker.

Plan # 731142

Dimensions: 28' W x 24' D

Levels: 1

Heated Square Footage: 475

Bedrooms: 1

Bathrooms: 1

Foundation: Slab

Material Take-off Included: Yes

Price Category: A

Images provided by designer/architect.

CAD FILE CAD AVAILABLE

Copyright by designer/architect.

GARAGE
28'-0" X 24'-0"

24'-0"

28'-0"

KITCHEN

LIVING ROOM
12'-5" X 13'-1"

BEDROOM
13'-9" X 9'-8"

BATH

24'-0"

19'-10"

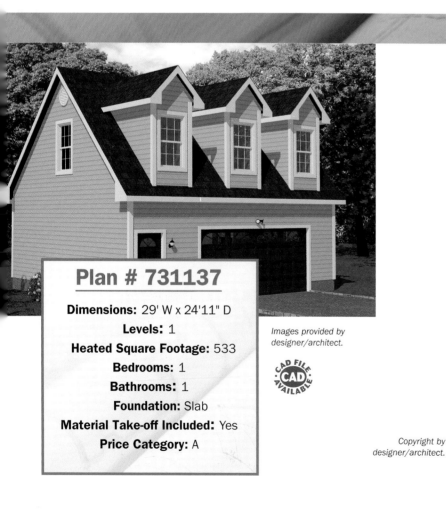

Plan # 731137

Dimensions: 29' W x 24'11" D

Levels: 1

Heated Square Footage: 533

Bedrooms: 1

Bathrooms: 1

Foundation: Slab

Material Take-off Included: Yes

Price Category: A

Images provided by designer/architect.

CAD FILE CAD AVAILABLE

Copyright by designer/architect.

29'-0"

STOR.
3'-6" X 10'-0"

GARAGE
24'-0" X 24'-0"

24'-11"

29'-0"

LIVING/KITCHEN
13'-8" X 10'-2"

BEDROOM
9'-10" X 15'-6"

BATH
7'-10" X 5'-0"

24'-11"

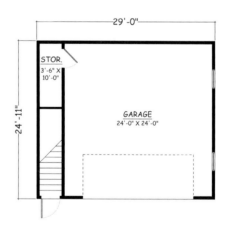

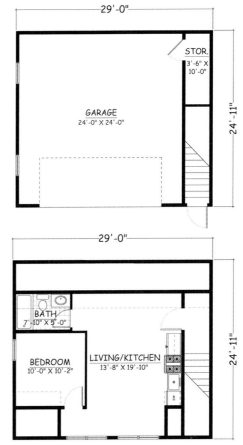

Plan # 731146

Dimensions: 29' W x 24'11" D

Levels: 1

Heated Square Footage: 556

Bedrooms: 1

Bathrooms: 1

Foundation: Slab

Material Take-off Included: Yes

Price Category: A

Images provided by designer/architect.

CAD FILE AVAILABLE

Copyright by designer/architect.

Plan # 731166

Dimensions: 28' W x 28' D

Levels: 1

Heated Square Footage: 616

Bedrooms: 1

Bathrooms: 1

Foundation: Slab

Material Take-off Included: Yes

Price Category: A

Images provided by designer/architect.

CAD FILE AVAILABLE

Copyright by designer/architect.

GARAGE
24'-0" X 28'-0"

28'-0"

28'-0"

Plan # 731141

Dimensions: 28' W x 28' D

Levels: 2

Heated Square Footage: 672

Bedrooms: 1

Bathrooms: 1

Foundation: Slab

Material Take-off Included: Yes

Price Category: A

Images provided by designer/architect.

CAD FILE AVAILABLE

LIVING ROOM
12'-9" X 13'-6"

KITCHEN
10'-0" X 8'-6"

NOOK
10'-0" X 5'-0"

HW

BATH

BEDROOM
13'-6" X 13'-3"

28'-0"

24'-0"

Copyright by designer/architect.

28'-6"

GARAGE
24'-6" X 24'-0"

24'-0"

FOYER
3'-6" X 4'-6"

PORCH
4'-0" X 2'-8"

Plan # 731138

Dimensions: 28'6" W x 24' D

Levels: 1

Heated Square Footage: 674

Bedrooms: 1

Bathrooms: 1

Foundation: Slab

Material Take-off Included: Yes

Price Category: A

Images provided by designer/architect.

CAD FILE AVAILABLE

28'-6"

LAUNDRY
5'-6" X 7'-10"

KITCHEN
11'-0" X 7'-10"

DINING
7'-0" X 7'-10"

BATH
5'-0" X 7'-0"

24'-0"

BEDROOM
10'-6" X 9'-6"

GREAT ROOM
13'-0" X 15'-4"

Copyright by designer/architect.

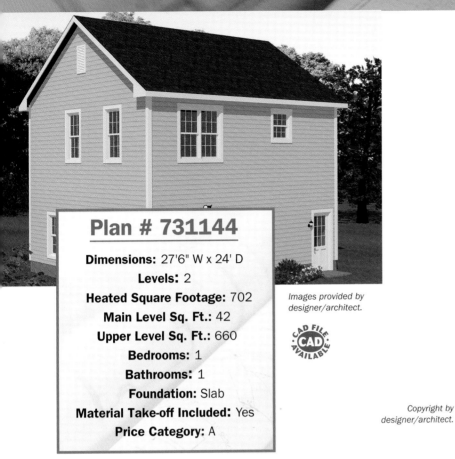

Plan # 731144

Dimensions: 27'6" W x 24' D

Levels: 2

Heated Square Footage: 702

Main Level Sq. Ft.: 42

Upper Level Sq. Ft.: 660

Bedrooms: 1

Bathrooms: 1

Foundation: Slab

Material Take-off Included: Yes

Price Category: A

Images provided by designer/architect.

CAD FILE AVAILABLE

Copyright by designer/architect.

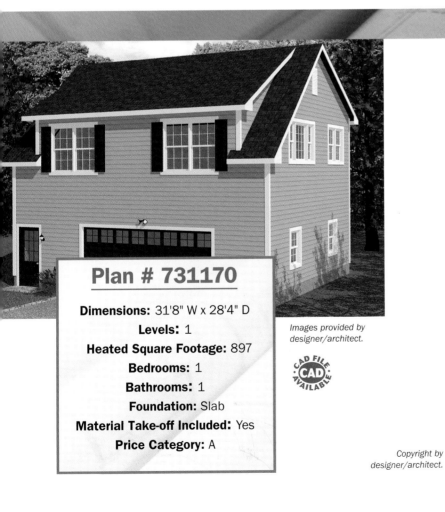

Plan # 731170

Dimensions: 31'8" W x 28'4" D

Levels: 1

Heated Square Footage: 897

Bedrooms: 1

Bathrooms: 1

Foundation: Slab

Material Take-off Included: Yes

Price Category: A

Images provided by designer/architect.

CAD FILE AVAILABLE

Copyright by designer/architect.

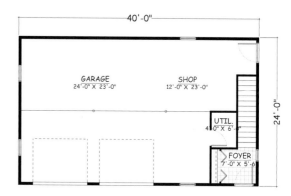

GARAGE
24'-0" X 23'-0"

SHOP
12'-0" X 23'-0"

UTIL.
4'-0" X 6'-0"

FOYER
7'-0" X 5'-6"

40'-0"

24'-0"

Plan # 731143

Dimensions: 40' W x 24' D

Levels: 2

Heated Square Footage: 960

Bedrooms: 2

Bathrooms: 1

Foundation: Slab

Material Take-off Included: Yes

Price Category: A

Images provided by designer/architect.

CAD FILE AVAILABLE

BED 2
13'-6" X 11'-6"

BATH
5'-0" X 7'-6"

FAMILY RM.
17'-0" X 11'-6"

BED 1
15'-6" X 11'-6"

DINING
9'-6" X 11'-6"

KITCHEN
10'-6" X 11'-6"

40'-0"

24'-0"

Copyright by designer/architect.

Plan # 731145

Dimensions: 30' W x 30' D

Levels: 2

Heated Square Footage: 988

Main Level Sq. Ft.: 88

Upper Level Sq. Ft.: 900

Bedrooms: 1

Bathrooms: 1

Foundation: Slab

Material Take-off Included: Yes

Price Category: A

Images provided by designer/architect.

CAD FILE AVAILABLE

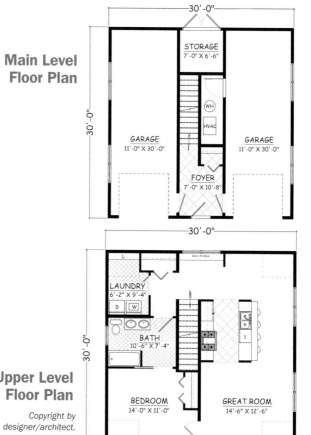

Main Level Floor Plan

30'-0"

30'-0"

STORAGE
7'-0" X 6'-6"

GARAGE
11'-0" X 30'-0"

GARAGE
11'-0" X 30'-0"

WH

HVAC

FOYER
7'-0" X 10'-8"

Upper Level Floor Plan

30'-0"

30'-0"

LAUNDRY
6'-2" X 9'-4"

D   W

BATH
10'-6" X 7'-4"

BEDROOM
14'-0" X 11'-0"

GREAT ROOM
14'-6" X 12'-6"

BUILT-IN DESK

Copyright by designer/architect.

Plan # 731140

Dimensions: 37' W x 34' D

Levels: 2

Heated Square Footage: 1,244

Main Level Sq. Ft.: 156

Upper Level Sq. Ft.: 1,088

Bedrooms: 2

Bathrooms: 1

Foundation: Slab

Material Take-off Included: Yes

Price Category: B

Images provided by designer/architect.

CAD FILE AVAILABLE

Main Level Floor Plan

Upper Level Floor Plan

Copyright by designer/architect.

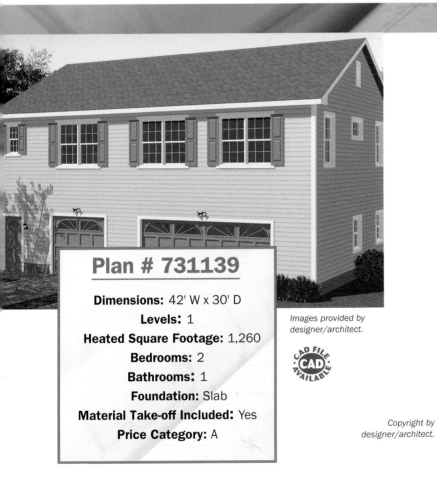

Plan # 731139

Dimensions: 42' W x 30' D

Levels: 1

Heated Square Footage: 1,260

Bedrooms: 2

Bathrooms: 1

Foundation: Slab

Material Take-off Included: Yes

Price Category: A

Images provided by designer/architect.

CAD FILE AVAILABLE

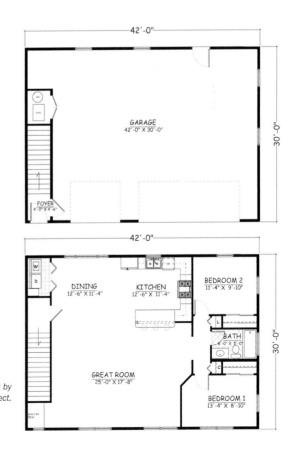

Copyright by designer/architect.

Images provided by designer/architect.

Plan # 731109

Dimensions: 55'1" W x 49'3" D

Levels: 1

Heated Square Footage: 1,508

Bedrooms: 4

Bathrooms: 2

Foundation: Crawl space, slab, or basement

Material Take-off Included: Yes

Price Category: C

Multiple dormers and an entry porch provide this two-bedroom duplex with additional curb appeal.

Features:

- Entry Porch: Columns and brick accents highlight the entry porches to this duplex.

Copyright by designer/architect.

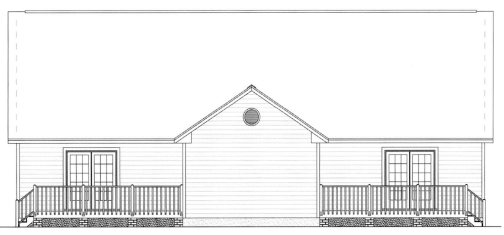

Rear Elevation

Left Elevation

Right Elevation

- Kitchen: Thoughtful design will allow each kitchen to be easily organized. The island area not only allows additional room for meal prep but also is large enough to sit and enjoy an informal meal or snack.

- Living Room: At the rear of each unit is this large living room. It is open to the kitchen on one side and features a sliding glass door that leads to a private rear deck.

- Bedrooms: Each of the two bedrooms in each unit features large windows, making the rooms bright and cheery. These bedrooms are also just steps away from a centrally located bathroom.

Plan # 731110

Dimensions: 50'9" W x 37'10" D

Levels: 1

Heated Square Footage: 1,512

Bedrooms: 4

Bathrooms: 2

Foundation: Crawl space, slab, or basement

Material Take-off Included: Yes

Price Category: C

Images provided by designer/architect.

A front porch featuring turned columns and brick accents gives this two-bedroom duplex its curb appeal.

CAD FILE AVAILABLE

Features:

- **Front Porch:** A combined front porch has the appearance of being a single family home.

- **Kitchen:** Each kitchen will be easily organized, thanks to its thoughtful design. Multitasking is also made easier with the addition of a small utility closet within the kitchen area.

- **Living Room:** Located at the rear of each unit is this expansive living room. With a multiple window unit and a sliding glass door that leads to a rear private deck, this room is both bright and airy.

- **Bedrooms:** In each unit are two bedrooms that have multiple windows, making the rooms light and cheery. Both bedrooms are located in close proximity to a full bathroom.

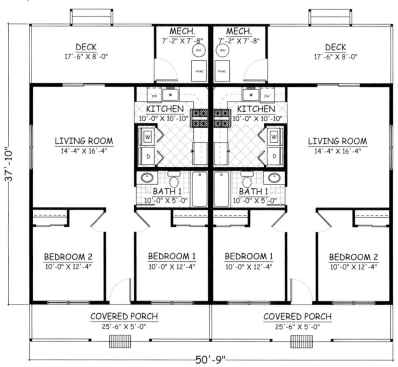

Copyright by designer/architect.

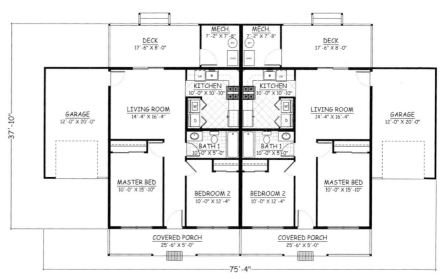

Images provided by designer/architect.

Plan # 731175

Dimensions: 75'4" W x 37'10" D

Levels: 1

Heated Square Footage: 1,512

Bedrooms: 4

Bathrooms: 2

Foundation: Crawl space, slab, or basement

Material Take-off Included: Yes

Price Category: C

Multiple dormers, turned columns, and brick accents invite you into this charming two-bedroom duplex.

Features:

- Kitchen: Thoughtful design will allow each kitchen to be easily organized. The inclusion of a utility closet that houses the washer and dryer makes multitasking easy.

- Living Room: Set at the rear of each unit is this spacious living room. It is open to the kitchen on one side and features a sliding glass door that leads to a private rear deck.

- Bedrooms: Each of the two bedrooms in each unit features large windows, making the rooms bright and airy.

Copyright by designer/architect.

Plan # 731111

Dimensions: 75'8" W x 40'1" D

Levels: 1

Heated Square Footage: 1,668

Bedrooms: 4

Bathrooms: 2

Foundation: Crawl space, slab, or basement

Material Take-off Included: Yes

Price Category: C

- Kitchen: Each tidy kitchen is well designed, providing ample counter and cabinet space for the preparation of meals.

- Bedrooms: Two moderately sized bedrooms and a full bathroom help to complete the private areas of each home.

This two-bedroom duplex features clean lines, giving it the look of a ranch-style single-family home.

CAD FILE AVAILABLE

Features:

- Front Porch: Simple square columns and brick accents give the front porches on the units an understated elegance.

- Dining Room: Open to both the living room and the kitchen, each dining room seems endless. The room also features a sliding glass door that leads onto a private rear deck, encouraging outdoor dining when the weather is warm.

DECK 17'-6" X 8'-0"

STORAGE/MECH 7'-6" X 7'-8"

STORAGE/MECH 7'-6" X 7'-8"

DECK 17'-6" X 8'-0"

DINING ROOM 10'-8" X 8'-0"

KITCHEN 12'-0" X 10'-10"

KITCHEN 12'-0" X 10'-10"

DINING ROOM 10'-8" X 8'-0"

LIVING ROOM 14'-4" X 13'-6"

LIVING ROOM 14'-4" X 13'-6"

BATH 1 10'-0" X 5'-0"

BATH 1 10'-0" X 5'-0"

40'-1"

BEDROOM 2 10'-0" X 12'-4"

BEDROOM 1 10'-0" X 12'-4"

GARAGE 12'-0" X 20'-0"

GARAGE 12'-0" X 20'-0"

BEDROOM 1 10'-0" X 12'-4"

BEDROOM 2 10'-0" X 12'-4"

COVERED PORCH 25'-2" X 5'-0"

COVERED PORCH 25'-2" X 5'-0"

75'-8"

Copyright by designer/architect.

Plan # 731101

Dimensions: 60' W x 40' D

Levels: 1

Heated Square Footage: 1,872

Bedrooms: 4

Bathrooms: 2

Foundation: Crawl space, slab, or basement

Material Take-off Included: Yes

Price Category: D

Images provided by designer/architect.

Outdoor living space is just one of the wonderful amenities featured in this two-bedroom duplex.

Features:

• Living Room: Step from a lovely private front porch on each unit into this living room. The room is gracious in nature and is centrally located, making it the perfect place for both entertaining and relaxing.

• Kitchen: Open to the living room, each efficiently designed kitchen also features a hinged patio door leading to a privatebrear deck, encouraging outdoor dining.

• Bedrooms: Each unit in this duplex features two bedrooms near a centrally located full bathroom. In addition to spacious closets, the larger of the two bedrooms includes a patio door that connects to the rear deck.

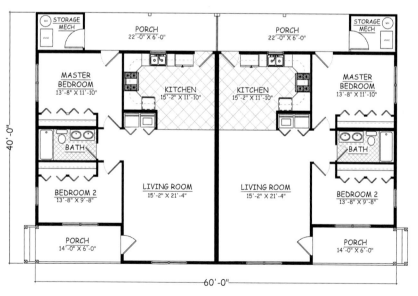

Copyright by designer/architect.

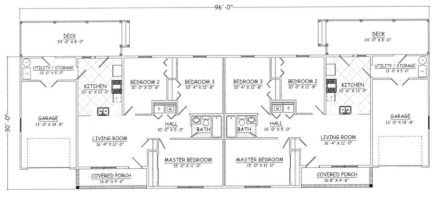

Images provided by designer/architect.

Plan # 731113

Dimensions: 96' W x 30' D

Levels: 1

Heated Square Footage: 1,932

Bedrooms: 6

Bathrooms: 2

Foundation: Crawl space, slab, or basement

Material Take-off Included: Yes

Price Category: D

This highly functional, attractive duplex provides plenty of door living space.

Features:

- **Living Room:** Step from the private front porch on each unit into this gen erously sized living room. Connected to the kitchen by the countertop eating area, the unit keeps the free-flowing feel of an open floor plan.

- **Kitchen:** With ample counter space and modern conveniences, each kitchen is sure to please the family cook. A countertop eating area open to the living room not only provides you with an area to eat, but also gives the cook additional prep space. At the rear of the room is a French door that leads out to a large deck, the perfect place to eat on warm summer nights.

- **Bedrooms:** Each of the units has three bedrooms—one master and two secondary bedrooms. All of the bedrooms are just steps away from the full bathroom.

Copyright by designer/architect.

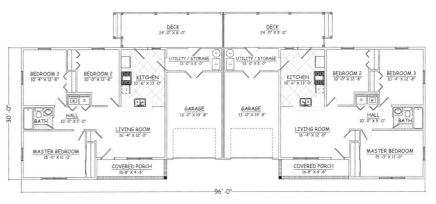

Images provided by designer/architect.

Plan # 731114

Dimensions: 96' W x 30' D

Levels: 1

Heated Square Footage: 1,932

Bedrooms: 6

Bathrooms: 2

Foundation: Crawl space, slab, or basement

Material Take-off Included: Yes

Price Category: D

This efficiently designed duplex features amenities the whole family will love.

CAD FILE AVAILABLE

Features:

- **Living Room:** Enter this generously sized living room from the front porch on each unit. Connected to the kitchen by the countertop eating area, the space will make you appreciate the free-flowing feel of an open floor plan.

- **Kitchen:** With ample counter space and modern conveniences, each kitchen is sure to please the family cook. A countertop eating area provides you with an area to eat and gives the cook additional prep space. A French door leads out to a large private deck, the perfect place to eat outdoors.

- Bedrooms: Each of the units has three bedrooms—one master and two secondary bedrooms. All of the bedrooms are located close to the full bathroom.

Copyright by designer/architect.

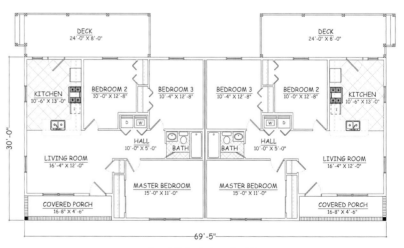

Images provided by designer/architect.

Plan # 731115

Dimensions: 69'5" W x 30' D

Levels: 1

Heated Square Footage: 1,932

Bedrooms: 6

Bathrooms: 2

Foundation: Crawl space, slab, or basement

Material Take-off Included: Yes

Price Category: D

Combined kitchen and living room spaces give this three-bedroom duplex an open and airy feel.

Features:

- Front Porch: Amply sized private front porches give both shelter and curb appeal to this duplex.

- Kitchen: Each simply designed kitchen has plenty of cabinet space for storage. The kitchen opens to the living room by way of a countertop eating area—this space not only gives you a place to eat, but also provides additional counter space. At the rear of the room is a lovely French door that leads to a large deck.

- Bedrooms: Each unit has a total of three bedrooms. The master bedroom is significantly larger than the other two bedrooms, providing you with a bit more comfort. All of the bedrooms are just steps away from the full bathroom.

Copyright by designer/architect.

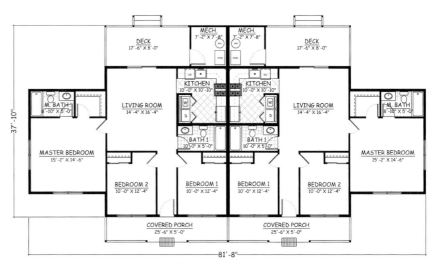

Plan # 731126

Dimensions: 81'8" W x 37'10" D

Levels: 1

Heated Square Footage: 2,160

Bedrooms: 6

Bathrooms: 4

Foundation: Crawl space, slab, or basement

Material Take-off Included: Yes

Price Category: D

Images provided by designer/architect.

• Master Suite: Extremely generous in its size, each master suite boasts both a walk-in closet and a private bathroom.

• Bedrooms: In addition to the master suite are another two bedrooms. The rooms feature large windows, making them bright and cheery. For convenience there is a full bathroom located in close proximity to the bedrooms.

Multiple dormers and covered entry porches provide this three-bedroom duplex with additional curb appeal.

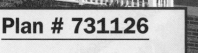

Features:

• Front Porch: Enter each unit from this lovely front porch that features turned columns and brick accents.

• Living Room: At the rear of each unit is this relatively large living room. It is located across from the kitchen and features a sliding glass door that leads to a private rear deck.

• Kitchen: A tidy space, each kitchen is located right off the living room. It features a utility closet, which houses the washer and dryer for the unit, enabling multi-tasking to occur quite easily.

Copyright by designer/architect.

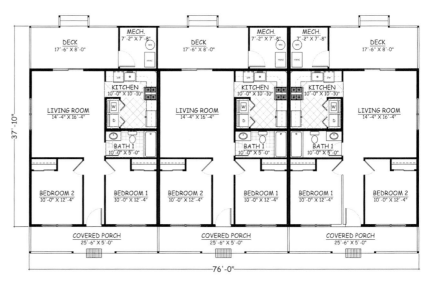

Plan # 731136

Dimensions: 76' W x 37'10" D

Levels: 1

Heated Square Footage: 2,268

Bedrooms: 6

Bathrooms: 3

Foundation: Crawl space, slab, or basement

Material Take-off Included: Yes

Price Category: E

Images provided by designer/architect.

Dormers and turned columns at the entry porch give this multi-family unit additional curb appeal.

Features:

- **Front Porch:** This lovely front porch spans the entire width of the building. The porch is wide enough for planters or a small sitting area, making it a cozy place to sit and relax.

- **Kitchen:** Organization will be a snap in each efficiently designed kitchen. In order to allow for multitasking, which is often required with today's active lifestyles, the kitchen also houses a utility closet with the washer and dryer.

- **Living Room:** Basked in natural light from the multiple window unit and sliding glass door, each lovely living room will certainly be the spot to unwind at day's end. At the rear of the living room is a sliding glass door that lead to a private rear deck, a lovely place to eat or relax on a nice evening.

- **Bedrooms:** Each unit has two moderately sized bedrooms with large windows. These rooms are placed in close proximity to a full bathroom.

Copyright by designer/architect.

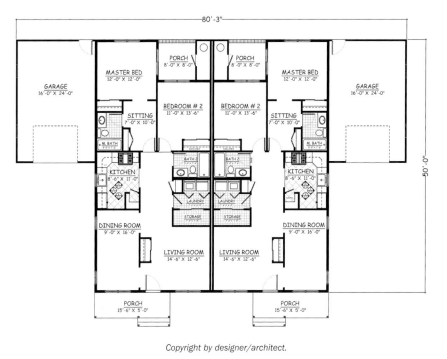

Images provided by designer/architect.

Plan # 731121

Dimensions: 80'3" W x 50' D

Levels: 1

Heated Square Footage: 2,290

Bedrooms: 4

Bathrooms: 4

Foundation: Crawl space, slab, or basement

Material Take-off Included: Yes

Price Category: E

The front facade of this two-bedroom duplex allows for it to blend in with residential surroundings.

CAD FILE AVAILABLE

Features:

- **Kitchen:** Efficiently designed, each tidy kitchen is given a bit more storage space, thanks to a handy pantry closet.

- **Laundry Room:** In addition to housing the washer and dryer, each laundry area includes a large storage closet, something that is often found lacking in duplex units.

- **Master Suite:** With a private bathroom, small sitting area, and sliding glass door leading to a private rear porch, each master suite will certainly leave you feeling relaxed and refreshed.

- **Secondary Bedroom:** In addition to the master suite, each unit has one moderately sized bedroom and a full bathroom.

Copyright by designer/architect.

Plan # 731124

Dimensions: 86'6" W x 41'5" D

Levels: 1

Heated Square Footage: 2,300

Bedrooms: 4

Bathrooms: 2

Foundation: Crawl space, slab, or basement

Material Take-off Included: Yes

Price Category: E

Images provided by designer/architect.

This charming single-story, two-bedroom duplex features attached garages that are situated in the middle of the units, making each feel as if it were a single-family home.

Features:

- Porch: Front porches with columns and brick accents grant access to each of the units while providing shelter from the elements.

- Living Room: Each cozy living room is a bit more enclosed, making it a wonderful place to relax in the evening.

- Dining Room: From the front door of each unit, step into this open dining room. The room has multiple windows and is connected to the kitchen by a large countertop eatng area. The eating area will provide space for more informal meals, while the dining room itself is large enough to accommodate a table for more formal meals.

- Kitchen: Each kitchen is chock-full of cabinet and counter space, ensuring that there is plenty of storage for dry goods and dishes, as well as areas for meal preparation. The countertop eating area connects the kitchen to the dining room, creating a cohesive nvironment.

Copyright by designer/architect.

Plan # 731112

Dimensions: 106'7" W x 40'1" D

Levels: 1

Heated Square Footage: 2,316

Bedrooms: 6

Bathrooms: 4

Foundation: Crawl space, slab, or basement

Material Take-off Included: Yes

Price Category: E

Images provided by designer/architect.

This three-bedroom, two-bathroom duplex has an open and airy atmosphere throughout the home.

CAD FILE AVAILABLE

Features:

- **Living Room:** From the front porch you are ushered back to the rear of each home and into this wonderful living room. The room is expansive and is open to the dining room on one side.

- **Dining Room:** A moderately sized space, each dining room has the appearance of being larger, as it is open to both the living room and the kitchen. A sliding glass door that leads to a generously sized private deck gives the room a feeling of openness. Whether you are dining indoors or out, this room will have you feeling relaxed as you enjoy your evening meal.

- **Kitchen:** Open to the dining room, each efficiently designed kitchen houses a utility room and can be reached directly from the garage.

- **Master Suite:** Each master suite features a large walk-in closet and a private bathroom, ensuring both comfort and privacy.

- **Bedrooms:** Each unit in this duplex features an additional two bedrooms and a full bathroom.

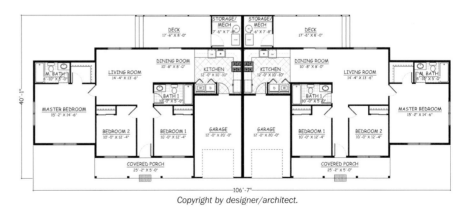

Copyright by designer/architect.

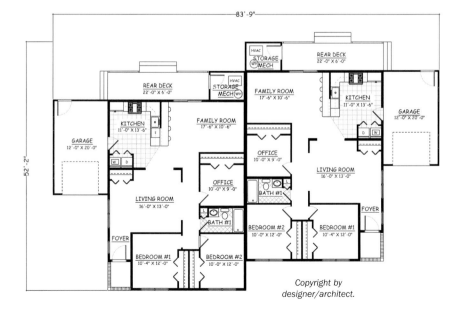

Images provided by designer/architect.

Plan # 731107

Dimensions: 83'9" W x 52'2 D

Levels: 1

Heated Square Footage: 2,332

Bedrooms: 4

Bathrooms: 2

Foundation: Crawl space, slab, or basement

Material Take-off Included: Yes

Price Category: E

The understated and simple facade of this two-bedroom duplex allows for it to blend in with its residential surroundings.

Features:

- **Living Room:** From each entry, step into this large and open living room. The room is centrally located and fea tures large cased openings, creating an open living atmosphere.

- **Kitchen:** Each, tidy kitchen boasts a large countertop eating area, has access to the garage, and houses a small utility room that features a washer and dryer. The space is also open to the family room, allowing for interaction between the cook and the rest of the family.

- **Family Room:** Large windows and a set of sliding glass doors leading out to an expansive private rear deck make this family room bright and inviting.

- **Bedrooms:** Two moderately sized bedrooms are located in each unit. Both bedrooms have ample closet space for storage and are located near a full bathroom.

- **Office:** In addition to the two bedrooms, each unit houses this small office area, perfect for keeping up with household expenses or even telecommuting.

Copyright by designer/architect.

Plan # 731105

Dimensions: 34'5" W x 45'6" D

Levels: 2

Heated Square Footage: 2,448

Main Level Sq. Ft.: 1,224

Upper Level Sq. Ft.: 1,224

Bedrooms: 4

Bathrooms: 4 Full, 2 Half

Foundation: Crawl space, slab, or basement

Material Take-off Included: Yes

Price Category: E

Images provided by designer/architect.

This traditionally styled two-story two-bedroom duplex features amenities all will love.

Features:

- Covered Porch: Each unit boasts a large porch that is large enough to place a seating area for enjoying a warm evening. While the units are mirrored, the designer has offset each unit, allowing for the porches, front and rear, to have complete privacy.

- Living Room: Step from the covered porch on each unit into this centrally located living room. The room has two sets of multiple window units, making it bright and airy.

- Kitchen: This efficiently designed galley kitchen is set between the living room and the dining nook.

- Dining Nook: At the rear of each unit is a spacious dining nook that features a sliding glass door leading to an out-door covered porch, making outdoor dining a common occurrence.

- Upper Floor: Located on each upper level are the bedrooms. Each of the rooms has large closets, and one of the rooms boasts a private bathroom. In addition to the private bathroom there is an additional full bathroom on this floor and a powder room on the lower level.

CAD FILE AVAILABLE

Upper Level Floor Plan

BEDROOM 1
13'-2" X 11'-8"

BATH 1
9'-6" X 5'-0"

BATH 2
9'-6" X 5'-0"

BEDROOM 2
13'-0" X 11'-10"

BEDROOM 1
13'-2" X 11'-8"

BATH 1
9'-6" X 5'-0"

BATH 2
9'-6" X 5'-0"

BEDROOM 2
13'-0" X 11'-10"

39'-6½"

34'-5"

Copyright by designer/architect.

Main Level Floor Plan

PORCH
9'-2" X 6'-0"

STORAGE MECH
7'-4" X 5'-8"

STORAGE MECH
7'-4" X 5'-8"

PORCH
9'-2" X 6'-0"

NOOK
13'-0" X 9'-2"

NOOK
13'-0" X 9'-2"

KITCHEN
9'-8" X 11'-8"

KITCHEN
9'-8" X 11'-8"

LIVING ROOM
16'-4" X 13'-10"

LIVING ROOM
16'-4" X 13'-10"

PORCH
17'-0" X 8'-0"

PORCH
17'-0" X 8'-0"

45'-6½"

34'-5"

Light Homes Efficiently

The Importance of Lighting

Good lighting is not only practical and contributes to a homeowner's overall safety, it is also a powerful decorating tool. The right lighting delivered by the right bulb and the right lighting fixture goes a long way to improving the look of a room. Selecting energy-efficient lighting is also a way to cut the energy used to run a home. Today's homeowner has a variety of choices when selecting the bulbs to light his or her home. There are improved incandescent bulbs as well as energy-stingy fluorescent and halogen bulbs.

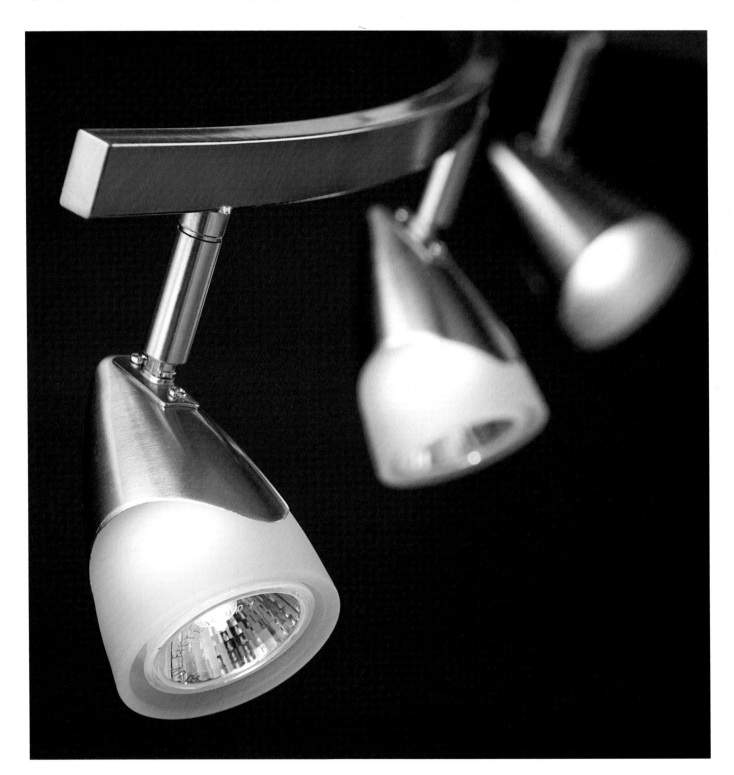

Indoor Lighting Solutions

We all remember a parent complaining about having every light in the house on. If you're paying electricity bills, you've probably said it at least once. Here are a few ways to take the edge off of those high energy costs:

- **Compact-fluorescent lightbulbs** use about one-quarter the energy of regular incandescent bulbs to produce the same number or more lumens. They also last about ten times longer than regular bulbs. Some compact fluorescents are warranted for eight years. Compact fluorescents cost a bit more initially, but the long-term savings more than offset the initial difference in price. A compact fluorescent that gives the same amount of light as a 100-watt regular bulb can save more than $80 over the life of the bulb.
- **Task lighting** concentrates the light where it's needed. Task lighting doesn't waste energy casting light in spaces where it isn't needed. Also, a task light doesn't annoy others in the area with an intrusively bright light. When a homeowner uses task lighting, he or she can use a lower watt bulb to accomplish the desired result.
- **Three-way bulbs** in touch lamps or regular three-way lamps are also good ways to save energy on interior lighting. The bulb allows for only as much light as needed but gives the option of brighter light when required.

Outdoor Lighting Solutions

Lighting isn't limited to the inside of the home. Most homes have at least a light at the front door and some way to illuminate the walkway to the house.

- **Motion detectors** are great energy saving devices for exterior needs. They come on automatically and stay on as long as motion is detected in the area. With motion detectors there is no need to leave a light burning while the occupants are out. It will come on automatically to light their way when they return home.
- **Low-voltage lighting** can be used to light walkways with significantly less power than regular incandescent bulbs. One 60-watt string of lights can illuminate up to 100 feet of walkway. You can also install timers and sensors that turn the lights on at dusk and shut them off after a specific time.
- **Solar exterior lights** charge all day in the sunlight, and then come on as darkness falls. Solar lights are slightly more expensive than regular low-voltage lights, but they don't require any electricity or cords. You can place solar lights anyplace that receives sunlight.

Take a walk around the house, and see where you can make a change to save some change. It's not just money or energy you're saving. It's also the environment. Invest in a few lightbulbs or fixtures, and consider it an investment in the future as well.

Energy Star Lighting

ENERGY STAR lighting uses about 75 percent less energy than a standard incandescent bulb and lasts up to 10 times longer, while providing the same high quality light. The energy-efficiency performance of ENERGY STAR lighting also means savings of at least $25 in energy costs over the life of each ENERGY STAR bulb that replaces an incandescent bulb. Consider purchasing ENERGY STAR lighting to help save money on utility bills through superior designs that require less money and less energy to keep your home bright!

With incandescent, fluorescent, compact fluorescent (CFL) or halogen bulbs, you have more choices than ever when it comes to buying lightbulbs. The following information will help you understand the types of bulbs available.

Lightbulb Lingo

Like most aspects of home improvement and home building, the lighting industry has developed its own language. Here are a few of the industry's most often used terms:

- **Watts** are standard units of measure in electricity. One watt is equal to 1/746 horsepower. If you are switching from standard incandescent bulbs to CFLs or if you are simply replacing an incandescent bulb, it's important to know the wattage of the old bulb. A CFL uses less wattage and produces more light.
- **Lumens** are the standard measure of light produced by a bulb. Standard 100-watt bulbs produce about 1,600 lumens.
- **Incandescent** lightbulbs have a filament that's heated to the point of glowing. The glowing filament produces the bulb's light.
- **Fluorescent** bulbs or tubes are filled with mercury vapor that emits ultraviolet light when electricity is applied. The bulbs/tubes have a coating inside that turns the ultraviolet rays into visible light.
- **Life** is usually listed in the estimated number of hours a lightbulb will last. By comparing the lumens and life of different bulbs of the same wattage, you can select the lightbulb that provides the best combination of light output and length of life.

SAFETY NOTE: Never exceed the maximum wattage recommended for a lamp!

Bulb Colors

Incandescent and some fluorescent bulbs are available in a variety of colors to change and enhance the look of a room:

- **Soft White:** Enrich the interior design and give it a hint of softness to enhance mood; combine with spotlights to highlight a particular object or feature.
- **Yellow:** Bug lights are available that don't attract as many bugs as regular bulbs. Insects can't see the yellow light as well as they can see blue or ultraviolet light.
- **Amber:** This color replicates the light from a natural gas flame.
- **Clear:** Clear bulbs offer a brilliant light.
- **Light Blue:** Special bulbs are available with a coating to filter out the yellows in the color spectrum to produce a crisper light.
- **Black Light:** These provide special effects for glow-in-the-dark items and are good for parties or kids' rooms.

A variety of novelty colors are available for party lights.

Incandescent Bulbs

An incandescent bulb is the most common type of bulb. They are inexpensive and available in a variety of colors and styles. Incandescent lamps are popular for their warm, pleasing color that complements skin tones.

- **Most incandescent bulbs range from 15 to 150 watts.**
- **Incandescent bulbs are less expensive than halogen and fluorescent.**
- **Can be used with dimmer switches.**

A-Line: Standard light bulb shape available in a variety of wattages, clear, frosted/pearl, and colored/pastel styles. Colored/pastel styles create a soft light with a gentle hint of color to add the finishing touches to your home. Some are available in a shatter-resistant material.

Globe: A round bulb that is used when a light fixture has no shade (such as vanity lighting). Globe bulbs are available in varying sizes.

Specialty Globe: Used to highlight a vanity fixture.

Candle: A decorative bulb that creates the mood of romance. Candle bulbs can be used with dimmers for accent lighting and in chandeliers.

Flicker: The filament in the bulb resembles a flickering flame. These bulbs are used in chandeliers and candelabras.

Bullet/Torpedo: A decorative bulb shaped like a bullet. This type of bulb is often seen in night lights.

Flame: Flame-shaped bulb with wrinkled glass usually used with dimmers for accent lighting.

OTHER INCANDESCENT BULBS

Reflector: An indoor bulb used for directing light such as a spotlight or recessed light.

Tubular: Tube-shaped bulb used mainly in picture and undercabinet lighting.

Ceiling Fan: Specialty bulb made specifically for a ceiling fan. Ceiling fan bulbs are also available in bullet and flame shapes.

Parabolic Aluminized Reflectors (PAR): Outdoor flood bulb that is resistant to damp areas. PAR bulbs are used for spotlighting or as flood lights. PARs are also available in halogen.

Compact-Fluorescent Bulbs

Compact-fluorescent lightbulbs (CFL) are the most energy-efficient of all light bulbs. They use 67 percent less energy than standard incandescent bulbs and last longer.

- CFLs are available in medium bases to fit standard light sockets.
- CFLs use less wattage than incandescent bulbs. For example, a standard 75-watt bulb is comparable to a 20-watt CFL in light output.
- CFLs cost more than incandescent bulbs, but they last up to 16 times longer than incandescent bulbs.

- CFLs are available for outdoor use as well. Make sure the packaging indicates that the bulb is rated for outdoor use.
- CFLs may not hold up to the stress of power surges. So using them in areas such as workshops isn't advisable.
- If the outlet is wired for a dimmer or three-way bulb, make sure you purchase a CFL rated for the specific use.

Spiral: Great for table lamps. Lasts eight times longer than a regular A-line bulb. Spiral shape provides better light distribution than other CFLs.

Post: Has a shatterproof cover. Lasts 16 times longer than a 75-watt A-Line. Available in the buglight version that filters the wavelength of light that attracts bugs.

OTHER COMPACT-FLUORESCENT BULBS

3-way: Made for 3-way table lamps. This bulb last six times longer than standard A-line bulbs. Fits lamps with an 8-inch harp.

Dimmable: Made for incandescent dimming circuits. Dims to as low as 10-percent light output. It lasts 13 times longer than a 100-watt A-Line.

A-Line: Looks similar to an incandescent bulb, yet lasts six times longer than a 60-watt A-line. Fits most table lamps with an 8-inch harp.

Halogen Bulbs

Both incandescent and halogen lightbulbs use the same technology and filament to produce light. However, halogen bulbs are more efficient than incandescent bulbs, but cost a little more.

- Halogens last up to three times longer and produce almost 50 percent more light for the same amount of energy.
- Halogens produce the brightest, purest light and make tasks like reading easier.
- Always use a clean rag to handle a halogen bulb when changing. The oil from skin will cause the bulb to burn hotter and reduce its longevity.

Fluorescent Bulbs

Fluorescent lightbulbs have been traditionally a linear light source, but also come in u-shaped and circular. Fluorescent tubes will not work without a ballast. Fluorescent bulbs last longer than incandescent.

Color has been a big issue for many years with fluorescent bulbs. Now, you can get a wide variety of options to enhance your indoor environment:

- **Sunlight:** Good for residential or commercial areas where outdoor light is minimal.
- **Cool White:** Good for office, retail, school, basement, and workshop areas.
- **Soft White:** Enrich an interior design and give it a hint of softness to enhance mood; combine with spotlights to highlight a particular object or feature.
- **Natural Color:** Good for retail and commercial areas where high-color rendition is preferred.
- **Black Light:** Provides special effects for glow-in-the-dark items. Good for parties or kids' rooms.

Linear: Fluorescent tubes available in lengths of 24" to 48".

U-Shaped: Fluorescent bulb used in undercabinet light fixtures with a ballast on one end only.

Circular: Fluorescent lamps used in non-linear fixtures.

Grow Lights: Fluorescent bulbs specifically made to provide "natural" light to indoor plants. The light output contains blue, green, red, and orange spectrums to promote plant growth. The bulbs are available in 20 W and 40 W.

Aquarium: Specifically made for fish tanks. For tanks with fish only, the bulb should provide lighting that minimizes the growth of algae and maximizes the color of the fish. In tanks containing coral and plants, the spectrum of the light becomes a factor. There must be adequate amounts of red and blue light for photosynthesis.

A-Line: It provides all the benefits of halogen, such as longlife and good color, in the classic shape.

Parabolic Aluminized Reflectors (PAR): Outdoor flood bulb that is resistant to damp areas. PAR bulbs are used for spotlighting or as flood lights.

Exterior Lighting Buying Guide

One of the most economical ways to make your home safer and to highlight architectural features and landscaping is to install low-voltage outdoor lights or solar lighting. Installing low-voltage lighting or solar lighting is an easy project. No special skills or tools are needed, and most installation can be done in under an hour using only a screwdriver. Low-voltage systems are shockless and safe for use around children and pets.

Low-Voltage Lighting Systems

Low-voltage lighting systems consist of the following:

- **A power pack** (or transformer) supplies the electricity. The power pack plugs into a standard outlet and reduces the regular household current (120 volts) to a safe 12 volts. Power packs have an automatic timer allowing lights to go on and off at preset times.
- **A low-voltage lamp** is the source of light. Lamps are available in a variety of brightness levels, ranging from 4 watts up to 50-watts halogen.

Selecting Cable Size

The low-voltage cable transmits the electricity. Low-voltage cable is a weather-resistant, self-sealing, insulated stranded copper wire that is available in 12-, 14- and 16-gauge sizes. The gauge required for lighting is determined by the amount of watts required to operate the system:

- ~~16-gauge cable can carry 150 watts~~
- 14-gauge cable can carry 200 watts
- 12-gauge cable can carry 300 watts

Use the following table to determine the correct size cable needed based on the length of the runs.

Total Wattage of Power Pack	150 watts 16-gauge cable	200 watts 14-gauge cable	300 watts 12-gauge cable
88 watts	100 ft.	125 ft.	150 ft.
121 watts	100 ft.	125 ft.	150 ft.
200 watts	100 ft.	125 ft.	150 ft.
300 watts	100 ft.	150 ft.	200 ft.
600 watts	100 ft. x 2	150 ft. x 2	200 ft. x 2

The maximum number of garden lights that can be connected is determined by the total wattage of all the fixtures attached to the system. The transformer is 100-watt. Therefore, the total wattage must not exceed 100 watts. For example:

10 garden lights with 10-watt bulbs=100 watts

A standard, multifunctional 100-watt transformer has a dusk to dawn manual on/off switch as well as an auto on with a 4-, 6-, or 8-hour timer.

Solar Lighting

Sun-powered, solar accent lighting puts out enough light at night to mark and outline the locations of dark areas. Solar lighting should be used where a regular source of electricity is unavailable or difficult to access. No wiring is required, and solar lighting is easier to install than low-voltage lighting.

The solar-collection panel absorbs energy from sunlight and converts it into electrical power that is stored in efficient, rechargeable batteries. As the sun sets, the solar lights turn on. In ideal situations, fully charged solar lights remain on for up to 15 hours.

All solar-powered lighting requires a sufficient amount of sunlight to recharge the batteries. Solar-lighting performance is based on the amount of sunlight received during the day.

Number of Lights

The number of lights used and the distance placed between them greatly changes the overall lighting effect. Generally, it is better to use fewer lights, placed closer together (within 10 feet of each other) than to use many lights, scattered too far apart. For more information on planning your outdoor lighting, visit the Lowe's website at www.lowes.com.

In high-maintenance areas, be sure to select the proper lighting: lawnmowers, power trimmers, and other equipment can destroy your lights.

Different Finishes

Choose verdigris and black for fixtures that you want to blend in with surrounding foliage. For fixtures with higher visibility, choose styles and colors that best complement the home's exterior design and landscape theme. The following are available finishes:

- **Antique copper**
- **Black**
- **Pewter**
- **Antique brown**
- **Polished copper**
- **Verdigris**
- **Brass**

ILLUMINATE LANDSCAPING

Taller fixtures allow light to disperse over a larger area providing more illumination to surrounding surfaces.

Tall fixtures are preferred for single accent lights.

A wide variety of shapes and sizes is available. Each style casts its own unique light pattern to provide decorative accent lighting.

HIGHLIGHT ARCHITECTURAL SURFACES

- **Floodlights** direct light upwards at controllable angles to illuminate statuary and highlight landscaping fences and architectural surfaces.
- For hedges, try **tier lights** with the tops removed, directing the light straight up and down.
- **Well lights** throw light up and out to highlight a garden structure or wall.

WALKWAYS AND STEPS

A wide variety of shapes and sizes is available. Each style casts its own unique light pattern to provide decorative accent lighting.

Tier lights direct light downward on the ground or shrubs and minimize glare, making them ideal for lighting walks and steps.

Alternate lights from side to side to avoid the "runway" look.

FLOWER AND ROCK GARDENS

A wide variety of shapes and sizes is available. Each style casts its own unique light pattern to provide decorative accent lighting.

SECURITY

Light areas of your landscape where would be intruders could hide:

- A remote photo-control accessory automatically turn lights on and off when needed.
- A photo-sensor accessory deters trespassers. When motion is detected, the outdoor lights come on for five minutes.

OTHER USES FOR EXTERIOR LIGHTS
SURFACE MOUNT/DECKS

Surface/deck lights are mounted directly onto the surfaces of walls, fences, decks etc. These lights help to direct foot traffic around steps, benches, railings, and more.

Deck lighting can be built into posts or steps to create a visual effect and add an extra measure of safety.

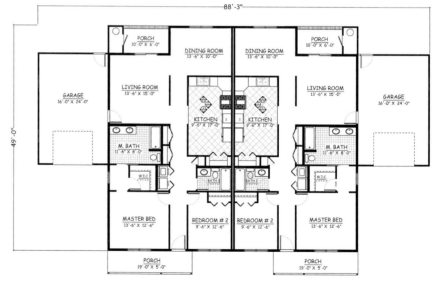

Plan # 731120

Dimensions: 88'3" W x 49' D

Levels: 1

Heated Square Footage: 2,600

Bedrooms: 4

Bathrooms: 4

Foundation: Crawl space, slab, or basement

Material Take-off Included: Yes

Price Category: F

Images provided by designer/architect.

This two-bedroom duplex is designed with amenities everyone will appreciate.

CAD FILE AVAILABLE

Features:

- Front Porch: Turned columns add grace and charm to the front porch of each unit.

- Kitchen: Thoughtful design allows for easy organization in each kitchen. While there is plenty of cabinet and counter space, the room also features a pantry for additional storage.

- Living Room: Many evenings will be spent relaxing in this generously sized living room. Each room is across from the kitchen and features a sliding glass door leading out to a covered patio.

- Master Suite: Each master suite features a private bathroom and a large walk-in closet, adding comfort and privacy to an already lovely space.

- Secondary Bedroom: In addition to the master suite, each unit has one moderately sized bedroom and a full bathroom.

Copyright by designer/architect.

Images provided by designer/architect.

Plan # 731122

Dimensions: 59'4" W x 37'6" D

Levels: 2

Heated Square Footage: 2,600

Main Level Sq. Ft.: 1,300

Upper Level Sq. Ft.: 1300

Bedrooms: 4

Bathrooms: 4 Full, 2 Half

Foundation: Crawl space, slab, or basement

Material Take-off Included: Yes

Price Category: F

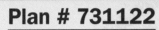

This charming two-story two-bedroom duplex includes front porches and paneled shutters, ensuring that it will fit right into a residential area.

Features:

- Porch: The entry to each unit includes this lovely front porch that features stately columns and brick accents.

- Living Room: Step from either unit's front porch or garage into this spacious living room. It is connected to the kitchen through a large opening, giving the home a feeling of continuity.

- Kitchen: Each galley-style kitchen has plenty of cabinet and counter space

for preparing meals, while the large cased openings leading to both the living room and the dining room allow the space to feel open and airy.

- Upper Level: On the upper level of each unit you will find two substantially sized bedrooms, each with large closets and one with a private bathroom. The floor also has a hall bathroom, ensuring enough private space for all.

Main Level Floor Plan

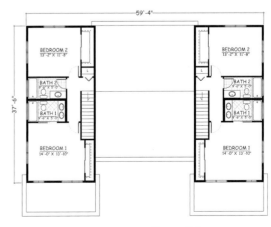

Upper Level Floor Plan

Copyright by designer/architect.

Plan # 731134

Dimensions: 89' W x 37'6" D

Levels: 2

Heated Square Footage: 2,600

Main Level Sq. Ft.: 1,300

Upper Level Sq. Ft.: 1300

Bedrooms: 4

Bathrooms: 6 Full, 3 Half

Foundation: Crawl space, slab, or basement

Material Take-off Included: Yes

Price Category: F

This attractive two-story, two-bedroom triplex is given additional curb appeal with its charming front porches and paneled shutters.

Images provided by designer/architect.

Features:

- Porch: While the front porches provide shelter from the elements, they also give each unit the appearance of being a single-family dwelling.

- Living Room: This spacious living room can be entered from either the front porch or the garage of each unit. At the rear of the room is a large opening that connects you to the kitchen, creating cohesive atmosphere.

- Kitchen: Plenty of cabinet and counter space is found in each galley-style kitchen, and the large cased openings leading to both the living room the and dining room continue the home's continuity.

- Upper Level: The upper floors each have two large bedrooms, one with a private bathroom, and a hall bathroom.

Main Level Floor Plan

Copyright by designer/architect.

Upper Level Floor Plan

order direct: 1-800-523-6789

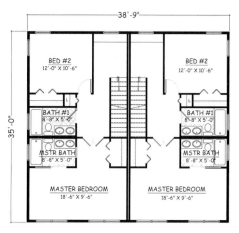

Plan # 731125

Dimensions: 38'9" W x 39' D

Levels: 2

Heated Square Footage: 2,646

Main Level Sq. Ft.: 1,287

Upper Level Sq. Ft.: 1359

Bedrooms: 4

Bathrooms: 4

Foundation: Crawl space, slab, or basement

Material Take-off Included: Yes

Price Category: F

Images provided by designer/architect.

The exterior details of this two-story duplex give the unit the appearance of being a single-family dwelling.

CAD FILE AVAILABLE

Features:

- Porch: Simple front porches provide you with shelter from the elements, while a rear porch invites you to spend an evening relaxing or dining outdoors.

- Living Room: Step through a cased opening in each unit into this lovely living room. The room has a triple-window unit, making it bright and inviting.

- Dining Room: Entering each unit, step into a simple foyer area with a coat closet, leading back to this open dining room. The room has two double-hung window units, providing lots of natural light.

- Kitchen: Each U-shaped kitchen has plenty of cabinet and counter space, while the countertop eating area opens it up to the dining room, providing a place to sit for a light meal or afternoon snack.

Main Level Floor Plan

Upper Level Floor Plan

Copyright by designer/architect.

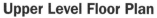

Images provided by designer/architect.

Plan # 731108

Dimensions: 83'10" W x 31'10" D

Levels: 1

Heated Square Footage: 2,665

Bedrooms: 4

Bathrooms: 4

Foundation: Crawl space, slab, or basement

Material Take-off Included: Yes

Price Category: F

Dormers and a gracious front porch add charm to this bright and airy two-bedroom duplex.

Features:

- **Entry Porch:** This shared entry porch gives the duplex continuity and the appearance of being a single-family dwelling.

- **Living Room:** Step from the entry porch directly into each expansive living room. The room features large openings that lead to the dining room and back to the private areas of the home.

- **Dining Room:** Bright and airy, each dining room will certainly be used for everyday family meals as well as

intimate dinner parties. The space also features a sliding glass door leading out to a rear deck, encouraging outdoor dining.

- **Master Suite:** Featuring a generously sized walk-in closet and a private bathroom, each spacious master suite is

sure to please. The bathroom features a dual-sink vanity, an oversized tub, and a separate shower, providing you with the comfort and privacy you seek.

- **Secondary Rooms:** Each unit also features a moderately sized second bedroom, utility closet, and full bathroom, ensuring plenty of space for all.

Copyright by designer/architect.

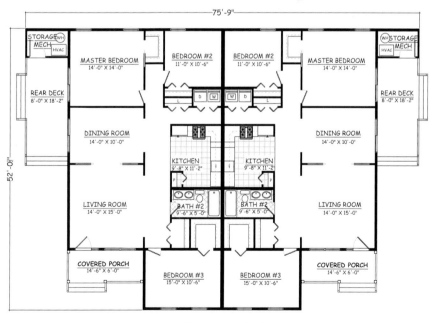

Images provided by designer/architect.

Plan # 731106

Dimensions: 75'9" W x 52" D
Levels: 1
Heated Square Footage: 2,789
Bedrooms: 6
Bathrooms: 2
Foundation: Crawl space, slab, or basement
Material Take-off Included: Yes
Price Category: F

This charming three-bedroom duplex features units that are spacious and have plenty of storage room.

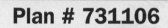

Features:

- Living Room: From the entry porch of each unit, step into this spacious and centrally located living room, which will certainly be the main gathering spot.
- Kitchen: Cabinet and counter space abound in each L-shaped kitchen, which features a large panty and is situated directly across from the dining room.

- Dining Room: Across from the kitchen, each moderately sized dining room features a sliding glass door leading to an expansive private deck, ensuring that many meals will be enjoyed outdoors.

- Deck: With entry through sliding glass doors from either the dining room or master bedroom, this expansive deck will provide a wonderful place for dining and relaxing throughout the year.

Copyright by designer/architect.

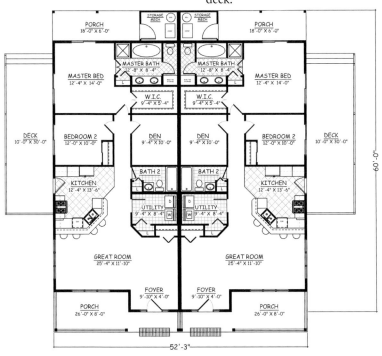

Plan # 731103

Dimensions: 52'3" W x 60" D

Levels: 1

Heated Square Footage: 2,796

Bedrooms: 4

Bathrooms: 4

Foundation: Crawl space, slab, or basement

Material Take-off Included: Yes

Price Category: F

Images provided by designer/architect.

There is an abundance of space in this thoughtfully designed two-bedroom duplex featuring front and rear covered porches.

Features:

- **Great Room:** From each porch, step into this centrally located and generously sized great room, connected to the kitchen by the countertop eating area and to the outdoors via a sliding glass door. The sliding door leads to a private deck, a perfect area for relaxing or dining alfresco.

- **Kitchen:** Featuring ample counterspace and modern conveniences, each kitchen is sure to please the family cook. The adjacent dining room is a just steps away, while the countertop eating area is perfect for a more informal meal. The room also features a French door leading to the private deck.

- **Master Suite:** Each large master suite features a large walk-in closet, a private bathroom, and two sets of sliding glass doors. The private bathroom features an oversize tub and a private toilet area, giving you a sense of luxury. Sliding glass doors in this room lead you to

a deck that will be shared by the rest of the household and to a private covered porch area.

- **Secondary Bedroom:** A more moderate-size bedroom in each unit is located near the main bathroom and features a sliding glass door leading out to the deck.

Copyright by designer/architect.

Images provided by designer/architect.

Plan # 731118

Dimensions: 106'2" W x 30" D
Levels: 1
Heated Square Footage: 2,840
Bedrooms: 6
Bathrooms: 4
Foundation: Crawl space, slab, or basement
Material Take-off Included: Yes
Price Category: F

You'll feel right at home in this three-bedroom, two-bathroom duplex, built with comfort and efficiency in mind.

CAD FILE AVAILABLE

Features:

- **Living Room:** From the front door of each unit, step into this spacious living room. The room serves as a central gathering spot in the home, both for spending time together as a family and entertaining friends.

- **Kitchen:** Each L-shaped kitchen is designed with efficiency in mind. The kitchen is open to the breakfast nook, helping to provide a continuous flow between the rooms.

- **Breakfast Area:** n each unit, you'll love enjoying meals in this cozy breakfast nook. Continuity is added by having the space completely open to the adjacent kitchen area and living room.

- **Master Suite:** Each gracious master suite, which features a private bathroom and a large walk-in closet, will be a welcome retreat after a long day. The bathroom contains a whirlpool tub, a dual-sink vanity, and a separate shower.

Copyright by designer/architect.

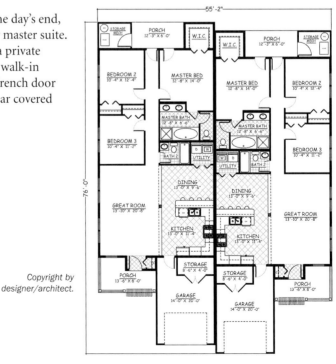

Images provided by designer/architect.

Plan # 731104

Dimensions: 55'2" W x 76' D

Levels: 1

Heated Square Footage: 2,872

Bedrooms: 6

Bathrooms: 4

Foundation: Crawl space, slab, or basement

Material Take-off Included: Yes

Price Category: F

Multiple gables give this three-bedroom duplex home additional character.

CAD FILE AVAILABLE

Features:

- **Front Porch:** A tidy brick entry porch provides a charming entrance to each of the units.
- **Great Room:** From the entry foyer of each unit, step into this expansive great room, which is open to both the kitchen and the dining room, allowing for an easy flow from room to room.
- **Kitchen:** Each U-shaped kitchen with a countertop seating area is adjacent to the dining room and open to the great room. The well-planned space contributes to efficient organization.

- **Dining:** While the kitchen has a countertop area for seating, each moderately sized dining room offers you the ability to sit for a more formal meal. It is open to both the kitchen and great room, making the room feel larger.
- **Master Suite:** At the day's end, relax in this lovely master suite. The room boasts a private bathroom, a large walk-in closet, and has a French door leading out to a rear covered porch.

- **Secondary Rooms:** Two secondary bedrooms and a full bathroom complete each unit.

Copyright by designer/architect.

Images provided by designer/architect.

Plan # 731129

Dimensions: 104' W x 30' D

Levels: 1

Heated Square Footage: 2,898

Bedrooms: 9

Bathrooms: 3

Foundation: Crawl space, slab, or basement

Material Take-off Included: Yes

Price Category: F

CAD FILE AVAILABLE

Combining the kitchen and living room into one continuous space helps to give this three-bedroom triplex an open and airy feel.

Features:

Front Porch: Separate ample-sized front porches provide a wonderful space to greet guests in each unit.

Living Room: From the front entry door of each unit, step directly into this large living room. A countertop eating area connects the living room to the kitchen, keeping with the continuity of a free-flowing floor plan.

• Kitchen: Each kitchen has been designed with plenty of cabinet space for storage and is open to the living room by way of a countertop eating area. The eating area not only provides an area to enjoy a meal but also gives you additional counter space for meal preparation. At the rear of the room, a French door leads onto a deck, a perfect place for dining or just relaxing outdoors in the warm weather.

• Bedrooms: Each unit has a total of three bedrooms. The master bedroom is significantly larger than the other two bedrooms, providing you with a bit more comfort, while all of the bedrooms are just steps away from the full bathroom.

Copyright by designer/architect.

Plan # 731119

Dimensions: 137'7" W x 29'6" D

Levels: 1

Heated Square Footage: 3,014

Bedrooms: 6

Bathrooms: 4

Foundation: Crawl space, slab, or basement

Material Take-off Included: Yes

Price Category: G

Stately columns and brick accents grace the covered entry porches to this three-bedroom duplex.

CAD FILE AVAILABLE

Images provided by designer/architect.

Features:

- **Great Room:** From the front porch of each unit, step into this expansive great room. The room is bright and airy, and connects to both the kitchen and the dining room.

- **Kitchen:** Each wonderfully designed kitchen is sure to please the family cook. It not only has an abundance of cabinet space but also features a countertop seating area that is sure to be used quite often for weekday breakfasts or afternoon snacks.

- **Utility Room:** Located directly off each kitchen, this utility room houses the washer and dryer, making the multi-tasking that is often required with today's active family lifestyle much easier.

- **Master Suite:** Each lovely master suite features its own bathroom, which will provide privacy. The bathroom has a tub, a separate shower, and a dual-sink vanity, continuing the comfortable feeling of an already delightful space.

- **Secondary Bedrooms:** In addition to the master suite, each unit has two moderately sized bedrooms and a full bathroom.

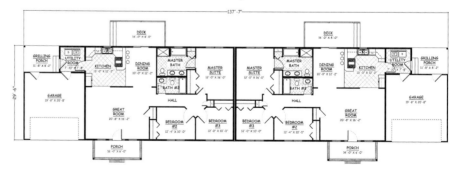

Copyright by designer/architect.

Images provided by designer/architect.

Plan # 731174

Dimensions: 101'3" W x 37'10" D

Levels: 1

Heated Square Footage: 3,024

Bedrooms: 8

Bathrooms: 4

Foundation: Crawl space, slab, or basement

Material Take-off Included: Yes

Price Category: G

This multifamily building unit is given additional curb appeal with turned columns, dormers, and brick accents.

CAD FILE AVAILABLE

Features:

- **Front Porch:** A combined front porch has the appearance of being a single family home.

- **Kitchen:** Each kitchen will be easy to organize due to its simple design. Multitasking is also made easier with he addition of a small utility closet within the kitchen area.

- **Living Room:** Located at the rear of each unit is this expansive living room. The room has a multiple window unit and a sliding glass door that leads to a rear deck.

- **Bedrooms:** Each unit houses two moderately sized bedrooms. Both bedrooms are located close to a full bathroom.

Copyright by designer/architect.

Images provided by designer/architect.

Plan # 731128

Dimensions: 131'10" W x 37' D
Levels: 1
Heated Square Footage: 3,231
Bedrooms: 6
Bathrooms: 3
Foundation: Crawl space, slab, or basement
Material Take-off Included: Yes
Price Category: G

A single-story, two-bedroom triplex has an open floor plan, giving each unit a feeling of continuity and spaciousness.

Features:

- Front Porch: Each private porch is a wonderful space that will provide a perfect place for sitting on a warm summer evening.

- Living Room: Step through the front door of each unit and be welcomed immediately into this living room, the heart of the home. The room is open to the dining room, creating a spacious living area.

- Dining Room: Open to the kitchen via a countertop eating area, each dining room also features a sliding glass door that leads onto a large deck, perfect for outdoor dining.

- Kitchen: Each well-designed kitchen has a fantastic amount of storage space, making it easy to organize. The kitchen also features a countertop eating area and a utility closet that houses the washer and dryer.

- Bedrooms: Each unit houses two generously sized bedrooms with large closets and a centrally located full bathroom. One of the bedrooms has a French door that leads to the rear deck.

Copyright by designer/architect.

Plan # 731123

Dimensions: 30'5" W x 60' D
Levels: 2
Heated Square Footage: 3,284
Main Level Sq. Ft.: 1,642
Upper Level Sq. Ft.: 1,642
Bedrooms: 4
Bathrooms: 4
Foundation: Crawl space, slab, or basement
Material Take-off Included: Yes
Price Category: G

Images provided by designer/architect.

The front elevation of this two-story duplex gives it the appearance of being a single-family dwelling.

Features:

- Great Room: Each great room features multiple window units and a countertop seating area, which connects the room to the kitchen, giving the space a feeling of continuity.

- Kitchen: The wraparound countertop seating area that is open to the great room provides each kitchen with not only an area for dining but additional counter space for meal preparation.

- Master Suite: At the rear of each unit is the master suite, which houses a private bathroom, a large walk-in closet, and a sliding glass door that leads out onto a covered patio. Note that while the first-floor unit has a covered porch, the upper unit also has a sun porch off of the master suite.

- Secondary Rooms: In addition to the master suite, each unit features a separate formal dining room, a moderately sized bedroom, a full bathroom, and laundry facilities, in addition to plenty of closet space and outdoor storage.

**Main Level
Floor Plan**

**Upper Level
Floor Plan**

Copyright by designer/architect.

Plan # 731132

Dimensions: 72'4" W x 50' D

Levels: 1

Heated Square Footage: 3,384

Bedrooms: 6

Bathrooms: 6

Foundation: Crawl space, slab, or basement

Material Take-off Included: Yes

Price Category: G

Images provided by designer/architect.

Reverse gables at the front elevation accentuate the welcoming entries to each unit in this multifamily dwelling.

Features:

- Living Room: Located directly across from the dining room in each unit is this spacious living room, the perfect spot to relax at day's end.

- Dining Room: Multiple window units will bathe each dining room in natural light, making it both bright and inviting.

- Kitchen: Each tidy kitchen is given a bit more storage space by a moderately sized pantry.

- Master Suite: Each lovely master suite is a welcome retreat at the end of the day. The suite houses a private bath room, a small sitting area, and a sliding glass door that leads you out to a rear porch with mechanical room/storage area.

- Secondary Bedroom: In addition to the master suite, each unit has one moderately sized bedroom and a full bathroom.

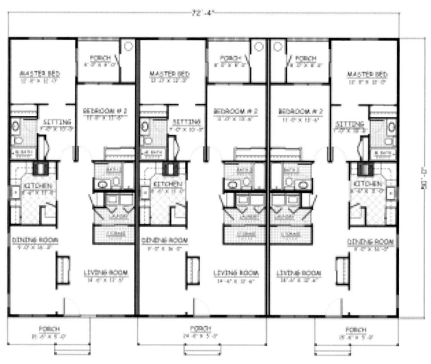

Copyright by designer/architect.

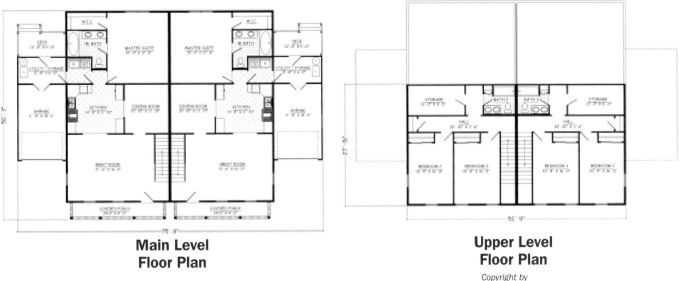

Images provided by designer/architect.

Plan # 731117

Dimensions: 75' 9" W x 50'3" D

Levels: 2

Heated Square Footage: 3,836

Main Level Sq. Ft.: 2,408

Upper Level Sq. Ft.: 1,428

Bedrooms: 6

Bathrooms: 2

Foundation: Crawl space, slab, or basement

Material Take-off Included: Yes

Price Category: H

Thoughtful design makes this two-story three-bedroom duplex a delightful place to call home.

CAD FILE AVAILABLE

Features:

- **Covered Porch:** Each unit has an expansive brick front porch with stately columns. This porch provides not only shelter from the elements but also a place to sit on a warm evening.

- **Great Room:** Through the front entry door of each unit, step into this expansive great room, the perfect place to relax in the evening. Cased openings at the rear of the room lead you to the kitchen or the dining room.

- **Master Suite:** Located at the rear of each unit is this spacious master suite. The suite houses a private bathroom that features a dual-sink vanity and an over-size tub, adding additional comfort and privacy.

- **Upper Level:** On the upper level of each unit are an additional two bedrooms, a full bathroom, and a large storage closet.

Main Level Floor Plan

Upper Level Floor Plan

Copyright by designer/architect.

Plan # 731116

Dimensions: 76' 1" W x 50'3" D

Levels: 2

Heated Square Footage: 3,846

Main Level Sq. Ft.: 2,418

Upper Level Sq. Ft.: 1,428

Bedrooms: 6

Bathrooms: 2

Foundation: Crawl space, slab, or basement

Material Take-off Included: Yes

Price Category: H

Images provided by designer/architect.

An expansive covered front entry porch is the perfect place to sit and relax on a warm summer evening.

CAD FILE AVAILABLE

Features:

- Great Room: Step from the front porch of each unit directly into this gracious

great room the perfect place to gather with friends or just relax after a long day. At the openings—one leads to the kitchen, the other to the dining room.

- Dining Room: Whether you are enjoying the evening family meal or have decided to host a dinner party, each dining room is sure to fit the bill. It can be accessed through cased openings from both the kitchen and great room.

- Kitchen: Organization will be made easy in each well-designed kitchen.

There is sure to be enough cabinet and counter space to please the family cook.

- Master Suite: Situated at the rear of the unit and featuring a private bathroom, this master suite provides additional privacy. The bathroom features an over-size tub and a dual-sink vanity.

- Upper Level: On this upper level, each unit has two additional bedrooms, a full bathroom, and a large storage area. With multiple units, storage is often lacking; however, in this duplex, each unit has ample storage.

Main Level Floor Plan

Upper Level Floor Plan

Copyright by designer/architect.

Images provided by designer/architect.

Plan # 731127

Dimensions: 51'10" W x 37'6" D

Levels: 2

Heated Square Footage: 3,888

Main Level Sq. Ft.: 1,944

Upper Level Sq. Ft.: 1,944

Bedrooms: 6 Full, 3 Half

Bathrooms: 2

Foundation: Crawl space, slab, or basement

Material Take-off Included: Yes

Price Category: H

Reverse gables and front porches allow this two-story, two-bedroom triplex to fit right into a residential area.

CAD FILE AVAILABLE

Features:

- **Porch:** Stately columns and brick accents add charm to the entry porch of each unit.

- **Living Room:** From the front entry porch of each unit, step directly into this spacious living room. The room is connected to the kitchen through a large opening.

- **Kitchen:** Cabinet and counter space abound in each galley-style kitchen, which has large cased openings leading to both the living room and dining

- **Additional Rooms:** A dining room, laundry facilities, and a powder room round out the first floor of each unit; while the upper level houses two moderately sized bedrooms. Each room has large closets and one of the rooms has a private bath room. A centrally located hall bathroom ensures enough private space for all.

Main Level Floor Plan

Upper Level Floor Plan

Copyright by designer/architect.

Paint Buying Guide

 Learn what you need to know when buying paint. Lowe's provides a guide to selecting interior paint that will last longer and provide a foolproof decorating tool.

Getting Started

- Size up the room. How you use color depends on where you use color. Each room has its own unique elements and function. First think about the structure of the room. Consider its shape and size. A lighter color can make a small room feel more spacious, while a darker color can help an immense room seem cozier.

- Take into account any architectural details, such as molding, trim, columns, and brackets. What's attractive and what's not? Varied intensities and hues can complement architecture, furnishings, and art. Remember, paint can accentuate a room's features or hide them.

- Your choice of color also depends largely on function. Will the main purpose of the room be eating, sleeping, working, entertaining, or something else entirely? A warm hue in the living room creates an inviting atmosphere.

Interior Paint

- Before choosing paint, think about where the room fits into the scheme of things. Where is it situated in relation to other rooms? Is it a high- or low-traffic area? Flat paint, for instance, is best suited for ceilings, walls, surface imperfections, and anywhere else that a muted low-reflecting surface is desired. Because it takes more effort to remove stains from this type of paint, a flat finish is best suited for the low-traffic areas of the home.

- Use low-luster, satin, and eggshell paint on areas where a sheen is desired. These paints are easier to clean than flat paint, and they hold up better under repeated washings. They withstand the wear and tear of high-traffic areas, such as hallways, kitchens, baths, and children's rooms.

- Semigloss and high-gloss paint and enamel are best suited for banisters, railings, shelves, kitchen cabinets, furniture, doorjambs, windowsills, and any other surface you wish to accentuate. But be careful—the higher the gloss, the more it emphasizes any surface imperfections.

Choosing a Color Palette

- Having trouble deciding on the paint palette? Choose a design direction. If you've already chosen an interior décor, focus on a favorite fabric color, piece of art or furniture, or other object. If you still can't settle on a color you like, we offer free computerized paint matching and custom color mixing.

- Have color confidence—don't be afraid to paint bold and bright. If the room is unfurnished, a vibrant color can fill it until it is fully furnished.

- Consider the homeowner above all. Paint color should reflect their mood and personality. What are their favorite colors? If they are having trouble selecting a color, ask them to look in their closet. The colors they enjoy wearing are the ones that make them feel good. They are the ones who have to live with the color, so they should love the shades selected.

Decorating is a great way to give the home some personality. There are many elements that go into decorating, but the most important is color. The color wheel is a valuable tool that can help you decorate the home. Thousands of color combinations are possible, but you can use basic color information to create the color scheme best suited for the home and your clients' personal taste.

The Color Wheel

The color wheel identifies color families and how they relate.

Primary Colors

All colors, with the exception of white and black, come from primary colors. Blue, yellow, and red are the primary colors. Combinations of these three colors produce other colors. Mix all three together in equal amounts to produce brown.

Secondary Colors

Mix equal amounts of two primary colors to create secondary colors. The results are violet (red and blue), green (blue and yellow), and orange (red and yellow).

Tertiary Colors

Mix one primary color with larger amounts of another primary color to create tertiary colors. For example, mix one part blue with two parts red to make red-violet.

Basic Color Terms

- The hue of a color is the basic color. For example, blue is the hue in light blue and dark blue.
- Tone describes the color's density and reflective quality. Tone is important when choosing a color scheme.
- The value of a color describes the amount of white or black in the color. The value ranges from light to dark on a gray scale.
- The saturation of a color refers to its pureness and boldness.

The Effects of Color

Different colors affect our moods in different ways. You've decided emerald green, your favorite color, is going to be the main focus in a room. Before you buy five gallons of emerald green paint, consider the effect it will have on the appearance and mood of the room. Use the following descriptions as guides to create color combinations:

Warm and Cozy Colors

Warm and cozy colors, as shown in the paint swatches below, convey a message of togetherness and strength:

- Varying shades of red are commonly found in dining rooms and libraries but are becoming popular in kitchens and bedrooms as well.
- Pure orange is an extremely warm color. It's very hard to tone down and is often used as an accent color only.

- Yellow has different effects depending on its tone and value. A sharp yellow can create a feeling of deterrence, as with police tape at a crime scene. But a pale yellow, such as buttercup, can create a bright and pleasing environment.

Cool and Soothing Colors

Cool and soothing colors, as shown in the photo above, provide a sense of calm and feelings of trust:

- As you may have noticed, most hospitals and doctors' offices decorate with green. Green is one of nature's most prominent colors and blends easily with any room.
- Blue is generally a peaceful color. Light blue can make a room appear bright and refreshing, while a deep blue can create a sober mood. Use blue in any room of the house.
- Violet is getting more and more recognition due to its connection to romance. Violet is also being used in bedrooms and living rooms to communicate an air of serenity.

Pastel Colors. Pastel colors are the result of adding a large amount of white to colors. Because of the lightness of the color, there's little concern of clashing. Pastels create a comfortable, airy feeling in any room.

Neutral Colors. Neutral colors include shades of white, gray and black. Neutral colors are the easiest colors to use for one obvious reason; they blend easily with most surroundings. Builders typically use neutral colors on the interior of a home to accommodate the new homeowners' wide range of tastes. Neutral colors can be stylish and dramatic. For instance, black and white are neutral colors that create a wonderful palette for additional colors.

Various Color Schemes. A color scheme is any set of colors that work together to create a visually appealing layout. Experiment with paint swatches to determine how different colors work together in different light levels.

Making Your Purchase

- **Water versus oil.** When selecting an interior finish, try choosing a water-based enamel instead of an oil-based gloss paint. Water-based gloss enamels have less odor than conventional oil-based paints. They are much easier to clean up, and they wear better over time.
- **Don't purchase low-quality paint.** High-quality paint performs better for a longer period of time. It's less prone to yellow as it ages, goes on smoother, and won't leave brush marks. It is also dirt-resistant. High-quality paint will save time and money in the long run.
- **Purchase test quarts** to review the color and finish selections on-site. Paint a piece of scrap material such as cardboard, or even a portion of the wall, to study the effects of various light conditions.

Types of Exterior Paint

Increase the home's curb appeal with a coat of high-quality paint. Learn the tricks to distinguishing the best exterior paint or primer for your house. Lowe's Exterior Paint-Buying Guide provides information on paint finishes, types of paint, and what characteristics to look for.

- **Solvent-based (oil or alkyd):** In oil-based paint, the liquid solvent is mineral spirits. Oil-based paint dries more slowly than latex—usually taking 24 hours to cure. It cleans up with turpentine or paint thinner.
- **Water-based (latex):** The liquid is water. An advantage of latex paint is that it dries relatively fast, which may or may not be desirable in hot weather or direct sunshine. Cleanup is faster, requiring only soap and water.

Paint Finishes

Sheen is the term used to describe the degree of light reflection paint has. Usually the less sheen paint has, the less stain-resistant it is. Different manufacturers may have various trade names for them, but in general sheens are classified as:

- **Gloss** is the toughest. It cleans easily and resists scuffs better. Therefore, it's a good choice for areas of high traffic or constant use, like doorjambs and window casings. For shutters and other trimwork, gloss paint provides a sleek, eye-catching look. Gloss paint will, however, show imperfections in the surface more than other sheens.
- **Semigloss** paints are also durable and easy to clean but have less shine than gloss. They are just as suitable for trimwork and casings.

- **Satin** (sometimes referred to as **eggshell** or **low luster**) offers a good combination of easy-clean and moderate sheen. Satin is a good choice for siding that is in good condition.
- **Flat paint** is the best choice for vinyl and aluminum siding that is scratched or dented because it hides imperfections well and spatters less when applied. It's also easier to touch up.

If you want to change colors, buy a small quantity of your color choice. Try it out before purchasing several gallons. Paint a small area, and wait a few days. Paints can react to each other and cast reflections that may change the appearance. Changes in light can also affect the look of the paint color.

Characteristics of Quality Exterior Paint

- **Hiding power** is the ability of the paint to sufficiently cover or conceal the surface where it's applied. Hiding power comes from the paint's pigment and is affected by the manner and thickness of the application.
- **Color retention** refers to tinted paints only. The paint's ability to maintain its original color during exposure determines its color retention.
- **Chalking resistance** prevents the white chalky powder from forming on the surface and lightening the color of the paint. Chalking occurs over a period of time by the binder slowly degrading. The telltale streaking of paint (chalk run down) is one consequence of using a paint that isn't chalk resistant.
- **Blister resistance** will keep excessive moisture from coming through the substrate and affecting the paint layer. If paint is applied over a damp or wet surface, blistering is inevitable.

Primer

A primer will help paint adhere to the surface, providing a more uniform appearance. Use a primer when painting over new wood, bare wood, or existing bright or dark colors. Ask your salesperson, and read the labels before making this decision.

Before You Buy

Once you have decided on the color scheme and type of paint, measure the area you are painting, including the door and window areas. Take these measurements with you when you go shopping.

Primer Purpose

Choose the right primer for the job. Learn how primer works with paint and what primer you should use for different surfaces. (See "Primer Selection," opposite.) Primer improves a paint job. The right primer

- Provides a uniform and attractive paint finish.
- Blocks tannin, water, grease, and smoke stains that can bleed through the topcoat.
- Improves adhesion of the topcoat. The paint will last longer and look better.

Primer Selection

Before you use any primer, properly clean the surface.

- **New wood.** If the wood isn't seriously stained, use a high-quality latex primer or an oil-based primer. If the wood is stained or you are painting redwood or cedar, use a stain-blocking primer.

- **Painted wood.** If the paint is in very good condition, a primer may not be needed. However, if there is exposed wood, chalking, or chipped paint, use an oil-based primer. Before you prime, scrape away as much chipped paint as possible, and wash off any chalk. (Just because you are using a primer doesn't mean you get to skip surface preparation.)

- **Weathered wood.** Use a high-quality latex or oil-based primer. Sand and scrape away as much paint as possible. When you start to see new wood fibers, start priming.

- **Masonry block.** Fill a fresh surface with block filler before painting. If repainting, scrape off any loose or peeling paint, and cover with latex paint. Use a block filler only if the paint has been completely scraped off of the surface.

- **Aluminum and galvanized steel.** If the surface is rusty, remove the rust and apply a latex or oil-based, corrosion-resistant primer. If the surface is new and rust-free, you can apply a high-quality latex paint and no primer.

- **Drywall.** Use a latex primer. Don't use an oil-based primer unless you are putting up wallpaper or covering a stain. Oil-based primers raise the grain of the drywall and make the finish look uneven.

- **Stains.** Crayons, water, smoke, and grease can bleed through the topcoat. Prime these areas with a stain-blocking or stain-killing primer. Oil-based stain killers work the best on water stains and for spot priming. Latex stain-blocking primers work better on large areas and hold up better on exterior surfaces. Pigmented-shellac primer works well to block smoke and soot damage as well as to block animal urine smells.

- **Shiny surfaces.** Bonding primers will stick to glass, tile, formica, and previously painted surfaces. Use bonding primers for interior surfaces only. They tend to crack when exposed to the elements because they aren't flexible.

Images provided by designer/architect.

Plan # 731133

Dimensions: 93'4" W x 42'5" D

Levels: 1

Heated Square Footage: 3,945

Bedrooms: 6

Bathrooms: 6

Foundation: Crawl space, slab, or basement

Material Take-off Included: Yes

Price Category: H

Dormers and porches dress up the front of this multifamily dwelling, welcoming you and your guests inside.

Features:

- **Front Porch:** A combination front porch has the appearance of being a single family home.

- **Kitchen:** Each kitchen is designed with efficiency in mind. It is conveniently located next to the breakfast nook and includes a utility closet that houses the washer and dryer.

- **Breakfast Nook:** Each cozy breakfast nook is located right off the kitchen and has a single French door at the rear of the room that leads you out to a lovely rear deck.

- **Master Suite:** Set at the rear of the home, each master suite features a large walk-in closet, a private bathroom, and a French door that also leads to the rear deck.

Copyright by designer/architect.

Plan # 731135

Dimensions: 63'11" W x 46'6" D

Levels: 2

Heated Square Footage: 4,962

Main Level Sq. Ft.: 2,483

Upper Level Sq. Ft.: 2,479

Bedrooms: 6

Bathrooms: 9

Foundation: Crawl space, slab, or basement

Material Take-off Included: Yes

Price Category: I

CAD FILE AVAILABLE

Brick accents, along with paneled shutters and columns, give this two-bedroom triplex a traditional appearance.

Images provided by designer/architect.

Features:

- **Porch:** At the entry to each unit is a lovely porch that will provide you with a bit of shelter from the elements.

- **Living Room/Dining Room:** This open area in each unit combines the living and dining areas, creating a feeling of continuity in the home. At the rear of the living room is a sliding glass door that leads out onto a large deck. Each unit has a mechanical room at the deck area that provides you with extra storage space.

- **Kitchen:** Designed with efficiency in mind, each kitchen offers you plenty of counter space for preparing meals. Also in conjunction with the cabinetry, the room has a large pantry for additional storage, as well as a utility closet that houses a washer and dryer, making multitasking much easier.

- **Upper Level:** In the upper floor of each unit you will find this spacious master bedroom with a private bathroom, as well as a large secondary bedroom and full bathroom.

Copyright by designer/architect.

Main Level Floor Plan

Upper Level Floor Plan

Images provided by designer/architect.

Plan # 731171

Dimensions: 69'3" W x 37'6" D

Levels: 2

Heated Square Footage: 5,192

Main Level Sq. Ft.: 2,596

Upper Level Sq. Ft.: 2,596

Bedrooms: 8

Bathrooms: 8 Full, 4 Half

Foundation: Crawl space, slab, or basement

Material Take-off Included: Yes

Price Category: J

Paneled shutters, stately columns, and brick accents make this lovely two-story two-bedroom quadplex even more inviting.

CAD FILE AVAILABLE · CAD

Features:

- Porch: A front porch grants access to each of the units while providing shelter from the elements.

- Living Room: Each gracious living room is sure to be the central gathering spot for all. It is connected at the rear to the kitchen through a large opening.

- Kitchen: Each galley-style kitchen has an abundance of cabinet and counter space. Large cased openings

at each end connect it to both the living room and dining room.

- Upper Level: With a dining room, laundry facilities, and a powder room on the first floor, the upper levels of the units house two moderately sized bedrooms. Each room has large closets with one of the bedrooms having a private bathroom, while a centrally located hall bathroom ensures enough private space for all.

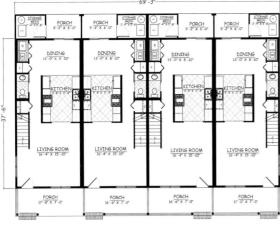

Main Level Floor Plan

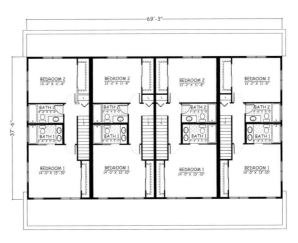

Upper Level Floor Plan

Copyright by designer/architect.

Plan # 731167

Dimensions: 70' W x 42'5" D

Levels: 2

Heated Square Footage: 5,260

Main Level Sq. Ft.: 2,630

Upper Level Sq. Ft.: 2,630

Bedrooms: 12

Bathrooms: 8

Foundation: Crawl space, slab, or basement

Material Take-off Included: Yes

Price Category: J

Images provided by designer/architect.

This two-story four-unit multifamily home includes many features everyone will love.

CAD FILE AVAILABLE · CAD

Features:

- **Living Room:** Step from entry hall of each unit into this cozy living room, which is the perfect place to entertain.

- **Kitchen:** Each kitchen is wonderfully designed with ample counter space and an abundance of cabinets, along with a utility closet that houses the washer and dryer, making the design extremely efficient.

- **Breakfast Nook:** Located right off each kitchen is this breakfast nook, which

features a French door that leads you out to a generously sized rear deck, a perfect spot for summer meals.

- **Master Suite:** Set at the rear of the home each comfortable master suite features a large walk-in closet, a private bathroom, and a French door leading to the rear deck.

- **Secondary Rooms:** In addition to the master suite, each unit houses two moderately sized bedrooms and full bathroom.

Uppper Level Floor Plan

Copyright by designer/architect.

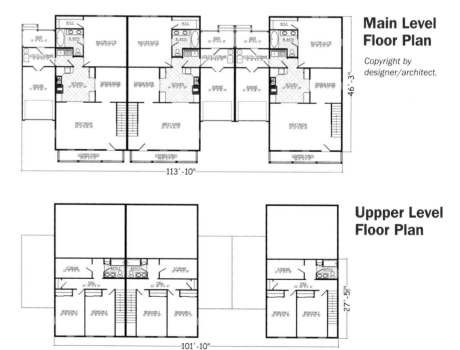

Plan # 731130

Dimensions: 113'10" W x 50'5" D

Levels: 2

Heated Square Footage: 5,748

Main Level Sq. Ft.: 3,606

Upper Level Sq. Ft.: 2,142

Bedrooms: 9

Bathrooms: 6

Foundation: Crawl space, slab, or basement

Material Take-off Included: Yes

Price Category: J

With such features as a front porch, a spacious rear deck, and a private master suite, this two-story, three-bedroom triplex unit will make everyone in the household happy.

Features:

- **Great Room:** Unwind and relax after a long day in each expansive great room. Cased openings at the rear of the room lead you through to the kitchen and the dining room.

- **Kitchen:** You will never lack cabinet countertop space in each well-designed kitchen. The utility room, which houses the washer and dryer, is close by, allowing for multitasking to easily take place.

- **Master Suite:** Each spacious suite features a private bathroom and is located at the rear of the first floor. The private bathroom has a dual-sink vanity and an oversize tub, providing additional comfort and privacy.

- **Upper Level:** In addition to two bedrooms and a full bathroom in each unit, each upper level features a large storage closet.

Main Level Floor Plan

Copyright by designer/architect.

Uppper Level Floor Plan

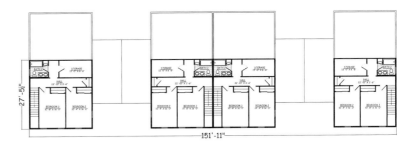

Images provided by designer/architect.

Plan # 731131

Dimensions: 152' W x 46'3" D

Levels: 2

Heated Square Footage: 7,664

Main Level Sq. Ft.: 4,808

Upper Level Sq. Ft.: 2,856

Bedrooms: 12

Bathrooms: 8

Foundation: Crawl space, slab, or basement

Material Take-off Included: Yes

Price Category: L

This attractive two-story, three-room multifamily building uses efficient design to incorporate features that everyone in the home will appreciate.

Features:

- **Entry Porch:** Each unit has its own entry porch. These porches feature formal columns, giving the facade of the building a more traditional look.

- **Great Room:** At the end of the day, each spacious great room will be the perfect place to gather with friends and family. Located at the rear of the room are two cased openings leading you back to the kitchen and the dining room.

- **Kitchen:** Centrally located on the first floor of each unit is this well-designed kitchen. The kitchen has plenty of cabinet and countertop space for both storage and meal preparation. The room can be reached from the dining room or the great room.

- **Master Suite:** At the rear of each first floor level is this spacious master suite. The room features a private bathroom with a dual-sink vanity and an oversize tub, providing additional comfort and privacy.

- **Upper Level:** There are two bedrooms and a full bathroom on the upper level of each unit, as well as a large storage closet, something that is often found lacking in a multi-family building.

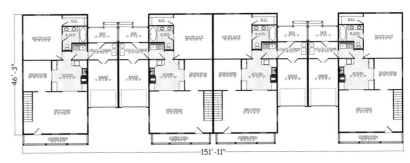

Main Level Floor Plan

Uppper Level Floor Plan

Copyright by designer/architect.

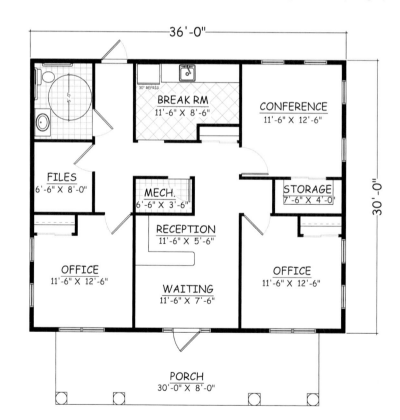

Plan #731150

Dimensions: 36' W x 30' D

Levels: 1

Heated Square Footage: 1,080

Offices: 2

Restrooms: 1

Foundation: Crawl space, slab, or basement

Material Take-off Included: Yes

Price Category: B

This freestanding office is designed with both the staffs' and the clients' needs in mind.

CAD FILE AVAILABLE

Features:

- Waiting/Reception: Step from a covered entryway directly into this combined waiting/reception area. The area is open to the rest of the office space, creating a continuous traffic pattern.

- Offices: There are two private offices, a conference room, and a file room, as well as a generously sized break room.

- Restroom: A wheelchair-accessible restroom is located in the rear of the building.

Images provided by designer/architect.

36'-0"

30'-0"

BREAK RM
11'-6" X 8'-6"

30" REFRIG

CONFERENCE
11'-6" X 12'-6"

FILES
6'-6" X 8'-0"

MECH.
6'-6" X 3'-6"

STORAGE
7'-6" X 4'-0"

RECEPTION
11'-6" X 5'-6"

OFFICE
11'-6" X 12'-6"

WAITING
11'-6" X 7'-6"

OFFICE
11'-6" X 12'-6"

PORCH
30'-0" X 8'-0"

Copyright by designer/architect.

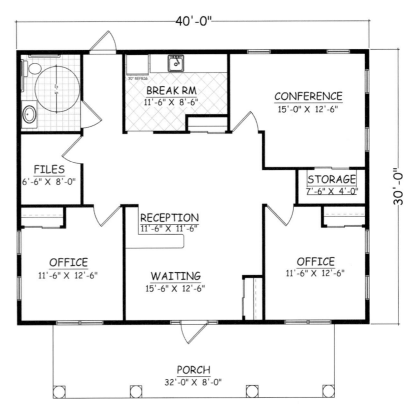

Plan #731148

Dimensions: 40' W x 30' D

Levels: 1

Heated Square Footage: 1,200

Offices: 2

Restrooms: 1

Foundation: Crawl space, slab, or basement

Material Take-off Included: Yes

Price Category: B

Images provided by designer/architect.

Brick siding and a front porch provide this professional office building with additional curb appeal.

Features:

- Reception/Waiting Area: Combining the reception and waiting areas gives this space feeling of continuity.

- Office: There are two private offices, as well as a moderately sized conference room, a file room, a wheelchair-accessible restroom, and an employee break room.

Copyright by designer/architect.

Images provided by designer/architect.

Plan #731153

Dimensions: 51'10" W x 24' D

Levels: 1

Heated Square Footage: 1,244

Offices: 4

Restrooms: 1

Foundation: Crawl space, slab, or basement

Material Take-off Included: Yes

Price Category: B

Features:

- Waiting Room: This moderately sized waiting room will make patients feel comfortable while waiting to be seen.

- Reception Area: Centrally located, this reception area is generously sized, allowing the receptionist to complete office tasks and greet patients.

- Offices: In addition to a large private office, the building houses three independent offices for exams, along with an X-ray room and a wheelchair-accessible restroom.

Simply designed, this ranch-style medical building will provide all the space needed for your a physician's private practice.

CAD FILE AVAILABLE

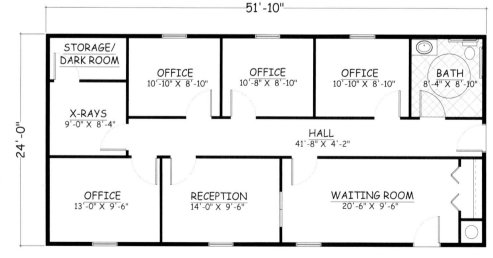

Copyright by designer/architect.

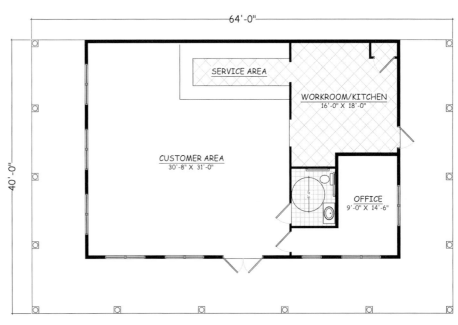

Images provided by designer/architect.

Plan #731155

Dimensions: 64' W x 40' D

Levels: 1

Heated Square Footage: 1,536

Offices: 1

Restrooms: 1

Foundation: Crawl space, slab, or basement

Material Take-off Included: Yes

Price Category: C

This freestanding restaurant would make the perfect ice cream shop or specialty sandwich shop.

CAD FILE AVAILABLE

Features:

- **Porch:** This large porch will increase your table space on warm days.

- **Customer Area:** This large, inviting area welcomes your customers into your restaurant. There is plenty of room for tables and take-out service customers.

- **Kitchen:** This large area can be adapted to any configuration of appliances and worktables. The side door provides easy access for deliveries.

SERVICE AREA

WORKROOM/KITCHEN
16'-0" X 18'-0"

CUSTOMER AREA
30'-8" X 31'-0"

OFFICE
9'-0" X 14'-6"

64'-0"

40'-0"

Copyright by designer/architect.

Plan #731154

Dimensions: 60' W x 30' D

Levels: 1

Heated Square Footage: 1,800

Offices: 1

Restrooms: 1

Foundation: Crawl space, slab, or basement

Material Take-off Included: Yes

Price Category: D

This office building's uncomplicated design makes it the perfect space for growing business.

CAD FILE AVAILABLE

Features:

- Covered Entrance: The facade of the building includes this covered entrance with columns, giving the building a bit of character.

- Office Space: This wide-open office space allows your client to configure the interior of the office the way that works the best for his/her company, while a conference room provides the private space needed for client meetings.

- Additional Areas: The remainder of the office space has a break room, a storage closet, and a wheelchair-accessible restroom.

60'-0"

BREAK ROOM 13'-8" X 9'-6"	STORAGE 10'-0" X 9'-6"	BATHROOM	OFFICE AREA 26'-0" X 14'-0"

30'-0"

CONFERENCE ROOM 24'-0" X 14'-0"

WAIING AREA 23'-0" X 14'-0"

OFFICE 11'-6" X 14'-0"

PORCH 17'-0" X 8'-0"

Copyright by designer/architect.

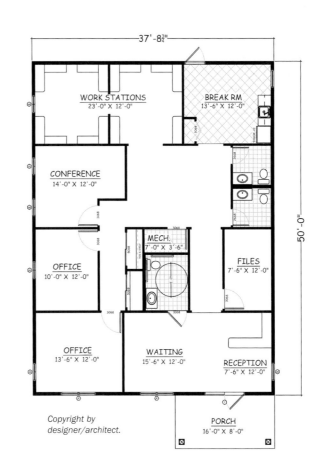

Plan #731149

Dimensions: 37'9" W x 50' D

Levels: 1

Heated Square Footage: 1,884

Offices: 2

Restrooms: 3

Foundation: Crawl space, slab, or basement

Material Take-off Included: Yes

Price Category: D

Images provided by designer/architect.

A front porch offers shelter from the elements for both employees and clients in this well-designed office space.

Features:

- Reception/Waiting Area: This reception and waiting area is combined, creating an open and airy space sure to make clients comfortable.

- Office: There are two private offices, a conference room, and a larger space toward the rear of the building that can be set up to accommodate eight additional workstations.

- Employee Area: Employees will appreciate the thoughtfully placed break room and private restroom at the rear of building, while the waiting area has a restroom for clients.

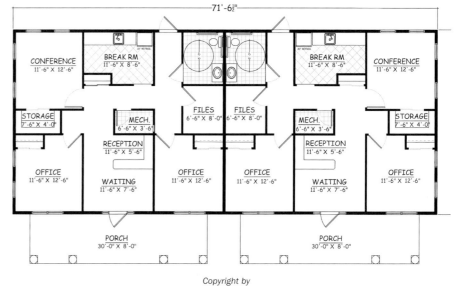

OFFICE SUITE ONE   OFFICE SUITE TWO

Plan #731151

Dimensions: 71'6½" W x 30' D

Levels: 1

Heated Square Footage: 2,160

Offices: 4

Restrooms: 2

Foundation: Crawl space, slab, or basement

Material Take-off Included: Yes

Price Category: D

With the appearance of a long ranch, this professional office building houses two independent office spaces.

CAD FILE AVAILABLE

Features:

- Covered Entrance: Each of the offices has a covered entry porch, which will shelter both employees and clients from the elements.

- Waiting/Reception: Step directly into this combined waiting/reception area from the covered porch. The waiting area in each office is open to the rest of the office, creating a continuous traffic flow.

- Offices: In each of the independent office spaces there are two private offices, a conference room, a file room, and a tidy break room as well as a wheelchair-accessible restroom.

71'-6½"

| CONFERENCE 11'-6" X 12'-6" | BREAK RM 11'-6" X 8'-6" | FILES 6'-6" X 8'-0" | FILES 6'-6" X 8'-0" | BREAK RM 11'-6" X 8'-6" | CONFERENCE 11'-6" X 12'-6" |

STORAGE 7'-6" X 4'-0"

MECH. 6'-6" X 3'-6"

RECEPTION 11'-6" X 5'-6"

OFFICE 11'-6" X 12'-6"

WAITING 11'-6" X 7'-6"

OFFICE 11'-6" X 12'-6"

OFFICE 11'-6" X 12'-6"

MECH. 6'-6" X 3'-6"

RECEPTION 11'-6" X 5'-6"

WAITING 11'-6" X 7'-6"

STORAGE 7'-6" X 4'-0"

OFFICE 11'-6" X 12'-6"

PORCH 30'-0" X 8'-0"

PORCH 30'-0" X 8'-0"

Plan #731102

Dimensions: 60' W x 46' D

Levels: 1

Heated Square Footage: 2,760

Exam Rooms: 6

Restrooms: 3

Office: 1

Foundation: Crawl space, slab, or basement

Material Take-off Included: Yes

Price Category: B

Images provided by designer/architect.

- Exam Rooms: Six ample-size exam rooms will ensure patients are seen in a timely manner.

- Employee Area: Employees will appreciate the thoughtfully placed break room and private bathroom.

An entry porch and a generously sized waiting room will certainly make patients who enter this doctor's office feel at ease. This efficiently designed office space offers all that a private practice doctor will require to care for his or her patients.

Features:

- Front Porch: This covered porch offers shelter from the elements for both employees and patients.

- Waiting Room: This generously sized waiting room will allow patients to feel more at ease while waiting to be seen.

- Reception Area: The central area for the business, this reception area is open and airy, with easy access to all areas of the building.

Copyright by designer/architect.

Plan #731152

Dimensions: 73'5" W x 54'11" D

Levels: 1

Heated Square Footage: 3,767

Offices: 3

Restrooms: 3

Foundation: Crawl space, slab, or basement

Material Take-off Included: Yes

Price Category: H

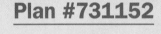

For someone looking to expand his or her professional office space, this building is sure to fill the bill.

Features:

- Covered Entrance: Stately columns grace this covered entrance to the professional office space.

- Waiting/Reception Area: This understated reception and waiting room has a wheelchair-accessible restroom for convenience.

- Offices: In addition to three private offices and a generously sized conference room, this office space features two sections for cubicles. The cubicles offer a bit of private space for calls and work, but they also allow employees to interact, creating a team environment.

- Additional Areas: The remainder of the office space has a file room, a break room with kitchen, and two employee-only restrooms.

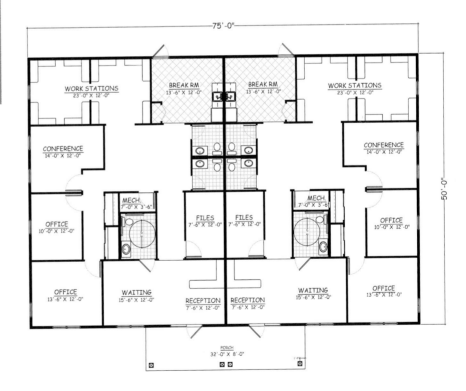

OFFICE DUPLEX

Images provided by designer/architect.

Plan #731168

Dimensions: 75' W x 50' D

Levels: 1

Heated Square Footage: 3,768

Offices: 4

Restrooms: 6

Foundation: Crawl space, slab, or basement

Material Take-off Included: Yes

Price Category: H

This simply designed office building houses two completely separate office suites, ideal for a small professional or medical office.

Features:

- Reception/Waiting Room: This combined waiting and reception area is open and airy, ensuring that clients and patients will feel comfortable.

- Offices: In addition to two private offices, each suite houses a conference room, three restrooms—one which is wheelchair accessible—an employee break room, and a spacious workstation area at the rear of each unit.

Copyright by designer/architect.

Plan #731147

Dimensions: 75' W x 60' D

Levels: 1

Heated Square Footage: 4,500

Exam Rooms: 12

Restrooms: 9

Foundation: Crawl space, slab, or basement

Material Take-off Included: Yes

Price Category: I

Images provided by designer/architect.

Copyright by designer/architect.

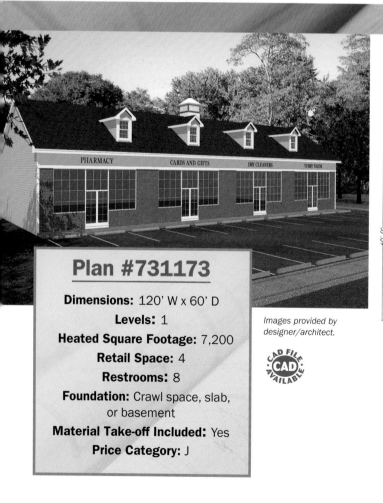

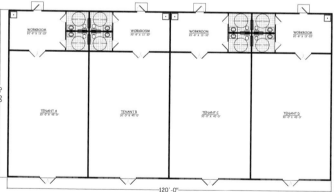

Plan #731173

Dimensions: 120' W x 60' D

Levels: 1

Heated Square Footage: 7,200

Retail Space: 4

Restrooms: 8

Foundation: Crawl space, slab, or basement

Material Take-off Included: Yes

Price Category: J

Images provided by designer/architect.

Copyright by designer/architect.

Let Us Help You Plan Your Dream Home

As a builder, you know that time is money. So are an architect's design services, which could be up to 15 percent of the cost of construction. That's a hefty premium for any building project.

A pre-designed plan and a Material Take-off from our Builder Portfolio of Easy-to-Build Plans can help get your project started quickly and without the cost of an architect. So here's a better idea; save time and money by selecting a plan from among the 175 unique designs shown in our collection.

What Does Creative Homeowner Offer?

In this book, Creative Homeowner provides 175 plans that you won't find in any other book or magazine. Our designs are among the most popular available. By using this book or visiting our Web site, **ultimateplans.com,** you will be sure to find the design best suited for your project. Our plan packages include detailed drawings to help you construct your next project. **(See page 232.)**

Can I Make Changes to the Plans?

Creative Homeowner offers three ways to help you achieve a truly unique design. Our customizing service allows for extensive changes to our designs—a custom plan for thousands of dollars less. **(See page 233.)** We also provide reverse images of our plans, or we can give you the tools for making minor changes on your own. **(See page 236.)**

Can You Help Me Manage My Costs?

To help you stay within your budget, Creative Homeowner has teamed up with North America's leading estimating company to provide, free, one of the most accurate, complete, and reliable building material take-offs in the industry when you buy your plans. **(See page 234.)** If you want an idea of costs before you commit to buying a plan, we can provide you with general construction costs based on the zip code for where you plan on building. **(See page 236.)** Then you can decide whether you want to buy the plan later.

How Can I Begin the Building Process?

To get started building your next project, fill out the order form on page 237, call our order department at **1-800-523-6789,** or visit our Web site, **ultimateplans.com.** To help keep up with changes in the construction industry or to keep tabs on your subcontractors, we offer best-selling building and design books at **creativehomeowner.com.**

Our Plans Packages Offer:

"Square footage" refers to the total "heated square feet" of this plan. This number does not include the garage, porches, or unfinished areas. All of our plans are the result of many hours of work by leading architects and professional designers. Most of our plans include each of the following:

Frontal Sheet
This artist's rendering of the front of the house gives you an idea of how the house will look once it is completed and the property landscaped.

Detailed Floor Plans
These plans show the size and layout of the rooms. They also provide the locations of doors, windows, fireplaces, closets, stairs, and electrical outlets and switches. Also included are full structural plans

Foundation Plan
A foundation plan gives the dimensions of basements, crawl spaces, and slab construction. Each house has a chioce of one of these three foundations.

Roof Plan
In addition to providing the pitch of the roof, these plans also show the locations of dormers, skylights, and other elements.

Exterior Elevations
These drawings show the front, rear, and sides of the house as if you were looking at it head on. Elevations also provide information about architectural features and finish materials.

Interior Elevations and Details
Interior elevations show specific details of such elements as fireplaces, kitchen and bathroom cabinets, built-ins, and other unique features of the design.

Cross Section
This shows the structure as if it were sliced to reveal construction requirements, such as insulation, flooring, and roofing details.

Frontal Sheet

Floor Plan

Foundation Plan

Roof Plan

Cross Section

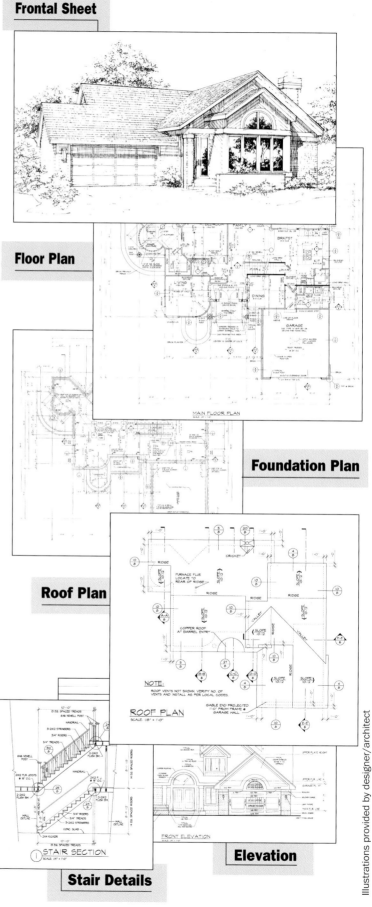

Stair Details

Elevation

Illustrations provided by designer/architect

Customize Your Plans in 4 Easy Steps

1 **Select the plan** that most closely meets your needs. Purchase of a reproducible master, PDF file, or CAD file is necessary in order to make changes to a plan.

2 **Call 1-800-523-6789 to place your order.** Tell our sales representative that you are interested in customizing your plan, and provide your contact information. Within a day or two you will be contacted (via phone or email) to provide a list or sketch of the changes requested to one of our plans. There is no consultation fee for this service.

3 **Within three business days** of receipt of your request, a detailed cost estimate will be provided to you.

4 **Once you approve the estimate,** you will purchase either the reproducible master, PDF file, or CAD file, and customization work will begin. During all phases of the project, you will receive progress prints by fax or email. On average, the project will be completed in two or three weeks. After completion of the work, modified plans will be shipped. You will receive one set of blueprints in addition to a reproducible master or CAD file, depending on which package you purchased.

Modification Pricing Guide

Categories	Average Cost For Modification
Add or remove living space	Quote required
Bathroom layout redesign	Starting at $150
Kitchen layout redesign	Starting at $120
Garage: add or remove	Starting at $600
Garage: front entry to side load or vice versa	Starting at $300
Foundation changes	Starting at $220
Exterior building materials change	Starting at $200
Exterior openings: add, move, or remove	$75 per opening
Roof line changes	Starting at $600
Ceiling height adjustments	Starting at $280
Fireplace: add or remove	Starting at $90
Screened porch: add	Starting at $300
Wall framing change from 2x4 to 2x6	Starting at $250
Bearing and/or exterior walls changes	Quote required
Non-bearing wall or room changes	$65 per room
Metric conversion of home plan	Starting at $495
Adjust plan for handicapped accessibility	Quote required
Adapt plans for local building code requirements	Quote required
Engineering stamping only	Quote required
Any other engineering services	Quote required
Interactive illustrations (choices of exterior materials)	Quote required

Note: *Any home plan can be customized to accommodate your desired changes. The average prices above are provided only as examples of the most commonly requested changes, and are subject to change without notice. Prices for changes will vary according to the number of modifications requested, plan size, style, and method of design used by the original designer. To obtain a detailed cost estimate, please contact us.*

Terms & Copyright

These home plans are protected under the terms of United States Copyright Law and may not be copied or reproduced in any way, by any means, unless you have purchased reproducible masters, which clearly indicate your right to copy or reproduce. We authorize the use of your chosen home plan as an aid in the construction of one single-family home only. You may not use this home plan to build a second or multiple dwellings without purchasing another blueprint or blueprints, or paying additional home plan fees.

Architectural Seals

Because of differences in building codes, some cities and states now require an architect or engineer licensed in that state to review and "seal" a blueprint, or officially approve it, prior to construction. Delaware, Nevada, New Jersey, New York, and some other states require that all plans for houses built in those states be redrawn by an architect licensed in the state in which the home will be built. We strongly advise you to consult with your local building official for information regarding architectural seals.

Before Customization

After

Turn your client's dream home into reality

Material Take-off and LOWE'S FOR PROS

When purchasing one of the plans featured in this book, you get, at no additional cost, one of the most complete materials lists in the industry.

1 What comes with a Material Take-off?

Building Materials

- When you purchase one of the plans featured in this book, you get one of the most complete material list in the industry.

In-Store Selections

- In-Store Selection pages guide you through the selection of products to finish off the project's interior spaces

Quote

- Basis of the entire estimate.

- Detailed list of all the framing materials needed to build your project, listed from the bottom up, in the order that each one will actually be used.

Kitchen Design

- Included with your quote is your kitchen design packet. Work with your kitchen designer to choose your new cabinets and countertops.

Express List

- A combined version of the Quote with SKUs listed for purchasing the items at your local Lowe's.

- Your Lowe's Commercial Sales Specialist can then price out the materials list.

Appliance Advantage

- Take advantage of Lowe's large selection of appliances. The skilled appliance specialists are trained and certified by the manufacturer and Lowe's

Millwork Report

- A complete count of the windows, doors, molding, and trim.

Bathroom and Lighting Fixtures

- Save money and maintain design control by choosing your plumbing and lighting fixtures

Man-Hour Report

- Calculates labor on a line-by-line basis for all items quoted and presented in man-hours

Finish and Decor Checklist

- A room-by-room checklist that will help you account for all of the final finish and decor choices you will have to make.

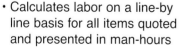

2 Why a Material Take-off?

Accurate. Professional estimators break down each individual item from the blueprints using advanced software, techniques, and equipment.

Timely. You will be able to start your project quickly—knowing the exact framing materials you need and how to get them with Lowe's.

Detailed. Work with your Lowe's associate to select with the remaining products needed for your project and get a final, accurate quote.

3 So how much does it cost?

Material Take-off pricing is normally determined by the total square feet of the plan—including living area, garages, decks, porches, finished basements, and finished attics. For the collection in this book, the Material Take-off is included in the price of the plans:

Square Feet Range	Price
Up to 5,000 total square feet	~~$345.00~~ Included
5,001 to 10,000 total square feet	~~$545.00~~ Included

Call our toll-free number (800-523-6789), or visit ultimateplans.com to order your Material Take-off (also called Ultimate Estimate online). A free material Take-off is not included with an order of a Study Set.

4 What else do I need to know?

When you purchase your products from Lowe's you may receive a gift card for $345 or $545, the regular price of a Material Take-off (even though it was included in your plan price) as an added value. Please go to UltimatePlans.com and select Ultimate Estimate located under "Quick Links" for complete details of the program.

The Lowe's Advantage:

What's more, you can save an additional 10% (up to $500.00) on your first building material purchase.* You will receive details on this program with your order.

Turn a dream project into reality.

*Good for a single purchase of any in-stock or Special Order merchandise only up to $5,000 (maximum discount $500). Not valid on previous sales, service or installation fees, the purchase of gift cards, or any products by Fisher & Paykel, Electrolux, John Deere, or Weber.

Decide What Type of Plan Package You Need

How many Plans Should You Order?

Standard 8-Set Package. We've found that our 8-set package is the best value for someone who is ready to start building. The 8-set package provides plans for you, the subcontractors, mortgage lender, and the building department.

Minimum 5-Set Package. If you are in the bidding process, you may want to order only five sets for the bidding round and reorder additional sets as needed.

1-Set Study Package. The 1-set package allows you to review your plan in detail. The plan will be marked as a study print, and it is illegal to build from a study print alone. It is a violation of copyright law to reproduce a blueprint without permission.

Buying Additional Sets. If you require additional copies of blueprints for your construction project, you can order additional sets within 60 days of the original order date at a reduced price. The cost is $50.00 for each additional set. For more information, contact customer service.

Reproducible Masters

If you plan to make minor changes to one of our plans, you can purchase reproducible masters. These plans are printed on bond paper. They clearly indicate your right to modify, copy, or reproduce the plans. Reproducible masters allow you, an architect, or designer to alter our plans to give you a customized design. This package allows you to print as many copies of the modified plans as you need for the construction of one building.

PDF Files

PDF files are a complete set of plans in electronic file format sent to you via email. These files cannot be altered electronically; once printed, changes can be hand drawn. A PDF file has the license to modify the plans to fit your needs and build one building.

CAD (Computer-Aided Design) Files

CAD files are the complete set of home plans in an alterable electronic file format. Choose this option if there are multiple changes you wish made to the plans and you have a local design professional able to make the changes.

Right-Reading Reverse

Plans can be printed in reverse—we can "flip" plans to create a mirror image of the design. This is useful when the building would fit your site or personal preferences if all the rooms were on the opposite side than shown. All plans in this collection are available in right-reading reverse; this feature will show the plan in reverse, and the writing on the plan will be readable. A $150.00 fee per plan order will be charged for right-reading reverse (regardless of the number of right-reading reverse sets ordered).

EZ Quote® : Cost Estimator

EZ Quote® is our response to a frequently asked question we hear from customers: "How much will this building cost me to build?" EZ Quote®: Cost Estimator will enable you to obtain a calculated building cost to construct your building, based on labor rates and building material costs within your zip code area. This summary is useful for those who want to get an idea of the total construction costs before purchasing sets of plans. It will also provide a level of comfort when you begin soliciting bids. The cost is $29.95 for the first EZ Quote® and $19.95 for each additional one in the same order. Available only in the U.S. and Canada.

3-D Framer's Walk-Through

Step-by-step 3-D framing instructions from foundation sill plate to roof sheathing are available for all plans in this collection at a cost of $545. This plan-specific "slide show" will be deliverd in PDF format for easy viewing. The 3-D framer's walk-through enables you to "virtually tour" your new project in the framing stage of construction. This is a valuable tool when framing the building, and it can save you time and money. It will show you stud lengths, plate heights, header size and location, plus girder size and location.

Lowe's Material Take-off (See page 234.)

Material Take-off may take 2 to 3 weeks for delivery.

Order Toll Free by Phone
1-800-523-6789
By Fax: 201-760-2431

Orders received 3PM ET, will be processed and shipped within two business days.

Order Online
www.ultimateplans.com
Mail Your Order
Creative Homeowner
Attn: Home Plans
24 Park Way
Upper Saddle River, NJ 07458

Canadian Customers
Order Toll Free 1-800-393-1883
Mail Your Order (Canada)
Creative Homeowner Canada
Attn: Home Plans
113-437 Martin St., Ste. 215
Penticton, BC V2A 5L1

Before You Order

Our Exchange Policy

Blueprints are nonrefundable. However, should you find that the plan you have purchased does not fit your needs, you may exchange that plan for another plan in our collection within 60 days from the date of your original order. The entire content of your original order must be returned before an exchange will be processed. You will be charged a processing fee of 20% of the amount of the original order, the cost difference between the new plan set and the original plan set (if applicable), and all related shipping costs for the new plans. Contact our order department for more information. Please note: reproducible masters may only be exchanged if the package is unopened. PDF files and CAD files cannot be exchanged and are nonrefundable.

Building Codes and Requirements

All plans offered for sale in this book and on our Web site (www.ultimateplans.com) are continually updated to meet the latest International Residential Code (IRC). Because building codes vary from area to area, some drawing modifications and/or the assistance of a professional designer or architect may be necessary to comply with your local codes or to accommodate specific building site conditions. We strongly advise you to consult with your local building official for information regarding codes governing your area.

Multiple Plan Discount

Purchase **3** different plans in the **same order** and receive **5% off** the plan price.

Purchase **5** or more different plans in the **same order** and receive **10% off** the plan price. (Please Note: Study sets do not apply.)

Blueprint Price Schedule

Price Code	1 Set	5 Sets	8 Sets	Reproducible Masters or PDF Files	CAD	Material Take-off
DD	$135	$1==	N/A	$2"0	$500	included
A	$431	$494	$572	$693	$1,181	included
B	$488	$567	$646	$777	$1,376	included
C	$551	$651	$730	$861	$1,549	included
D	$604	$704	$782	$914	$1,654	included
E	$656	$767	$845	$971	$1,759	included
F	$725	$830	$908	$1,040	$1,890	included
G	$756	$861	$940	$1,071	$1,937	included
H	$767	$872	$950	$1,097	$1,995	included
I	$1,045	$1,150	$1,229	$1,355	$2,216	included
J	$1,250	$1,355	$1,433	$1,565	$2,415	included
K	$1,255	$1,360	$1,439	$1,570	$2,415	included
L	$1,302	$1,402	$1,481	$1,612	$2,520	included

Note: All prices subject to change

Lowe's Material Take-off (MT Tier)

Price

~~$345~~	Included
~~$545~~	Included

Shipping & Handling

Shipping & Handling	1–4 Sets	5–7 Sets	8+ Sets or Reproducibles	CAD
US Regular (7–10 business days)	$18	$20	$25	$25
US Priority (3–5 business days)	$35	$40	$45	$45
US Express (1–2 business days)	$45	$60	$80	$50
Canada Express (3–4 business days)	$100	$100	$100	$100
Worldwide Express (3–5 business days)	** Quote Required **			

Note: All delivery times are from date the blueprint package is shipped (typically within 1-2 days of placing order).

Order Form
Please send me the following:

Plan Number: _____ **Price Code:** _____ (See Plan Index.)

Indicate Foundation Type: (Select ONE. See plan page for availability.)

❏ Slab   ❏ Crawl space   ❏ Basement

Basic Blueprint Package   Cost

❏ CAD Files $_____
❏ PDF Files $_____
❏ Reproducible Masters $_____
❏ 8-Set Plan Package $_____
❏ 5-Set Plan Package $_____
❏ 1-Set Study Package $_____
  (Material Take-off and free garage not included)
❏ Additional plan sets:
  __ sets at $50.00 per set $_____

❏ Print in right-reading reverse: $150.00 per order $_____
  *Please call all our order department
   or visit our website for availibility*

Important Extras

❏ Lowe's Material Take-off $_Included_
❏ 3-D Framer's Walk-Through: $545.00 $_____
❏ EZ Quote® for Plan #_____ at $29.95 $_____
❏ Additional EZ Quotes® for Plan #s_____ $_____
  at $19.95 each
❏ Free Detached Garage Plan: Any home plan
  purchased from this book, except Study Sets,
  qualifies for a free detached garage plan
  Detached Garage Plan Number _____ $__Free__

Shipping (see chart above) $_____
SUBTOTAL $_____
Sales Tax (NJ residents only, add 7%) $_____
TOTAL $_____

Order Toll Free: 1-800-523-6789   By Fax: 201-760-2431
Creative Homeowner (Home Plans Order Dept.)
24 Park Way
Upper Saddle River, NJ 07458

Name _____
(Please print or type)

Street _____
(Please do not use a P.O. Box)

City _____ State _____

Country _____ Zip _____

Daytime telephone ( ) _____

Fax ( ) _____
(Required for reproducible orders)

E-Mail _____

Payment   ❏ Bank check/money order. No personal checks.
Make checks payable to Creative Homeowner

❏ VISA   ❏ MasterCard   ❏ AMERICAN EXPRESS Cards   ❏ DISCOVER

Credit card number _____

Expiration date (mm/yy) _____

Signature _____

Please check the appropriate box:
❏ Building home for myself   ❏ Building home for someone else

SOURCE CODE **LA526**

Index

For pricing, see page 237.

Plan #	Price Code	Page	Total Finished Sq. Ft.	Material Take-off
731001	C	77	2174	Y
731002	E	109	2927	Y
731003	C	74	1651	Y
731004	F	117	2795	Y
731005	B	58	1924	Y
731006	E	107	2789	Y
731007	C	70	1786	Y
731007	C	71	1786	Y
731008	E	115	2827	Y
731009	B	61	1831	Y
731010	F	118	3147	Y
731011	D	101	2696	Y
731012	G	134	4030	Y
731013	C	75	2532	Y
731014	G	131	4125	Y
731015	C	66	1688	Y
731016	F	118	2972	Y
731017	C	75	2594	Y
731018	E	113	3556	Y
731019	C	67	2540	Y
731020	F	119	3816	Y
731021	D	80	2690	Y
731022	F	119	3658	Y
731023	B	60	2366	Y
731024	E	109	3288	Y
731025	C	76	2090	Y
731026	G	130	3632	Y
731027	D	99	2778	Y
731028	H	135	4426	Y
731029	D	77	2354	Y
731030	G	132	3984	Y
731031	C	76	2198	Y
731032	E	111	3058	Y
731033	C	72	2298	Y
731033	C	73	2298	Y
731034	E	107	3029	Y
731035	D	100	3151	Y
731036	G	133	4504	Y
731037	B	45	1844	Y
731038	C	78	2418	Y
731038	C	79	2418	Y
731039	D	96	3202	Y
731039	D	97	3202	Y
731040	D	81	2690	Y
731041	D	104	2776	Y
731041	D	105	2776	Y
731042	G	128	3809	Y
731043	B	37	2013	Y
731044	D	86	2860	Y
731044	D	87	2860	Y
731045	B	33	2053	Y
731046	B	14	1381	Y
731047	B	17	1632	Y
731048	B	56	1960	Y
731048	B	57	1960	Y
731049	B	60	1680	Y
731050	B	34	1919	Y
731050	B	35	1919	Y
731051	B	38	2107	Y
731051	B	39	2107	Y
731052	C	68	2124	Y
731052	C	69	2124	Y
731053	B	19	2062	Y
731054	B	46	2416	Y
731054	B	47	2416	Y
731055	B	36	1584	Y
731056	B	63	2192	Y
731057	B	65	2093	Y
731058	B	45	2056	Y
731059	B	64	1932	Y
731060	B	20	1700	Y
731060	B	21	1700	Y
731061	B	30	1368	Y
731061	B	31	1368	Y
731062	B	43	1710	Y
731063	B	13	1686	Y
731064	B	44	1957	Y
731065	B	59	1992	Y
731066	D	84	2458	Y
731067	D	82	2489	Y
731068	D	106	2821	Y
731069	E	106	2408	Y
731070	B	83	2381	Y
731071	B	18	1832	Y
731072	C	74	2053	Y
731073	B	40	1563	Y
731074	F	116	3453	Y
731075	F	117	2915	Y
731076	E	108	2414	Y
731077	B	62	2046	Y
731078	B	42	2460	Y
731079	B	44	2230	Y
731080	B	32	2380	Y
731081	I	137	5496	Y
731082	E	108	3304	Y
731083	F	116	2737	Y
731084	B	61	2170	Y
731085	B	15	1895	Y
731086	B	58	2208	Y
731087	B	42	1975	Y
731088	E	112	3189	Y
731089	D	98	2645	Y
731090	D	103	2856	Y
731091	D	102	2670	Y
731092	D	85	2540	Y
731093	B	59	1988	Y
731094	G	129	3704	Y
731095	H	136	4420	Y

Index

For pricing, see page 237.

Material Take-off
The fastest way to get started building your next project— and it's Included!

One of the most complete materials lists in the industry. Work with your Lowe's associate to get all the products you need.

LOWE'S FORPROS

To learn more, see page 234 or go to UltimatePlans.com and select Ultimate Estimate located under "Quick Links" for complete details on this program.

Copyright Notice

All plans sold through this publication are protected by copyright. Reproduction of these, either in whole or in part, including any form and/or preparation of derivative works there-of, for any reason without prior written permission is strictly prohibited. The purchase of a set of plans in no way transfers any copyright or other ownership interest in it to the buyer except for a limited license to use that set of plans for the construction of one, and only one, building. The purchase of additional sets of the plans at a reduced price from the original set or as a part of a multiple-set package does not convey to the buyer a license to construct more than one building.

Similarly, the purchase of reproducible plans (sepias, mylars, bond), PDF files, and CAD files carry the same copyright protection as mentioned above. It is generally allowed to make up to a maximum of 10 copies for the construction of a single building only. To use any plans more than once, and to avoid any copyright license infringement, it is necessary to contact the plan designer to receive a release and license for any extended use. Whereas a purchaser of reproducible plans, PDF file, or CAD file is granted a license to make copies, it should be noted that because blueprints are copyrighted, making photocopies from them is illegal.

Copyright and licensing of plans for construction exist to protect all parties. Copyright respects and supports the intellectual property of the original architect or designer. Copyright law has been reinforced over the past few years. Willful infringement could cause settlements for statutory damages to $150,000.00 plus attorney fees, damages, and loss of profits.